The Literature of Penance
in Anglo-Saxon England

The Literature of Penance

in Anglo-Saxon England

Allen J. Frantzen

Rutgers University Press

New Brunswick, New Jersey

PR
179
.P44
F7
1983

Publication of this volume has been assisted by a grant
from Loyola University of Chicago.

Jacket illustration, folio 1r of Bodley 718, courtesy
Bodleian Library, Oxford.

Library of Congress Cataloging in Publication Data

Frantzen, Allen J., 1947–
    The literature of penance in Anglo-Saxon England.

    Bibliography: p.
    Includes index.
    1. Anglo-Saxon literature—History and criticism.
2. Christian literature, Anglo-Saxon—History
and criticism.   3. Penance in literature.
4. Penance—History.   5. Penitentials.   I. Title.
PR179.P44F7   1983   829'.09'382   81–23367
ISBN 0-8135-0955-6   AACR2

To my parents,
and to G. R. P.

Contents

Preface   ix

Acknowledgments   xiii

Abbreviations   xv

Chapter One
An Introduction to Penitentials and Penance   I

Chapter Two
Early Ireland and the Origins of Private Penance   19

Chapter Three
Penance and Prayer in Eighth-Century England   61

Chapter Four
Irish, Anglo-Saxon, and Frankish Penitentials
in the Ninth Century   94

Chapter Five
The Penitential Tradition in Tenth-Century England   122

Chapter Six
Teaching Penance: Old English
Homilies, Handbooks, and Prayers   151

Chapter Seven
Penance as Theme and Image in Old English Poetry   175

Epilogue
A Look Ahead to New Questions   198

Bibliography   209

Index   229

Preface

THE subject of this study is the handbook of penance, also known as the penitential, a guide for the priest in hearing confession and prescribing acts of atonement proportionate to the offenses acknowledged. Developed in Ireland in the sixth century, the penitential was subsequently introduced to England and the continent, where its success was both immediate and lasting. Although once unknown outside the missions of Irish monks, the handbook eventually became indispensable to early medieval pastoral work.

As the handbook was adopted by non-Irish cultures, it was altered in both form and substance. But these revisions only gave new life to the text and ultimately ensured that the penitential, however altered, would endure. Even the moral theologians of the twelfth century, so different in spiritual outlook from the Irish, English, and Frankish clerics studied here, found the handbook essential, although in a form revised to suit more exacting standards. Five early Irish penitentials require some seventy pages in a modern edition, while a single manual for confessors from the thirteenth century consumes nearly three hundred. Yet this long and complex document is also called a *liber paenitentialis*, and like the shorter handbooks it guided the priest in inducing candor, determining guilt, and prescribing remedies for sin.

A study of a topic so broad and varied necessarily entails certain limitations which are best acknowledged at the outset. Although they are no longer so neglected as they once were, handbooks of penance still present a formidable challenge to scholarship. All but a few of the early penitentials are known only in editions more than a century old and long out of date. Those more recently edited must be joined by commentary to make plain their significance for medieval life and literature. For some time I have wondered how best to write a book about these materials which neither labors too much of what is already known nor lingers over highly specific and indeed arcane matters. Specialists in some of the fields I survey here will wish for a more detailed discussion, but others will perhaps find the broader outlines of the topic more useful in guiding their research. Like all compromises mine is to some extent bound to be unsatisfactory, but like most compromises it is necessary. Rather than write a book which explores the full historical, sociological, and literary meaning of penitentials and penance, I have chosen to write about the sources themselves, the textual and contextual problems which they raise, and their relevance to the literature of Anglo-Saxon England. For this was the first vernacular literature in which penitentials and penance loomed large.

My study draws on handbooks written between the late sixth century, when the first Irish penitentials appeared, and the late eleventh century, the date of the last penitentials in Old English. During most of this period, the penitential was a modest document, usually devoting one chapter to each of several serious sins. Some handbooks were short and simple enough to have been memorized. The earliest examples supplement the lists of sins and punishments with instructions for the priest but otherwise remain silent on the ceremony of confession or the performance of acts of penance. Hence, much about the confessional encounter and its practical consequences can be seen only indirectly in the handbooks. Other kinds of literature, such as homilies, prayers, and legislation, are useful in describing clearly and fully what penance and penitentials meant to medieval Christians.

Following an introductory chapter about penitentials and the system of confession and penance they provided for, I analyze the handbooks of Irish, Anglo-Saxon, and Frankish origin. These three chapters identify the characteristic features of the penitentials written in each region and show how the handbook was modified as it passed through and became part of each culture. The survey stresses the continuity of the penitential in both form and function and links it to other pastoral literature, native legal traditions, and relevant narrative sources. The next three chapters concern English vernacular texts of the tenth century. Struggling to restore the administrative and educational system destroyed by the ninth-century invasions, English ecclesiastics began to gather disciplinary and catechetical texts, penitentials among them, from continental centers. Much of this material was then translated into the vernacular. From it I have selected the handbooks, related prose, and certain poems and used these texts to assess the Anglo-Saxon penitential tradition.

Although they tackle some questions of literary form, these latter chapters stress the historical development of penance and penitentials in England. The handbooks and other texts written there are seen as a part of Old English literature, not merely as a background to it. My comments on "penitential poetry"—certainly the only literature related to penance to which Anglo-Saxonists have given much attention—assume a context of penitentials and penance for the poems. My objective has been to approach poetry as evidence of ecclesiastical history as well as a reflection of it.

By nature penance relates to a large field of interests. The penitential is, among other things, an image of early medieval society, a world which sometimes appears in the handbooks at its worst. No one would attempt to study a culture in terms of its sins, of course, or even its proposed cures for them. But it is surprising to see how close to medieval life the penitentials can bring us as we begin to understand them better. They reflect marriage customs and sexual mores, suggest the value of different kinds of property, and offer insight into matters we might not otherwise contemplate: how could one tell if a monk had sinned willingly or unwillingly in his sleep? was it permitted to eat honey from bees which had stung someone to death? how was a woman who committed abortion to know if the fetus was older or younger than forty days? (The penance assigned for killing a fetus older than forty days was much graver.) But we should not overemphasize such curiosities as these. Most of the offenses listed in the handbooks concerned grave matters treated gravely, without legalistic quibbling. They were in the main sins which had been committed and confessed, although some of them may have been included in a given penitential only because they were automatically copied from the compiler's source, without regard for their relevance to his own milieu. The penitentials are most usefully studied not in isolation, as lists of sins, but in the context of contemporary law and literature—their cooperation with secular law, their relation to homilies and catechetical texts, and their integration with prayer. They had kin in nearly every family of medieval ecclesiastical literature and abundant secular relations as well. The penitentials were, before all else, the key to penitential practice. By approaching them in this, their first function, and then relating them to subsidiary literature, I have sought to illuminate the reality which the handbooks established in early medieval England.

Acknowledgments

I N the course of researching and writing this study, I have acquired many debts; I hope the most important of them are acknowledged here. Early stages of my research were supported
by the American Council of Learned Societies, the American Philo-
sophical Society, Oberlin College, and Loyola University of Chicago. The first draft was written during a leave of absence generously
funded by the Alexander von Humboldt Foundation in 1979. I am
especially grateful for the foundation's support and for the kind assistance of Professor Raymund Kottje in arranging my stay at the
University of Augsburg.

Several scholars made specific suggestions for revision and offered criticism which helped to clarify my understanding of many
complex issues. In particular I wish to thank David W. Burchmore,
Patrick O'Neill, and Robert C. Rice, who read an early version of the
manuscript and commented generously on it, and Milton McC.
Gatch, whose reading of the near-final draft contributed substantially
to its improvement. I am also grateful to Barbara Rosenwein, my
colleague at Loyola, for her stimulating interest in my research. I owe
a long-standing debt to James W. Earl and V. A. Kolve, who directed
the University of Virginia dissertation which formed the kernel of
this study, and to Alan Bliss, T. P. Dolan, and Proinsias Mac Cana,
my teachers at University College, Dublin.

In editing and revising the manuscript I was most capably assisted by Virginia Krause and Elizabeth El Itreby, my graduate students at Loyola. The staff of Rutgers University Press handled both
this manuscript and its author with care and dispatch, and I am especially grateful to Herbert F. Mann, Phyllis Lanz, and Leslie Mitchner
for their patient and good-natured supervision. I also wish to ac-

knowledge the cooperation of the Dublin Institute for Advanced Studies, which granted permission to quote from *The Irish Penitentials* and *Sancti Columbani Opera*, and that of Columbia University Press, which granted permission to quote from *Medieval Handbooks of Penance*.

My greatest debts are to Dr. and Mrs. Gerd Wollburg, whose kindness and generosity have made my every visit to Augsburg a happy and memorable one, and to G. R. Paterson, who has dispensed comfort, good counsel, and encouragement at every stage of this project and whose relief at its completion may rival my own.

Abbreviations

ASE	*Anglo-Saxon England*	*MGH* (cont.)	
ASPR	Anglo-Saxon Poetic Records	*Conc*	*Concilia*
		Epp	*Epistolae*
BAP	Bibliothek der angel-sächsischen Prosa	*SRM*	*Scriptores Rerum Merovingicarum*
EETS	Early English Text Society	*MS*	*Mediaeval Studies*
		N&Q	*Notes and Queries*
EHD	*English Historical Documents*	*NM*	*Neuphilologische Mitteilungen*
EHR	*English Historical Review*	*PG*	J.-P. Migne, ed., *Patrologia Graeca*
ES	*English Studies*	*PL*	———, *Patrologia Latina*
JEGP	*Journal of English and Germanic Philology*	*PMLA*	*Publications of the Modern Language Association*
JEH	*Journal of Ecclesiastical History*	*PQ*	*Philological Quarterly*
JTS	*Journal of Theological Studies*	*RB*	*Revue Bénédictine*
MÆ	*Medium Ævum*	*RES*	*Review of English Studies*
MGH	*Monumenta Germaniae Historica*	*SN*	*Studia Neophilologica*
Cap	*Capitularia*	*SP*	*Studies in Philology*

The Literature of Penance
in Anglo-Saxon England

Chapter One

An Introduction to Penitentials and Penance

F EW controversies in the history of penance are more interesting than the debate about the Venerable Bede's authorship of the penitential attributed to him in many manuscripts of the ninth and tenth centuries; perhaps no controversy tells us more about scholarly attitudes toward penance itself. Delivering himself of a stout opinion against Bede's authorship, Plummer wrote:

> The penitential literature is in truth a deplorable feature of the medieval church. Evil deeds, the imagination of which may perhaps have dimly floated through our minds in the darkest moments, are here tabulated and reduced to system. It is hard to see how anyone could busy himself with such literature and not be the worse for it.[1]

Replying to Plummer, McNeill and Gamer asserted that Bede was of the same clay as other men and hence not incapable of acquaintance with the sins listed in the penitential.[2] Others, including Laistner, have argued that Bede was too intelligent and too good a Latinist to have written the handbook which claims his authorship.[3] Some issues in this dispute are comparatively commonplace: we know, for example, that medieval attitudes toward authorship were freer than our own, and that the evidence of manuscripts is especially unreliable

1. Charles Plummer, ed., *Venerabilis Baedae Opera Historica*, pp. clvii–clviii.

2. John T. McNeill and Helena M. Gamer, *Medieval Handbooks of Penance*, p. 217; they survey the authorship question on pp. 217–221.

3. M. L. W. Laistner, "Was Bede the Author of a Penitential?" pp. 166–170. See also H. J. Schmitz, *Die Bussbücher und die Bussdisziplin der Kirche*, pp. 555–556.

in this regard. But the argument about this penitential has involved another and more revealing issue—the subjectivity of those participating in the debate. Whether attacking or defending the case for Bede's authorship, these historians agree that the penitential is literature of a low level; they disagree only in setting a small part of Bede's reputation on that level or above it. Not surprisingly, their *ad hominem* arguments have failed to resolve the controversy and in the process have reinforced a contempt for penitentials which has long been a cliché in medieval studies.

Anyone who has busied himself with the handbooks of penance knows the prejudices with which they are traditionally regarded. Plummer's dark vision of their content seems to have inspired the design which decorates recent reprints of two early editions: a ghoulish figure, crudely sketched, swoons over a skull and crossbones, a whip ominously nearby.[4] The design represents a bizarre attempt to make the penitentials relevant if not sensational by linking them to morbidity, masochism, and possibly the occult. However misguided, it refreshingly reversed a hardy tradition suppressing anything in the handbooks which might be considered pornographic or scandalous. For decades translators have shied away from those parts of the penitentials which discuss sexual offenses. Sometimes these passages have been translated from the vernacular into Latin; sometimes they have been left in the original Latin, loosely paraphrased, or simply omitted.[5] The assumption behind such maneuvers

4. The editions are F. W. H. Wasserschleben, *Die Bussordnungen der abendländischen Kirche*, and H. J. Schmitz, *Die Bussbücher und das kanonische Bussverfahren*; both were reprinted in 1958 by Akademische Druk, Graz. The two-volume reprint of Schmitz's books is sedately bound in red.

5. Portions of the penitential in Old Irish are translated into Latin by E. J. Gwynn, "An Irish Penitential," and D. A. Binchy follows his lead in retranslating the text in *The Irish Penitentials*, ed. Ludwig Bieler, pp. 263–265. These passages deal with incest, homosexuality, and sperm libation, as well as the tamer offenses of adultery committed in the heart and other evil thoughts. McNeill and Gamer omit these passages from their reprint of Gwynn's translation, noting that the material is not "significant for any originality" (*Handbooks*, p. 157). Their translation of Theodore's penitential is equally evasive where sexual offenses are concerned. For example, where the Latin reads, "Si vir cum uxore sua retro nupserit," they translate, "In case of unnatural intercourse with his wife" (p. 197); it would, more accurately, be: "If a man enters his wife from the rear." They also translate "in tergo nupserit" as "a graver offense of this kind," but the meaning is plain, and "enter into the rectum" is a more accurate translation. (For Theodore's text, see Paul Willem Finsterwalder, ed., *Die Canones Theodori Cantua-*

is that anyone who can read about sins in a learned language will not be corrupted by them, a view both durable and *retardataire*: already in the ninth century—and probably earlier—alert officials sought to keep handbooks from the ignorant and unsophisticated.[6]

A fastidious desire to avoid the sexually explicit is now out of fashion, but another prejudice against the penitentials, directed at their use rather than their content, continues to thrive. This is the theory of social control, which holds that the chief function of penance was to ensure that the population obeyed the bishops' wishes in matters both spiritual and temporal. Penance would have been used to suppress what we might now call anti-social urges with the threat of severe punishment. Early advocates of this theory—Lea was perhaps the most influential—saw penance as oppressive; more recent discussions have been better balanced.[7] The theory of social control is unsatisfactory because it equates penitential practice with behavior modification and manipulation, exaggerating its restrictive influence. But penance was not a punishment: it was a cure. And the penitential was not only a list of sins and penalities for them; it was a blueprint

---

riensis und ihre Überlieferungsformen, p. 309, Book 1, 14. 21–22.) Bieler translates "in terga uero fornicantes" as "practicing homosexuality," but again the reference is clearly to anal intercourse (*Irish Penitentials*, pp. 74–75, from the penitential of Finnian, c. 2; and pp. 128–129, from Cummean's penitential, 10. 15). Hereafter citations of the penitentials give chapter and canon numbers if the work is divided into chapters, and canon numbers only if it is not: Cummean, 10. 15 refers to chapter 10, canon 15; Finnian, c. 2 is the second canon of Finnian's penitential.

6. In 866 Pope Nicholas responded to a request from the Bulgarian church for a penitential by noting that the text was not to fall into the hands of laymen because they did not have the power of judgment; for the text see Migne, *PL* 119:1008, translated by McNeill and Gamer, *Handbooks*, p. 407.

7. Henry Charles Lea, *A History of Auricular Confession and Indulgences in the Latin Church*, especially 2:107–110, where he remarks on the "punitive" quality of penance. Lea's views were quoted with approval by Thomas P. Oakley, *English Penitential Discipline and Anglo-Saxon Law in Their Joint Influence*, pp. 199–200, where penance is seen chiefly as a force to "civilise" the "rude inhabitants" and "barbarians" of the early Middle Ages. The theory of social control finds a sophisticated defense in Thomas N. Tentler's *Sin and Confession on the Eve of the Reformation*, pp. 20–22, 161–162, and elsewhere (see references to "discipline" in his index, p. 392); see also Tentler, "The Summa for Confessors as an Instrument of Social Control," and, for the counterargument that confession and penance were more closely linked to education than to the repression of anti-social behavior, see John Bossy, "The Social History of Confession in the Age of the Reformation."

for the sinner's conversion, didactic or catechetical as well as disciplinary. Mindful of the need to confess and repent, the medieval Christian no doubt became a more obedient and dutiful member of his society, but that was a side effect of penitential practice and not its central objective.

Controversies about the penitential inevitably involve attitudes toward the medieval church and even Christianity itself. It is not easy for the disinterested observer to get behind these controversies to the primary evidence, even with the aid of standard reference works.[8] Old editions of the handbooks are not always easily available, and editors in general seem to believe—rightly enough—that their duties do not include historical analysis of the texts. Historians, on the other hand, habitually defer such analysis to a time when better editions will be available. As a result, we are left with some large questions about the penitentials. We do not have a full understanding of how the penitential was used, how widely penance was practiced, or how the penitential interacted with other kinds of pastoral literature. No clear-cut answers to these questions are available, but enough is known about early Irish and Anglo-Saxon penitentials to warrant some preliminary analysis. That is the purpose of this study, which examines Irish, Anglo-Saxon, and Frankish handbooks, traces their chronological development, and seeks to explain how and why they are important to early English literature and history. Where this synthesis touches upon controversial matters, I have sought to clarify the points of contention rather than to take up one side or the other in a rather specialized debate. I seek to relate these controversies to the historical overview and have, in some cases, discussed their intricacies in separately published studies.

The study of penitentials must begin with the sacramental tradition to which they belong. This tradition is a vast one whose general outlines are much too well known to require rehearsal here.[9] My

8. Good introductions to the penitentials are G. Le Bras's article, "Pénitentiels," in *Dictionnaire de théologie catholique*, ed. A. Vacant, E. Mangenot, and E. Amann, vol. 12.1 (Paris, 1933), pp. 1160–1179, and H. Leclercq's article in the *Dictionnaire d'archéologie chrétienne et de liturgie*, ed. F. Cabrol and H. Leclercq, vol. 14.1 (Paris, 1939), pp. 215–251.

9. The early history of penance is analyzed by Josef A. Jungmann, *Die lateinischen Bussriten in ihrer geschichtlichen Entwicklung* and *The Early Liturgy to the Time of Gregory the Great*, trans. F. A. Brunner. Still useful is O. D. Watkins, *A History of Penance*.

study begins not with the scriptural background to penitential practice nor with the penitential tradition of the early church, but with penance in early Ireland.[10] The Irish penitentials present the first sharp break with the earliest form of penance known in the church, a public ritual presided over by a bishop.

In this ceremony, which sometimes began with a confession of sins before the assembly, sinners were enrolled in a class of penitents and expelled from the church to perform penance. Dismissed on Ash Wednesday, the penitents were readmitted on Holy Thursday and given absolution. This procedure was permitted only once in each sinner's lifetime, although there were exceptions.[11] Public penance was a response to the communal needs of the early church. It was a disciplinary system designed to maintain the purity of the community by excluding those who violated its standards. But to expel offenders permanently would have been to consign them to damnation; hence they were readmitted after they had atoned for their wrongdoing. The logic behind the public nature of the ceremonies of expulsion and absolution can be seen in Paul's letter to Timothy: "As for those who persist in sin, rebuke them in the presence of all, so that the rest may stand in fear" (1 Tim. 5:20). Public exposure was part of the punishment and a deterrent to other offenders.

Ceremonies somewhat similar to the public penitential ritual were observed in early Ireland, but an entirely new form of confession and penance existed there already in the sixth century.[12] This new method of reconciliation has its clearest antecedents in the communal discipline practiced in Irish monasteries. It entailed a private exchange between the confessor and the penitent in which confession was followed by the acceptance of a prescribed penance and

10. Biblical and patristic literature dealing with penance is surveyed by Stanislas Lyonnet and Leopold Sabourin, *Sin, Redemption, and Sacrifice: A Biblical and Patristic Study*; a brief synopsis of this literature is provided by McNeill and Gamer, *Handbooks*, pp. 4–18.

11. There was no single, uniform system of penitential practice in effect during the earliest Christian centuries; variations can be found in even the most widespread practices associated with public penance. See Cyrille Vogel, *La discipline pénitentielle en Gaule des origines à la fin du VIIe siècle*, and Bernhard Poschmann, *Die abendländische Kirchenbusse im Ausgang des christlichen Altertums*.

12. A good summary of the penitential traditions known in Ireland is Gerard Mitchell, "The Origins of Irish Penance." The topic is dealt with in the next chapter.

absolution. Although his penance might have kept the sinner from receiving the Eucharist for a certain period, and although his penitential acts might have indicated to others that he was performing penance (for example, that he was fasting), he was not publicly identified as a penitent, and he received absolution without benefit of a formal ceremony. Far less cumbersome than the older, public system, private penance had a further advantage of immense significance: it could be repeated as often as the sinner wished, or as often as his confessor required.

These two penitential systems were complementary rather than mutually exclusive. Although public penance declined in the later Christian era, it was not forgotten. In the early ninth century, when the penitentials and the private system were well established on the continent, Charlemagne called for a revival of public penance; subsequently, the church recognized a twofold division in the sacrament, requiring public penance for public sins and private penance for sins committed in private.[13] This dichotomy was maintained in Anglo-Saxon England, where in the late tenth century Archbishop Wulfstan of London and York vigorously insisted on both forms of reconciliation. Throughout the early medieval period, then, the public ritual coexisted with the private. A devout Anglo-Saxon Christian of Wulfstan's time could be expected to have known and observed both.

The differences between these penitential systems is of the utmost importance for history and literature, for they made different demands on the clergy and created different experiences for the laity. Public penance depended on the bishop's power, or that of his designated representative, exercised in a solemn liturgy. Its value to Charlemagne and Wulfstan can be seen not only in the discipline it enforced, but in the display of authority which accompanied it. Private penance required only a confessor with knowledge of the penitential, and a contrite sinner willing to cooperate with him. This method minimized public awareness of the sinner's misdeeds and maximized the priest's authority to forgive them. The benefits of private penance to missionary and pastoral activity are obvious. Pri-

13. The dual Carolingian system is summarized by Cyrille Vogel, Les "Libri Paenitentiales," pp. 39–43.

vate penance offered the church an opportunity to present its teachings to individuals rather than groups and to approach the faithful through the agency of a man known to them, perhaps raised among them and hence able to understand them and be understood by them.

The priest's guide in counseling penitents was the handbook of penance. Inevitably attacks on the system of private confession and penance came from bishops who doubted that priests were able to cope with this responsibility and believed that the penitential itself insufficiently supplemented the priests' training. The authors of the handbooks, themselves administrators (abbots and bishops), seem to have been fully aware of the penitential's liabilities and their priests' deficiencies. They often began the handbook by reminding the priest that the tariffs which followed were only a guide, to be used with discretion. These tariffs—a catalogue of sins and proportionate penances—constituted the bulk of the text; the following example, from the handbook attributed to Bede, shows the extent to which the priest would have had to use his own judgment before applying a specific tariff to a specific sin:

> Of manslaughter. 1. He who slays a monk or a cleric shall relinquish his weapons and serve God or shall do penance for seven years. 2. He who slays a layman with malice aforethought or for the possession of his inheritance shall do penance for four years. 3. He who slays to avenge a brother shall do penance for one year and in the two following years shall keep the forty-day fasts and other appointed fast days. 4. He who slays through anger and a sudden quarrel shall do penance for three years. 5. He who slays accidentally shall do penance for one year. 6. He who slays in public warfare shall do penance for forty days.[14]

14. Ed. Wasserschleben, *Bussordnungen*, pp. 224–225: "1. Qui occiderit monachum aut clericum, arma relinquat et Deo serviat vel annos VII peniteat. 2. Qui laicum odii meditatione vel possidende hereditatis ejus, annos IV peniteat. 3. Qui per vindictam fratris, I annum et in aliis duobus XLmas et legitimas ferias. 4. Qui per iram et rixam subitam, IIII annos. 5. Qui casu, I annum. 6. Qui in bello publico, XL dies." My policy concerning translations is as follows: unless otherwise indicated, the translation is my own or is based on an accurate published translation. The above passages are Bede 4. 1–6 (translated by McNeill and Gamer, *Handbooks*, pp. 224–225).

These tariffs assume that the priest has inquired about the circumstances of each offense and oblige him to consider those circumstances when he assigns penance. Accidental death entailed a much
lighter penance than the crime committed with passion (in anger),
while premeditated murder was, naturally, punished more severely
than either. The most important factor in determining guilt was the
penitent's awareness of his actions; one who sinned knowingly (*"sci-
ens," "volens"*) was always more heavily assessed than one who was
unaware that he had done wrong. The priest was required to know
more about penitents than this, however; the Bedan penitential
urges that the priest shall, "in everything which he finds here [in the
penitential], carefully distinguish the sex, the age, the condition, the
status, and the character of him who wishes to do penance, and shall
judge each sin one by one as it seems best to him." [15]

These passages should prompt us to reconsider statements
which dismiss the penitentials as primitive and mechanical instruments encumbered by "gross tariffs and clumsy casuistry," little more
than a "crude schedule of misdeeds and penances." [16] Without denying their limitations, it is easy to come to their defense. Compared to
the procedure outlined in confessional manuals of the later Middle
Ages, the system of penance outlined in the early handbooks does
seem unsophisticated. Before the scholastic period, penance was not
divided into the operations of contrition, confession, satisfaction,
and absolution, and the distinction between remote and proximate
matter had not yet been made. [17] These refinements enabled later confessors to determine culpability and judge the conscience more precisely than Irish or Anglo-Saxon confessors had done. But it is impossible to argue that the early penitentials neglected the sinner's

---

15. Ed. Wasserschleben, *Bussordnungen*, p. 220: "Ut universis que hic notata repperit,
sexum, aetatem, condicionem, statum, personam cujusque penitentiam agere volentis
ipsum quoque cor penitentis curiose discernet." Translation based on McNeill and
Gamer, *Handbooks*, p. 221.

16. See Stephan Kuttner, "Pierre de Roissy and Robert of Flamborough," *Traditio* 2
(1944): 493–494; and M.-D. Chenu, *Nature, Man and Society in the Twelfth Century*,
ed. and trans. Jerome Taylor and Lester K. Little, p. 229.

17. The development of a formal theology of penance is traced by Paul Anciaux, *La
théologie du sacrement de pénitence au xiie siècle*; see also F.-D. Joret, *Aux sources de l'eau
vive*, translated as *The Eucharist and the Confessional*.

interior disposition and routinely assigned one kind of act (fasting or almsgiving) to offset the effects of another (the sin). Both sins and sinners were differentiated by interior as well as exterior criteria: culpability depended not only on the sinner's social standing and physical well-being, but also on his frame of mind, his self-awareness.

We can see more of the confessor's office in the following description, taken from the seventh-century penitential of Cummean. The passage stresses the pedagogical as well as the judicial aspects of the priest's work:

> What is it, then, to cause a fault to be forgiven, unless you are said to cause forgiveness for his fault when you receive the sinner, and by warning, exhortation, teaching, and instruction lead him to penance, correct him of his error, amend him of his vices, and make him such that God is rendered favorable to him after his conversion? When, therefore, you are such a priest, and when such is your teaching and your word, there is given to you a share of those whom you correct, so that their merit may be your reward and their salvation your glory.[18]

This passage sums up both the early theology of penance and the private penitential system. Behind the power to forgive stands the simple command of Christ to the apostles: "Whatever you bind on earth shall be bound in heaven, and whatever you loose on earth shall be loosed in heaven" (Matt. 16:19). The "cause" of the forgiveness of sins is the action of the priest in correcting the sinner and converting him. The steps of the process are implied: the sinner, "received" by the priest, is admonished and instructed; thus "led to penance," he confesses his wrongdoing, and his vices are "amended," or cured, by acts of penance. The confessor was also a teacher, and the confessional encounter, more than simply a judgment of the sinner, was an opportunity for correction and instruction. The focus of this passage

18. Ed. Bieler, *Irish Penitentials*, p. 134. "Quid est autem repropitiare delictum, nisi, cum adsumpseris peccatorem [ad poenitentiam], admonendo, hortando, docendo, instruendo adduxeris eum ad poenitentiam, ab errore correxeris, a uitiis emendaueris et efficeris eum talem ut ei conuerso propitius fiat Deus, pro delicto repropitiare diceris?" Translation *ibid.*, p. 135, slightly modernized here.

is the sinner's conversion, not his punishment; hence, the priest's role as confessor was linked to his duties as a teacher and, in all probability, a preacher. All his pastoral skills converged in confession, and his guide in exercising them was the penitential.

The confessional encounter had more than judicial dimensions for the penitent as well as for the priest, but these too remain hidden if we consider only the "civilizing" or "socializing" influence of the penitentials on early medieval society. The penitentials inveigh against superficial or halfhearted conversion, the merely external submission to the confessor's directives. They demand a new inward disposition from the penitent: a submission of his will was to precede the submission of his body to penitential deeds.[19] To see this we need only to imagine how the penitent might have responded to the priest who received him using Cummean's penitential as his guide. For the penitent the confessional encounter must have been an awesome experience, no matter how warmly or kindly the priest welcomed him. Prodded and questioned by the confessor, the penitent was forced to overcome his reluctance to confess, to realize that his soul was in jeopardy, and to accept penance as the price of regaining his Saviour's favor. In all probability he had already been warned about the perils of sin on other occasions. But delivered by the priest specifically to the penitent in the privacy of confession, that message must have had greater impact. And it was more than a warning. The "teaching and instruction" mentioned by Cummean refers to the examination of faith which formed part of the penitent's confession. The priest asked the penitent about his beliefs as if he were a catechumen about to enter the church. To be sure that the penitent was prepared, it was necessary to catechize him—in short, to treat him as a pupil.

Christianity itself was a lesson which the penitent had to learn before he could be forgiven; confession and penance were opportunities to teach him and to test his fidelity to Christian values. In converting sinners and holding them to the faith, the church necessarily measured penitents against a moral standard at some points in

19. For the view that a transition from "vindictive to remedial penance" begins with the Irish, see Ludwig Bieler, "The Irish Penitentials: Their Religious and Social Background," pp. 333–336.

conflict with the accepted practices of pre-Christian society. Some of these conflicts are well known—for example, prohibitions against eating certain foods, against sexual intercourse during seasons of fasting, and against magic and divination. Other conflicts are less obvious. For example, the church's esteem for human life created protection for certain individuals whose rights were generally disregarded in secular law codes—women, children, and the poor in particular.[20] The church used a sinner's social standing, not his rights, to determine his degree of guilt; hence, a slave was less culpable than a free man, and a boy less culpable than a young man.[21] Certain social and sexual stereotypes were perpetuated by the church because they suited the church's own prejudices; as suspected instigators of the black arts and particularly heinous sexual abuses, women were at a disadvantage in both secular and church law.[22] But in its largest sense, the effect of penitential practice on a society in the process of conversion was to refine it. To the existing lists of crimes the church added lists of sins, with the result that old actions acquired new values and public morality became more exacting. Especially in the confessional encounter, the church brought believers to terms with the consequences—we might say with the meaning—of their thoughts, words, and deeds.

The heightened spiritual awareness achieved in confession was sustained by means of prayer, preaching, and poetry. These literary forms, discursive and devotional, were better able than the penitentials to supply themes and images to reinforce the sinner's conver-

20. This is Oakley's view; see *Penitential Discipline*, pp. 195–196. See also chapter three below.

21. In the chapter on homicide quoted above, n. 14 (from the penitential attributed to Bede), a slave who slew at his master's command was to do penance for forty days, but a free man who did so was to do penance for a year or more (see Wasserschleben, *Bussordnungen*, p. 225; Bede 4. 6–7). Cummean's penitential required a thief to do penance for one year unless he was a boy, in which case the penance was thirty or forty days; for Cummean 3. 1–2, see Bieler, *Irish Penitentials*, p. 116. (One became an adult at age twenty; see Cummean 10. 3, *ibid.*, p. 126.)

22. Jane Crawford, "Evidences for Witchcraft in Anglo-Saxon England," shows that women were not the exclusive targets of anti-witchcraft campaigns in England until the tenth century; but there is no doubt that in the penitentials women and not men were expected to have performed these evil acts.

sion. This was a renewable effort; after baptism the Christian's life was a cycle of temptation leading to sin and repentance leading to forgiveness and a fresh beginning. Much medieval literature seeks to guide its audience along this path, but only certain texts do so with explicit references to confession and penance, and these materials—homilies and prayers and poems—join with the handbooks to constitute "penitential literature." They are "penitential" to the degree that they depend, for form or theme, on confession and acts of penance as described in the handbooks.

This definition of penitential literature departs from current use of the term in two ways. First, such literature includes more than poetry, the category of Anglo-Saxon writing most often labeled penitential. Second, these texts relate specifically to the practice rather than the theory of penance. Penitential literature has to date been vaguely defined chiefly because penance has not been distinguished from repentance. This is a crucial distinction. Repentance, a state of mind in which one experiences and then expresses sorrow for sin, is an attitude endemic to the Christian consciousness. It is found frequently in scripture and, hence, in Christian literature of all ages and places. Universal rather than specific, this tradition is of relatively little value to the historian.

Penance, on the other hand, is an idea embodied in an act and has, as an ecclesiastical tradition, a high degree of specificity. Its administration depends on a certain formula, provided in the Middle Ages by the handbook, which both defined and controlled penitential practice. The parts of the process, and the logic behind it, had to be explained both to the priest and to the penitent. Hence, there is a connection of central importance between the acts of confession and penance and the texts—the penitentials, prayers, homilies, and poems—written about them. Private penitential practice did indeed have a unique relationship to literature. It depended for its administration on a new kind of text, the penitential, and the process delineated by the penitential provided both theme and form for other kinds of literature. The theme itself, that sorrow for sin could lead to confession and forgiveness, had long been familiar in western Christianity. But the expression of that theme in the ritual of private penance was new, and those texts which participated in that ritual, by means of exhortation to it or meditation on it, have as their subject and informing principle this same new process. Although initially concerned with his external deeds, private confession and penance defined a spiritual conflict within the sinner, articulated that conflict with the priest's assistance, and resolved it with the penitent's consent to perform penitential acts. This was a process ripe for literary exploration, for it was both formally explicit and limited, and it articulated anxieties which had long preoccupied Christian thought. Nowhere did the Anglo-Saxons realize the full import of confession as a model for literary imitation or a subject for imaginative exploration; that was left for Chaucer and Langland. In Anglo-Saxon literature the process of confession and penance is mirrored and explicated rather than investigated. There were many reasons for these limitations; at the moment I wish to establish only that they existed and that they gave Anglo-Saxon penitential literature its character.

The chief value of this literature is its testimony to confession and penance, particularly as they were presented to the lay population. Because private penance was a turning point in early medieval spirituality, texts which participate in it constitute a turning point in pastoral literature. Collectively, these texts amplified the penitential's emphasis on the individual and his need to assume responsibility for his spiritual welfare. The penitential ensured that the sinner understood his guilt and accepted the penance which atoned for it; homilies, prayers, and poems reinforced this awareness from different points of view. Very few of these texts, alas, tell us what we would most like to know: what the penitent himself thought of his encounter with the priest. Anglo-Saxon penitential literature was written from the administrator's point of view, rarely from the sinner's: we are forced to recreate the experience from the judge's point of view, not that of the accused. This perspective inevitably restricts our efforts to appreciate the impact of private confession and penance on early medieval spirituality.

Our chief witness remains the handbook of penance. Because we must rely so heavily on its testimony, a few words of caution are in order. Some discussions of the penitential imply that the long list of sins was less a mirror of society's evils than a schematic inventory compiled by clerics eager to ferret out every possible abuse. From this implication a second doubt about the practical value of the penitentials follows. The penances in the handbooks seem prohibitive, impossible to perform. Could a layman have performed penance for one, two, or seven years—intervals common in the handbooks? Would not such prolonged fasting or abstinence from sexual intercourse have had dire consequences for the workaday medieval world? Both reservations about the practice of penance raise valid questions about the penitentials as sources for historical inquiry. Are they in fact as fanciful and as impractical as some would have us believe?

We should note first that early Irish and Anglo-Saxon penitentials are neither overly long nor overly complex. We do not know the circumstances in which the first penitential was written, but I speculate in the next chapter that it was some cleric's attempt to record typical penitential decisions for future reference—an attempt at standardization and uniformity. Certainly the first penitential was not a record of an actual confession; it cannot therefore be interpreted as the record of an "event," in the way one might interpret the proceedings of an ecclesiastical synod (which resemble the minutes for a committee meeting).[23] Instead, the penitential probably was invented to serve as a reference book and, like other reference books, would have been used selectively. The penitentials themselves point this out: the priest was to ask the penitent only about those sins which he was likely to have committed. An unmarried penitent would not have been asked about sexual abuses characteristic of the married; a woman would not have been asked about sins expected of men. No penitential of the early period attempts to list all possible sins, and no penitential from either the late or early medieval period would have been applied in its entirety to a single sinner. The claim that the handbooks' lists are overly schematic is best dealt with in terms of the Irish penitentials, texts frequently described in that way. The claim that they constituted a guide for a detailed interrogation into the sinner's moral life contradicts the instructions for the priest in several early penitentials, as we shall see, and contradicts even

23. A stimulating study of "language and event" as the elements of an early church synod uncovers "violent group clashes" at the meeting; see Samuel Laeuchli, *Power and Sexuality*, especially pp. 1–16. The approach has its dangers, but this provocative study has not won the audience it deserves.

more plainly the objectives of penitential practice as the early church defined them.

One cannot reply to the second reservation about the practicality of the penitentials so readily. We do not know what percentage of the medieval population confessed, or how often confessions were made. Annual confession was not formally required until 1215, but it is amply clear that frequent confession was urged early in the medieval period and that annual confession was a desired norm at that time, if not a realized objective.[24] The lists of sins in the penitentials tell us that only the most serious offenses were confessed; homicide, theft, and perjury are all dealt with in less detail than sexual impurity (by far the most common category in the handbooks), but all of these sins are "major" rather than "minor," and they constitute the bulk of almost every early penitential. All except the sexual offenses would have had immediate and significant social consequences, and presumably sins as grave as homicide were not rampant in most early medieval societies. Where an ecclesiastical penance coincided with punishment for the violation of secular law, it is not unreasonable to suppose that the assigned penance was performed. In fact, the law codes sometimes specified that ecclesiastical penance was part of the offender's punishment.[25] The medieval church does not seem to have expected that every man, woman, and child would confess every act which was somehow sinful; on the other hand, the church demanded that serious sins be confessed immediately. It is difficult to argue, for the early period at least, that confession and penance were universally required. If we scale down our concept of the church's intentions for the penitential system, we may find it easier to believe that the penances listed in the handbooks were in fact undertaken by those most in need of correction. Certainly penance and prayer were traditions most likely to be taken up by the elite of any medieval society, but on balance it seems unwarranted to claim that the audience of the handbooks was so small as to be unrepresentative of medieval morality.[26] Although they are confined to

24. See Tentler, *Sin and Confession*, pp. 20–22.

25. See chapter five, nn. 9 and 91–95.

26. This is the view of John Boswell, *Christianity, Social Tolerance, and Homosexuality*,

major sins, the penitentials embrace the full range of medieval society—lord and lady, free man and slave, nun and priest, adult and child. And as the following pages will show, the penitentials are not our sole witness to the impact of private penance; in addition to a great many manuscripts of the handbooks themselves, we have ecclesiastical and civil legislation requiring their use and much complementary literature addressing the need to confess to the priest. We should not assume that this evidence, however difficult it may be to evaluate, merely constitutes window dressing.

Nor should we exaggerate the difficulties of performing the penances which the handbooks assign. Presumably the sinner confessed very few sins; one who had committed numerous grave offenses was not likely to confess at all. Admittedly the tariff for a single grave sin could be severe. But we should note that although penances were to last a number of years, they could be performed in various ways. To fast for one year, for example, may have meant that the sinner fasted intensely only for the specific seasons of fasting (the three "forty-day periods": Advent, Lent, and the forty days after Pentecost); or he may have fasted daily by reducing his consumption of food or doing without certain foods (such as meat) or without wine or beer.[27] Long periods of fasting could be shortened by means of substitution: intensive periods of prayer, almsgiving, or the saying of masses could reduce a penance of several years to weeks or even days. These arrangements obviously favored men and women of means, and their long-range effect on penitential discipline was not for the best.[28] We may even see them as accommodations of the practical difficulties of doing penance. The most severe penances demanded exile or entrance into a monastery, but these were reserved for the extremely grave sins—such as fratricide or the murder of a cleric—which would have involved a harsh penalty from the secular judges as well.

---

pp. 180–182; the handbooks say much more about homosexuality than Boswell allows, and their testimony should not be so heavily discounted.

27. See McNeill and Gamer, *Handbooks*, pp. 31–32, and Vogel, *Les "Libri,"* pp. 37–39.

28. It eventually became possible for wealthy penitents to pay others to do penance for them—a practice devastating to the integrity of the penitential system. See Cyrille Vogel, "Composition légale et commutations dans le système de la pénitence tarifée," and *Les "Libri,"* pp. 43–54.

We cannot deny that penitential practice was difficult, although neither can we deny that penance was in general undertaken voluntarily and that tolerance of the hardship it created was far greater in earlier times.

To delimit the foregoing generalizations, one should admit here that penitentials lend themselves to generalization less well than many other texts. As Oakley asserted long ago, there is no "typical" penitential.[29] The handbooks used by the Irish, Anglo-Saxon, and Frankish churches varied in both form and content. No single list of sins and no one set of instructions for the confessor prevailed. Indeed, even handbooks known by a single name—the penitential attributed to Bede, for example—existed in several distinct versions. These texts were frequently altered by interpolation or excerpted with a notable lack of system. Scribes executing the alterations rarely indicated their own part in composing the text. As a result, some penitentials are falsely attributed to those who did not write them, and many more are attributed to no one at all.

To some extent these variations reflect the role of the handbook in each region which adopted it, but it is surprising how often a tenth-century continental manuscript will cite a seventh-century English archbishop (Theodore) or one much less well known from the eighth century (Egbert). This combination of flexibility and conservatism obscures the evidence—what, we must ask, is "English" and what "continental" about a given penitential—and makes the handbooks difficult to study. Older penitentials were constantly reworked, combined with other forms, especially collections of canon law, or expanded with new material. Through the maze created by this ongoing process of revision, certain features remain relatively unchanged, and it is well to keep them in mind. The handbook often begins with prefatory material addressed to the priest; sometimes the preface reminded the priest of his duties or explained how the collection of tariffs which followed came to be compiled. The value of these passages for the literary history of penance is obvious.

The tariffs themselves are important not only for the code of conduct which they enforce, but for the organizational pattern

29. Thomas P. Oakley, "Some Neglected Aspects of the History of Penance," p. 308.

which shapes the list. Some penitentials followed a list of the chief sins;[30] others listed only the most common major offenses, such as homicide, fornication, theft, perjury, and drunkenness; still others seem to follow no clear structural design. Not every penitential concludes with a final reminder to the priest, as does Cummean's, but many supply material to supplement the tariffs. Very often these concluding passages provide a system for shortening the periods of penance—the practice of commutation—specified by the tariffs.

The penitential was designed as a self-contained text to guide every phase of the private penitential system, from the reception of the penitent by the priest to practical adjustments which enabled the sinner to perform the penance assigned to him. By tracing the development of this text from its origins in the Irish monastery to early Anglo-Saxon and then Frankish administrative centers and finally back to England in the tenth century, we discover more than the many points which distinguish the penitential standards of these cultures. We also discover a coherent literary history which demonstrates the great faith the medieval church invested in a small booklet. No amount of prejudice or controversy can obscure the remarkable vitality of the handbook of penance. Once the contours of its genesis are made plain, we may wish to reassess its standing among the humble and often overlooked texts which constitute early medieval pastoral literature.

30. The list of sins in Cummean's penitential, for example, included gluttony, lust, avarice, anger, dejection, languor, vainglory, and pride; this is the list compiled by Cassian. See Bieler, *Irish Penitentials*, p. 246, and Morton W. Bloomfield, *The Seven Deadly Sins*, pp. 69–78.

Chapter Two

Early Ireland and the Origins
of Private Penance

MANY kinds of literature older than the penitentials contain lists of sins, and some include corresponding penances for them. Most of these texts are canonical decrees
and synodical letters; those important to the development of the
Irish handbooks of penance appear to have originated in Wales and
to approximate both the form and the purpose of the penitentials
more closely than canonical collections do. The *Preface of Gildas on
Penance* and *Excerpts from a Book of David* are two "proto-penitential"
texts of the early Welsh church which may be seen as the first Celtic
penitential literature and, very probably, as the beginning of the literature of private penance in Ireland.[1] Neither text, however, is a penitential. Both are collections of penitential decisions rather than
guides for the priest's use in hearing private confession. It was
against the background created by canons, synodical decrees, and
other penitential *excerpta* that the Irish handbooks took shape. The
appearance of the first Irish penitential was the advent of a new literary form, fostered within the monastery but intended for the administration of penance in the pastoral rather than the cloistered context.
The Irish penitentials exhibit many traces of the monastic milieu in
which they were invented, and some of these signs persist in Anglo-
Saxon and Frankish handbooks developed from Irish models. We
cannot call all penitentials "Irish" merely because the Irish invented

1. Ed. Ludwig Bieler, *The Irish Penitentials*, pp. 60–65 and 70–73. For background see
James F. Kenney, *The Sources for the Early History of Ireland*, *1: Ecclesiastical*,
pp. 235–250.

them; relations between native Irish churches and the Irish missions to the continent produced so much mutual influence that only the very early penitentials are Irish in a strict sense. Nonetheless, had it not been for the missionary zeal of the Irish monks, western Christianity would have had neither the penitential nor the form of penitential practice which eventually became its principal method of ecclesiastical discipline.

It is difficult to speak of the "originality" of handbooks of penance because one is naturally reluctant to link originality to ecclesiastical literature whose integrity depends fundamentally on its debt to tradition. But we cannot speak of "penitentials" in non-Irish early medieval cultures even if we define that term broadly to include texts which listed sins and measured penances for them.[2] We must, therefore, admit that the Irish penitentials are original, even though the handbooks themselves attempt to conceal their originality behind claims to precedent in earlier literature, especially the Bible. Though not entirely false, these claims are certainly misleading. The authors of early Irish legislative texts, both canonical collections and penitentials, believed that they had received their materials from the venerable early fathers, in particular Augustine and Isidore. Under these and other names, the Irish transmitted many ideas having little to do with patristic precedent.[3] The penitentials illustrate this phenomenon perfectly in claiming to descend from sacred scripture, a source to which their connection was tenuous at best.

Such a claim is made in the prologue to Cummean's penitential, which lists the twelve remissions of sin and supports each with a biblical quotation:

> As we are about to tell of the remedies of wounds according to the ruling of the fathers before us, let us first, my most faithful brother, indicate in a concise manner the medicines of

2. Among the important canons listing sins are those of St. Basil (d. 379), St. Gregory of Nyssa (d. 395), St. Chrysostom (d. 407), and others; they are surveyed by Oscar D. Watkins, *A History of Penance*, 1:293–364.

3. Pseudo-anonymous traditions are studied by Paul Grosjean, "Sur quelques exégètes irlandais du VIIe siècle," *Sacris Erudiri* 7 (1955):67–98. Patristic libraries available in early Ireland would have been "scrappy and incomplete," according to Kathleen Hughes, *Early Christian Ireland: Introduction to the Sources*; see pp. 198–202.

Holy Scripture. The first remission then is that by which we are baptized in water, according to this (passage): *Unless a man be born again of water and of the Holy Spirit, he cannot see the Kingdom of God.* . . . The fifth is the confession of crimes, as the Psalmist testifies: *I said, I will confess against myself my injustice to the Lord, and thou hast forgiven the iniquity of my sin.*

The passage concludes with another assertion of scriptural authority:

Therefore, since these things are cited on the authority of the Canon, it is fit that you should search out, also, the decrees of the fathers who were chosen by the mouth of the Lord, according to this passage: *Ask thy father and he will declare unto thee, thy elders and they will tell thee*; moreover *Let the matter be referred to them.*[4]

This passage distinguishes "the authority of the Canon"—that is, scripture—from "the decrees of the fathers." Although the Bible is cited many times in the "twelve remissions," they derive from patristic sources. Who are "the fathers before us," those "chosen by the mouth of the Lord" and "thy elders"? They were not Augustine, Gregory, or Isidore, but the Greek exegete Origen and John Cassian, abbot of St. Victor of Marseilles.[5] The language of fatherhood in Cummean's prologue also refers to Irishmen before him who compiled penitentials—Finnian and Columbanus—and to Gildas, David, and other shadowy figures of early Celtic Christianity. Therefore, Cummean's penitential derives from a long and venerable tradition, but little in that tradition manifests the debt to scripture

4. Text and translation in Bieler, *Irish Penitentials*, pp. 108–111, cc. 1–6, 14: "De remediis uulnerum secundum priorum patrum diffinitiones dicturi sacri tibi eloqui, mi fidelissime frater, antea medicamina conpendi ratione intimemus. Prima itaque est remisio qua baptizamur in aqua secundum illud: *Nisi quis renatus fuerit ex aqua et Spiritu Sancto, non potest uidere regnum Dei.* . . . Quinta criminum confessio psalmista testante: *Dixi 'confitebor aduersum me iniustitiam meam Domino' et tu remisisti impietatem peccati mei.* . . . His ergo de canonis auctoritate prolatis patrum etiam statuta Domini ore subrogatorum inuestigare te conuenit secundum illud: *Interroga patrem tuum et adnuntiauit tibi, seniores tuos et dicent tibi*; item: *causa deferatur ad eos.*" (I have modified the translation slightly, using, e.g., "should" for "shouldst.")

5. For the works of Origen and Cassian used in Cummean's prologue, see p. 108, *ibid.*

which the prologue so strongly implies. The fathers most important to Cummean were most likely his elders in the Irish monastic tradition, from whom, in the best brotherly fashion, he took counsel.

If Cummean had sought scriptural support for the confession of sins and the priest's power to forgive them, he could have turned to those passages about binding and loosing or to episodes in which Christ forgave sinners—for example, the woman taken in adultery— or performed acts later understood to have prefigured confession, such as the raising of Lazarus.[6] But these exegetical traditions had little impact on the Irish penitentials because the handbooks were designed to answer the question how, not why: the theory of forgiveness is implicit in them, while the practice is explained in detail. Even the "twelve remissions" presented as the scriptural justification for the penitential are an index to methods of forgiveness, rather than a rationale for it.

The originality of the Irish system, and of the literature which accompanied it, has been the subject of extended controversy among those who seek to tie it closely to continental precedents, including public penance, and those who believed that it derives from pre-Christian, "Celtic" customs. This controversy is worth a summary because its poles, taken together—but only together—fully describe the backgrounds to Irish habits of penance.

Virtually alone in his position, John T. McNeill argued that Irish monks derived their penitential system from an "Indo-European" or so-called Celtic disciplinary tradition which existed in Ireland long before Christianity appeared there. The chief witness to this pre-Christian system was an Indian law code, the *Laws of Manu*, which McNeill saw as both spiritual and secular in nature.[7] This code required a spiritual director to assign wrongdoers "penances proportionate to their sins," including fasts, journeys into exile, and the recitation of lengthy religious verses. The code also provided a

6. The scriptual passages are discussed by Watkins, *A History*, 1:3–26; commentaries on these texts by Jerome, Ambrose, and Augustine are surveyed on pp. 365–465.

7. John T. McNeill, *The Celtic Penitentials and Their Influence on Continental Christianity*, more easily available as a series of articles entitled "The Celtic Penitentials" and published in *Revue Celtique* (references here are to the articles). His arguments are summarized in *Medieval Handbooks of Penance* (coauthored with Helena M. Gamer), pp. 25–44.

method for shortening long periods of penance which McNeill interpreted as a predecessor to the system of commutations found in the
penitentials.[8]

Reasoning by methods which now seem highly dubious,
McNeill believed that this penitential system survived in the Irish law
tracts, which share much common ground with the "Indo-European" legal tradition to which the *Laws of Manu* belong. What he
found in the Irish evidence corresponded very closely to the penitential system represented in the handbooks. This seemed to prove the
theory that "source materials analogous to the content of the penitentials" existed in Indo-European cultures, or the "Celtic" world;
that the Indo-European tradition of law in these cultures, Ireland
included, remained outside the influence of Roman law; and that
these ancient codes "made for the rise of the [Christian] penitential
literature and gave to it some of its prominent features."[9] What
McNeill was really looking at in the Irish laws were references to the
Christian penitential system inserted into the codes when they were
committed to writing; the laws were recorded after Ireland was converted and were probably written down by monks no earlier than the
seventh century. McNeill allowed for some monastic interference
when he conjectured that the Irish laws did not correspond more
closely to the *Laws of Manu* because the monks suppressed those
customs which did not conform to the Christian system. Nonetheless, his argument was circular: the only sources which supported the
pre-Christian penitential system he hypothesized for early Ireland
were late and thoroughly Christian.

One might have expected that a thesis so sweeping as McNeill's
would have generated a long and productive controversy, but such
was not the case—not because McNeill's argument did not require
refutation, but because scholarship on Irish law has proceeded
slowly, with others fearing to enter textual territory whose bound-
aries have only recently been made clear.[10] McNeill's belief that private confession was somehow uniquely Celtic was soon contra-

8. McNeill, "Celtic Penitentials," 40:89–93.

9. *Ibid.*, pp. 91–92.

10. There is a concise introduction to Irish law in the prefatory matter of *Corpus Iuris
Hibernici*, ed. D. A. Binchy. For additional background see Binchy, "The Linguistic
and Historical Value of the Irish Law Tracts."

dicted,[11] and the analogy he constructed between the system of commutations in the penitentials and the adjustment of penalties in the law codes was eventually demolished.[12] But there was only one challenge to McNeill's most important claim, which was that private confession and penance were more Celtic, and hence more Irish, than Christian.

This came from Thomas P. Oakley, who claimed that the Irish penitential system contained little not found in the homilies of Caesarius, a bishop of Arles in southern France, who died in 542. Suggesting that "many details of early Irish penitential discipline were derived from precedents in continental penance," Oakley showed that much in the penitentials appeared in the writings of Caesarius or John Cassian, both of whom lived and worked in and around a large monastery on the island of Lérins.[13] Oakley showed that Caesarius recommended private penance for certain sins, allowed penance to be repeated in certain circumstances, and classified sins according to structures also found in the handbooks. Since these customs vary from the procedures of public penance, Oakley concluded that while private confession and penance were indeed new, they were invented on the continent rather than in Ireland, and that they had little if anything to do with the pre-Christian world:

> Indeed, the long, elaborate lists of degrees of sins of thought and of action, and of the means for their remission, worked out by Caesarius of Arles, exerted so definite and strong an influence upon the Irish penitentials that one might almost conclude that the detailed elaboration of "tariffs" of penances by the Irish was largely developed from the principles and lists supplied by that prelate.[14]

11. See R. Pettazzoni, "Confession of Sins in the Classics."

12. See Binchy, "The Old-Irish Table of Penitential Commutations," and his remarks on the vernacular Irish handbooks in Bieler, *Irish Penitentials*, p. 51.

13. Thomas P. Oakley, "The Origins of Irish Penitential Discipline," and "Celtic Penance: Its Sources, Affiliations, and Influence." The penitential teachings of Caesarius are surveyed by H. G. J. Beck, *The Pastoral Care of Souls in South-East France during the Sixth Century*, and more briefly by Watkins, *A History*, 2:550–562.

14. Oakley, "Origins," p. 331.

Oakley's argument subtly shifted its ground before reaching this conclusion: it began by establishing precedents for certain parts of Irish penitential practice in the tradition of penance known to Caesarius, and ended by "almost" concluding that these precedents included the handbook of tariffs itself. The penitentials clearly derive material such as the "twelve remissions" from continental sources, including the homilies of Caesarius, the exegesis of Origen, and the *Institutes* and *Conferences* of Cassian. But none of these texts established a formal precedent to the handbook: a homily, scriptural commentary, or pastoral letter may discuss the forgiveness of sins and describe the process through which sins are to be punished and pardoned, but these forms were not intended to be used during confession. Immensely influential though his homilies were throughout the early Middle Ages, Caesarius was not a major influence on the penitentials, much less the inspiration behind them. Like Cassian's, his influence on the Irish penitentials is seen in their general principles rather than in their form.[15]

If McNeill overestimated the originality of private penance in native Irish culture, Oakley, who seemed to equate invention in such matters with heresy, erred in the opposite direction. However faulty, McNeill's argument has more to teach about the origins of Irish penitential discipline than Oakley's, for it focuses our attention on the missionary character of the early Irish church and so looks ahead to the contact between Irish monks and the laity, rather than back to the precedents for Irish monasticism itself. The penitential was originally Irish, but not in the way McNeill thought. It was an original solution to a problem confronting all missionary churches—the problem of extending Christian ideals to lay society without compromising their purity and, at the same time, without creating standards of conduct so high as to be all but impossible to maintain.

The ideals of Irish monasticism were derived from those of Egyptian monks, who retreated to the deserts and to a life of strict

15. Caesarius's catalogues of sins were incorporated into prayers and into one eighth-century penitential, probably of English origin; on the prayers see F. Hautkappe, *Über die altdeutschen Beichten und ihre Beziehungen zu Cäsarius von Arles*. A list of sins based on Caesarius appears in the penitential attributed to Egbert, analyzed in detail in the following chapter.

asceticism away from the urban world. The community formed by a group of Egyptian monks was loosely organized, but it involved confession to a senior brother as one of its disciplinary procedures. The custom of confession was observed and described by John Cassian when he visited Egypt, and it became part of the monastic life at Lérins. The *Institutes* and *Conferences* of Cassian, cited in the Irish penitentials, were one link between the Egyptian and Irish monastic traditions. How eastern monasticism became so strong an influence on early Ireland is not well understood, but two important channels of contact have been identified. One is commercial and monastic traffic between Ireland and the region of the Loire, where St. Martin of Tours had propagated an eremitical monasticism at the end of the fourth century.[16] The other channel of eastern ideas was through Iberia; Spain and the eastern Mediterranean region were in close contact, and evidence of Spanish influence on early Irish prayers suggests that Spain may have served as the route by which eastern monastic teachings reached Ireland.[17]

In the sixth century, the Irish church had established a strong presence on the continent which no doubt promoted the influence of continental traditions in Ireland. But such contact was naturally two-sided, and in order to understand the importance which it held for Irish penitential practice, it is necessary to focus on the missions of Irishmen abroad. Chief among them was Columbanus, whose two rules for monks are our fullest witness to early Irish monastic traditions. Columbanus died in 615 after a long career as a teacher in Ireland and as a zealous and often controversial exponent of Irish

16. Discussed by Henry Mayr-Harting, *The Coming of Christianity to England*, pp. 79–86, and, more fully, by Pierre Riché, *Education and Culture in the Barbarian West*, trans. John J. Contreni, pp. 324–336.

17. This view is taken by J. N. Hillgarth, "The East, Visigothic Spain and the Irish," and "Visigothic Spain and Early Christian Ireland," but Riché says only that "we have to suppose" contacts between Ireland and Spain at this time (*Education and Culture*, p. 320), and Mayr-Harting's reservations are worth quoting in full: "one may search the text and voluminous notes of the learned articles of Professor J. N. Hillgarth, who seeks to establish such links, without finding a single piece of evidence of travel or written correspondence or direct communication of any kind between Spain and Ireland in the seventh century" (*The Coming*, p. 127).

monasticism in France and northern Italy.[18] Both rules of Columbanus are known only in continental manuscripts, as are most of the
early Irish penitentials. But this offers no serious obstacle to inter-
preting these texts as evidence of monastic observance in Ireland,
especially in the case of Columbanus, whose fidelity to Irish customs
and whose defense of their integrity was nothing if not conten-
tious.[19] Both of Columbanus's texts, the *Monastic Rule*, which is a
theoretical statement, and the more detailed and practical *Communal
Rule*, belong to the sixth century, the period in which the first Irish
penitentials—among them that written by Columbanus—were taking shape.

These rules, unlike a penitential, are not lists of what is forbid-
den but guides to every aspect of the monk's daily existence. In early
Ireland nothing about that life could be described as easy or comfort-
able. Even prayer was rigorous: in Columbanus's monastery, the entire psalter would be recited in two days; later, the Benedictine *Rule*
allowed one week for the completion of this prayer cycle.[20] Modera-
tion was not considered a virtue, and watchfulness over the monk's
behavior was extreme. A monk who forgot to bless his spoon before
eating received six blows because "he who omits small things gradually declines." Standards were high because the goal of the monk's
life was extraordinary: one chapter of the *Monastic Rule* is entitled
"Of the Monk's Perfection."[21]

The monk pursued perfection through two closely related ave-
nues of discipline: taking counsel, which meant subjection of his will
to his superior's, and accepting correction for his infractions of the

18. For background on Columbanus and his mission, see G. S. M. Walker, ed. and
trans., *Sancti Columbani Opera*, pp. ix–xxxiv.

19. The letters of Columbanus are sometimes marvels of impudence. Writing to Gregory the Great, he defended Irish paschal customs against those known in Gaul (and
Rome), which had been authorized by Pope Leo; quoting scripture (Eccles. 9:4),
Columbanus said that in this dispute "a living dog is better than a dead Lion" (*ibid.*,
pp. 5–7, c. IV). What is striking is the Irishman's unshaken confidence in the liturgical
tradition he knew best and his refusal to see Roman ways as superior to Ireland's own.

20. Lowrie J. Daly, *Benedictine Monasticism: Its Formation and Development through the
Twelfth Century* (New York, 1965), p. 60.

21. Text in Walker, *Opera*, pp. 147 and 140–143.

monastery's behavioral code. Both forms of mortification required him to submit to the authority of his monastic father; Columbanus's *Monastic Rule* cites the same passage of Deuteronomy quoted later by Cummean: "Ask thy father and he will declare unto thee, thy elders and they will tell thee." The practice of taking counsel was fundamental to the monk's existence. "The chief part of the monks' rule is mortification," wrote Columbanus, "since indeed they are enjoined in Scripture, Do nothing without counsel. Thus if nothing is to be done without counsel, everything must be asked for by counsel." This chapter, "Of Mortification," continues:

> But though this training seem hard to the hard-hearted, namely that a man should always hang upon the lips of another, yet by those who are fixed in their fear of God it will be found pleasant and safe, if it is kept wholly and not in part, since nothing is pleasanter than safety of conscience and nothing safer than exoneration of the soul, which none can provide for himself by his own efforts, since it properly belongs to the judgement of others.

By learning to obey "without murmuring and hesitation," monks would curb their "proud independence" and acquire "lowliness of heart." Columbanus called such mortification the "bliss of martyrdom," for which the monks' model was Christ submitting in the Garden of Gethsemane: "Not as I will but as thou wilt." [22]

The monks observed another form of mortification identified as "martyrdom" when they were corrected after confessing their violations of specific rules of conduct. For example, a monk who spilled considerable amounts of food or drink while cooking was "corrected" before the assembled community in church. One who spilled

22. Text and translation *ibid.*, pp. 138–141, c. IX: "Maxima pars regulae monachorum mortificatio est, quibus nimirum per scripturam praecipitur, *Sine consilio nihil facias.* Ergo si nihil sine consilio faciendum, totum per consilium est interrogandum. . . . Sed licet duris dura videatur haec disciplina, ut scilicet homo semper de ore pendeat alterius, certis tamen deum timentibus dulcis ac secura invenietur, si ex integro et non ex parte conservetur, quia nihil dulcius est conscientiae securitate et nihil securius est animae impunitate, quam nullus sibi ipsi per se potest tradere, quia proprie aliorum est examinis." For the passage in Cummean's penitential, see Bieler, *Irish Penitentials*, p. III, c. 14.

only a small amount of food at the table confessed and was "corrected" in his place. Monks were sometimes assigned penances by their superiors; one who refused to submit to his superior's judgment, preferring to go to the father of the community or to other brothers not in immediate charge of him, "must be punished forty days in penance (on bread and water) unless he himself says (lying prostrate before the brethren) I am sorry for what I said."[23] A late seventh-century homily in Old Irish interprets the acceptance of such penance as another form of martyrdom; the second of the three kinds of martyrdom defined is "green martyrdom," known to one who "by means of [fasting and labor] . . . separates from his desires, or suffers toil in penance and repentance."[24] The *Communal Rule* shows that confession was not reserved for before meals or before retiring; the monks confessed whenever it was "opportune," or when a sin had been committed, and not at a fixed time.[25] The performance of the penance was the monk's own responsibility, a burden taken up after absolution had been received. Although neither the confession nor the penance was strictly private, this form of discipline was in fact private penance; the sinner was not expelled from the community or reconciled in a formal ceremony.

The practice of confession and penance described in the *Communal Rule* offers a model for the system of penance regulated by the handbooks and attested by other early Irish sources. There are in fact two levels of mortification seen in the monastic texts, one devotional, the other disciplinary. The taking of counsel was an exercise in humility independent of the correction of wrongdoing; it was the first form of what is often called "devotional confession," which expressed the sinner's piety by seeking forgiveness for the general

---

23. Walker, *Opera*, p. 147, c. II; and p. 152, c. VIII: "Qui ad praepositum audet dicere, Non tu iudicabis causam meam, sed noster senior aut ceteri fratres, sive, Ad patrem monasterii ibimus omnes, XL diebus castigari oportet in paenitentia, [in pane et aqua] nisi ipse dicat [prostratus coram fratribus] Paenitet me quod dixi."

24. Ed. and trans. Whitley Stokes and John Strachan, *Thesaurus Palaeohibernicus*, 2:247. On the date see Patrick O'Neill, "The Background to the *Cambrai Homily*." The forms of martyrdom named in the homily are also named in *The Old-Irish Penitential*, 3. 1 (in Bieler, *Irish Penitentials*; see pp. 265–266).

25. "Whenever it is opportune" to confess ("quandocumque fuerit facile dare"); Walker, *Opera*, pp. 146–147, c. I.

rather than particular failings of his moral being. The correction of
the monks' faults followed by the assigning of acts of penance proportionate to them was designed to ensure their moral well-being by
more specific means. Those actions which showed that the sinner
had failed to carry his cross, and hence had disobeyed the Father,
were both discouraged and atoned for; when he undertook penance,
the monk once more began to follow Christ in the difficult way to
perfection.

Such was the purpose of confession and penance within the
monastery. The twofold purpose of that discipline—counsel and correction—evolved into a penitential system intended for the laity and
adjusted to accommodate a weaker will to perfection. Indicating a
light penance for a layman who has intended to strike or kill his
neighbor, Finnian's penitential notes, "Since he is a man of this
world, his guilt is lighter in this world and his reward less in the
world to come." [26] In addressing a French synod, Columbanus set the
monks' standards higher than those expected even of bishops, whom
Jerome bade to imitate the apostles: monks Jerome had taught "to
follow the fathers who were perfect." [27] The monks seem consciously
to have modified their discipline before attempting to transfer it to
the lay population. To suppose that "by analogy with the monastic
rule" they "tried to make the law a 'rule of life' for Christians in the
world" is to overlook this modification and to interpret the rule itself
too narrowly as a restrictive influence. [28] Like monastic rules, the penitentials did more than punish sin: they also provided a system for
the giving of counsel.

We can see this intent expressed in the confessor's task as the
handbooks describe it. Three roles predominate: the confessor is a
physician, a judge, and a "fellow sufferer." All three emphasize his
duty to counsel. The physician could "treat with diverse kinds of
cures the wounds of souls, their sicknesses, [offenses], pains, ail-
ments and infirmities." No metaphor better establishes the "re-

26. Ed. and trans. Bieler, *Irish Penitentials*, pp. 76–77, c. 7: "quia homo seculi huius
est, culpa leuior in hoc mundo et premium minus in futuro."

27. Walker, *Opera*, pp. 20–21, c. VIII: "docuit sequi patres perfectos."

28. These remarks come from a stimulating discussion of the Irish penitentials by
Arthur Mirgeler, *Mutations of Western Christianity*, trans. Edward Quinn, pp. 69–71.

medial" nature of Irish penitential discipline, which sought "to re-store what is weak to a complete state of health."[29] In applying the remedies of penance to the wounds of sin, the priest was exhorted to exercise prudence, often by means of a second metaphor comparing him to a judge. By inquiring into the circumstances of each sin, the judge was able not only to determine the extent of the penitent's culpability, but also to view his offense with compassion. Cummean's epilogue states:

> this is to be carefully observed in all penance: the length of time anyone remains in his faults; what learning he has re-ceived; by what passion he is assailed; how great is his strength; with what intensity of weeping he is afflicted; and with what oppression he has been driven to sin.[30]

It was the priest's duty to bring the penitent's offenses to light, just as brothers in the monastery revealed each other's wrongdoing. Unlike the detractor, the monk—and the priest—called attention to an-other's sins so that they would be confessed and forgiven. If through his fault the sinner did not confess completely, the priest bore the guilt of the hidden sins and of his own sin in allowing another's to go unconfessed.[31]

The process of discriminating judgment brought the priest into close contact with the penitent and created an intimacy more explicit than that between judge and judged. The priest is also known as a "soul-friend" and a "fellow sufferer." These terms do not appear in the Irish penitentials but are used in other texts to describe the con-fessor's office, often as it was exercised by a saint. According to *The*

29. Text and translation in Bieler, *Irish Penitentials*, pp. 98–99: "ad integrum salutis statum debilia reuocare" (from the so-called B-prologue to the penitential of Colum-banus). The medical metaphor is discussed by John T. McNeill, "Medicine for Sin as Prescribed in the Penitentials."

30. Text and translation in Bieler, *Irish Penitentials*, pp. 132–133, c. 1: "in hoc omni paenitentia solerter intuendum est, quanto quis tempore in delictis remaneat, qua eruditione inbutus, qua inpugnatur passione, qualis existat fortitudine, qua uidetur adfligi lacrimabilitate, quali compulsus est grauatione peccare."

31. The *Monastic Rule* of Columbanus says that "the peril of the judge is greater than that of the accused" ("periculum *iudicantis* quam eius qui *iudicatur*"), a paraphrase of Matt. 7:1; text and translation in Walker, *Opera*, pp. 138–139, c. IX.

Martyrology of Oengus, a sinner without a soul-friend is like a body without a head.[32] According to a rule for reformed monks (probably contemporary with *The Old-Irish Penitential*), a penitent may visit a priest other than his usual confessor if "there happens to be a soul-friend whom he considers more learned in the Rules, in the way of the Scripture, and in the rules of the saints."[33] The soul-friend was not only a corrector, but also a counselor or spiritual adviser and a teacher. The Irish term for this office, *anmcharae*, is a native rather than a Latin or latinized expression, and it indicates an office older than that which it designates in the penitential system. It refers to one "under spiritual guidance" in *The Monastery of Tallaght*, but in the pre-Christian world it probably referred to the druid's role as both counselor and intercessor. The druid was succeeded in these offices by the saint and not by the confessor (the saints sometimes arbitrated public disputes, whereas confessors did not).[34] The term "soul-friend," while absent from the penitentials, is found in *The Old-Irish Table of Commutations*, where it clearly designates the confessor.[35] The authors of the penitentials may have avoided the term because it indicated judicial powers more extensive than the confessor's, but it is more likely that the omission occurred because the penitentials seem to have been confined, even at their most technical, to a purely Latin vocabulary.[36]

Even though the monks recognized the difference between their own forms of discipline and those which could reasonably be expected of lay people, the task of establishing church law outside the monastery cannot have been an easy one. We might expect the monks to have tried to ease the process by making the most of sim-

---

32. Quoted by Walker, *ibid.*, p. 139, n. 1.

33. William Reeves, "On the Celi-de, Commonly Called Culdees," *Transactions of the Royal Irish Academy* 24 (1873): 208.

34. On the jurisprudential function of the druid, see Eoin Mac Neill, *Early Irish Laws and Institutions*, pp. 68–75. See n. 42 below.

35. Ed. and trans. D. A. Binchy, "The Old-Irish Table of Penitential Commutations"; a translation also appears in Bieler, *Irish Penitentials*: see p. 278 for the "soul-friend," 6. 3.

36. Bieler finds few Celtic loan words in the penitentials' vocabulary; see *Irish Penitentials*, pp. 37–38.

ilarities between their disciplinary traditions and those native customs which seemed analogous to them. It would therefore have been in the monks' interest to emphasize the link between the confessor and the soul-friend in the penitentials, rather than to ignore it. In some areas the Christian literature of early Ireland exploits analogies between pagan and Christian traditions; the most famous examples are the lives of the saints, which show the holy men surpassing their pagan competition in various challenges, some of them—cursing contests, for instance—not very Christian.[37] On the other hand, the monks saw the necessity of preserving the integrity of their system, and it is doubtful that they ever made major concessions to the pagan religion of early Ireland. The analogy between the saint and the druid is well known, but how many other such analogies are there? As we study the Irish penitentials in the context of their native environment, few persuasive analogies emerge. We should remember the words of Columbanus, who asked that the Irish be allowed to maintain their own liturgical observances in France: the Council of Constantinople, Columbanus wrote, "decreed that churches of God planted in pagan nations should live by their own laws, as they had been instructed by their fathers."[38] This principle allowed for diversity within unity and should keep us from expecting too great a conformity between early Irish Christianity and the pagan world in which it emerged.

The growth of monasticism in Ireland was facilitated by the decentralized nature of government and the rural character of Irish society. During the establishment of Christianity in Ireland, which began in the fifth century, the centralized plan of the early Roman church, based on the authority of bishops, slowly gave way to a church of monastic and missionary character. In Irish monasteries, each of which had a specific character, an abbot was often also a

37. There are a good many instances cited by Charles Plummer, *Vitae Sanctorum Hiberniae*, 1:clxxiii–clxxiv; see pp. clxvii–xxxviii for a general discussion of druidical functions taken over by saints. (Plummer's views may be old-fashioned, but his references to the lives are thorough.) For a recent discussion of cursing in Irish literature, see Patrick O'Neill, "A Middle Irish Poem on the Maledictory Psalms."

38. Text and translation in Walker, *Opera*, pp. 24–25, c. III: "ecclesias Dei in barbaris gentibus constitutas suis vivere legibus, sicut edoctas a patribus, iudicantes." I am indebted to Francis John Byrne for the quotation.

bishop, and a bishop was sometimes subordinate to an abbot. Monasteries were not organized under central episcopal authority but existed in separate confederations with close ties to the secular world. Native society was organized into a "plethora of petty kingdoms" without a central administrative authority governing them all; monasticism "found a peculiarly congenial soil in the new Celtic environment."[39] If, as many believe, monasticism came into existence as an escape from urban society, then non-urban Ireland was a natural home for it. The monastery formed the center of the community. Lay people worked in the monastic fields and looked to the monastery for guidance. For the layman, this relationship to the church was probably not much different from his traditional subordination to the tribal prince. The church and the nobility were closely allied. Powerful abbots were frequently descended from royal households and ruled large federations of several monasteries. Aristocratic families sometimes established large monasteries on their lands, placing these houses in their debt. In this way political traditions influenced the introduction of the laity to monastic life; the result was that loyalty to a particular monastery was often an expression of loyalty to one's tribe.[40]

Laymen who lived near the monastery were known as *manaig*.[41] The monks also administered penance to those who journeyed from great distances, sometimes to accept penance from a monk famous

39. According to Kathleen Hughes, a bishopric was "limited to a narrow territorial area," whereas the monastic *paruchia* might continue to grow. As the *paruchia* gained pre-eminence over the bishopric, however, bishops did continue to function outside the monastery: see *The Church in Early Irish Society*, pp. 79–90. Comments about the "petty kingdoms" are taken from D. A. Binchy's review of Hughes's study in *Studia Hibernica* 7 (1967):219.

40. My overview is derived from Hughes, *The Church*, pp. 57–64; her reconstruction of monastic life is drawn largely from Adomnan's *Life of Columcille* (written between 688 and 692) and references to the laity in the penitentials. Monasteries were naturally bound to royal families which endowed—and evidently peopled—them; as Hughes notes, "the donors of the land retained a powerful interest in the property" (p. 77). See n. 44 below.

41. The *manaig*, "monastic clients," were recognized by the secular laws as "men who held the land and stock of the abbot," bound by contract to the monastery; *ibid.*, pp. 136–137.

for his wisdom and piety. Both categories of penitent seem to have sought spiritual guidance from the monks as well as the opportunity to confess specific wrongdoing. According to *The Monastery of Tallaght*, probably from the ninth century, if a layman "accepts spiritual direction, he is to keep himself from his wife" on Wednesday, Friday, Saturday, and—if possible—Sunday nights. This text, which claims to be a record of the regulations kept by a famous abbot, also mentions a layman and his wife living in lawful wedlock under the spiritual guidance of a particular monk.[42] These references suggest that lay people could attach themselves to monks who served as both confessors and counselors. Such a system established a degree of asceticism among the laity without interfering with their social and sexual functions. *The Monastery of Tallaght* provides explicit advice for the confessor in dealing with penitents. If they were suspected of concealing sins, they were to be dismissed without absolution, and if they exaggerated their offenses in the hope of receiving exceptionally great penances to prove their piety, their false confessions were to be rejected.[43]

How penance was administered to those who journeyed to the monastery from afar is seen in the lives of several early Irish saints. In the *Life of Columba*, pilgrims are seen arriving to confess to the saint. Columba sent one sinner to another monastery to do penance but accepted two brothers who came to Iona "to be pilgrims for a year."[44] In a much-quoted remark, Jonas of Bobbio refers to the faithful who "ran" to Columbanus to receive the "medicaments of penance."[45] Examples could be multiplied, but they do not always indicate whether these penitents continued to be thought of as laymen once they were in the monastery, or whether they became monks, as sometimes was the case. It was evidently true that "a monk

---

42. "The Monastery of Tallaght," ed. and trans. E. J. Gwynn and W. J. Purton, p. 132, c. 14, and p. 163, c. 86.

43. *Ibid.*, p. 153, c. 64.

44. A. O. and M. O. Anderson, ed. and trans., *Adomnan's Life of St. Columba*, pp. 266–267 and 270–272.

45. "Ad penitentiae medicamenta plebes concurrere"; *Ionae Vita Columbani*, ed. B. Krusch, *MGH: SRM* 4:76 (c. 10).

was simply a penitent," at least some of the time, "while a penitent frequently sought or was required to become a monk."[46]

Working from these two approaches to penitential practice among the laity, we can construct a general impression of how the system functioned. The *manaig* and pilgrim-penitents seem to have confessed more or less spontaneously, rather than according to the demands of a liturgical calendar. Columba heard confession in public and assigned penance on the spot. *The Monastery of Tallaght* contains a similar example of impromptu confession followed by penance.[47] Independence of liturgical context distinguishes private from public penitential discipline; although they sometimes confessed openly, neither monks nor laymen were normally enrolled in an order of penitents or formally reconciled. But the similarity between penance for the laity and penance for monks weakens after this point, both in the kind of infraction punished and in the penance assigned for it. The penitentials make these distinctions plain.

The penitential differed from the monastic rule in more than severity and scope. While no rule makes provision for the conduct of lay people, no penitential fails to consider it. This is the strongest indication that the penitential itself was a product of Irish missionary zeal, not simply Irish monasticism: the handbook was intended for an audience outside the community of monks. The Irish penitentials seem to mark stages of a progression toward greater concern for penance among lay people. The oldest Irish penitential is Finnian's, written in the sixth century. The penitential of Columbanus is also from the sixth century, but subsequent to Finnian's, which it cites. Cummean's penitential is from the seventh century.[48] The latest of the Irish penitentials in Latin, the *Bigotian Penitential*, was written on the continent in the form we now have it, but it is based on earlier material—specifically Cummean's penitential—and may safely be

46. Watkins, *A History*, 2:624–625.

47. Gwynn and Purton, "Monastery," p. 130, c. 7.

48. See Bieler, *Irish Penitentials*, pp. 3–4, for dating. Léon Fleuriot, "Le 'saint' Breton *Winniau* et le pénitentiel dit 'de Finnian'?" argues that Finnian's handbook is Breton. If this is true—and Fleuriot's argument awaits rejoinder—the earliest "Irish" penitential would have originated in a non-Irish but also "Celtic" church, like the penitential collections cited above, n. 1. The identification of the penitential with the early Irish

listed among the Irish penitentials for that reason; it also shows the influence of the only known penitential in the vernacular before the tenth century, *The Old-Irish Penitential*.[49]

The Irish penitentials differ substantially in their separation of penalties for monks, clerics, and lay people. The penitential of Columbanus divides into two sections, one chiefly for monks and another for clerics and laymen.[50] The first section seems to codify and clarify the *Communal Rule*; it is a systematic treatment of "correction" for "small matters of disorderly behaviour" and penances for "matters of importance," which included murder, theft, perjury, and sexual offenses. The second portion of the penitential follows the plan of the first but applies its tariffs to a broader segment of society and provides for a much more detailed weighing of the circumstances of each sin. If the second section of the penitential is later than the first, it is important to note the slight attention given to the laity in the first portion and to compare the detail with which penances for laymen are spelled out in the second. It has been suggested that the first section may reflect the earliest phase of Columbanus's mission to the continent, when he would have administered penance to a small, chiefly monastic community; the second may reflect the stage recorded by Jonas, when a greater diversity of cases was brought before Columbanus as he heard laymen's confessions.[51]

Finnian's penitential applies only to clerics and laymen; monks

church would remain unchanged, however, because Cummean and Columbanus were Irish, as were their penitentials, and it was the Irish mission—not monks from Brittany—who introduced them elsewhere. For Breton manuscripts containing Irish canons (most from the ninth and tenth centuries but some earlier), see Bieler, *Irish Penitentials*, pp. 20–21.

49. Bieler, *Irish Penitentials*, p. 10 and pp. 285–287, for a concordance comparing the contents of the Bigotian, Old Irish, and Cummean handbooks.

50. Section A contains twelve canons, section B thirty; ed. and trans. Walker, *Opera*, pp. 168–181, and Bieler, *Irish Penitentials*, pp. 96–107.

51. Walker believes that the penitential was written before the *Communal Rule*, since if the rule already existed when the handbook was composed, "no purpose could have been served . . . by any such fragmentary discussion of the discipline of monks" (*ibid.*, p. liv). However, section A is not a rule but a schedule of penances for monks to which four canons from the *Communal Rule* seem to have been added (cc. 9–12, pp. 170–171). For further discussion, see Jean Laporte, *Le pénitentiel de Saint Columban: introduction et édition critique*.

are omitted, although the first few provisions, which concern sins of the heart and inadvertent sins, may have been intended for them. The exclusion of monks strongly indicates that the penitential was neither an extension of the monastic rule nor a record of penance as the monks practiced it.[52] It was, instead, a schedule of penances intended for a new clientele. We would also know Finnian's penitential to be an early example of the handbook by its structural plan—or rather, its relative lack of plan. Like the handbook written by Columbanus, this penitential does not arrange the sins in any particular order; Finnian's also includes some statements which pertain not to penance, but to desired Christian conduct (for example, it urges the redemption of captives, support for the needy, and kindness to pilgrims).[53]

Cummean's, like *The Old-Irish Penitential*, shows the genre at an obviously more sophisticated stage of development. Both employ the eight chief sins as a structural guide and subdivide the sins systematically. Cummean's handbook, rich in advice for the priest, covers the broadest social range of any Irish penitential and provides penances for bishops and deacons as well as laymen and clerics; penalties for monks appear in this last category.[54] The world reflected in this penitential dwarfs that seen in Finnian's or Columbanus's: here the whole of Irish society is covered by the church's penitential code. *The Old-Irish Penitential* is equally inclusive and, like Cummean's, supplies the confessor with instructional information (although not with advice about the pastoral techniques required in

---

52. Watkins suggests that Finnian's penitential was written chiefly for those living—as monks, clerics, students, or penitents—within the confines of the monastery, and that in only two cases, both concerning women, was it extended beyond this community (*A History*, 2:606–608). But the penitential seems to have been intended for only a limited part of the monastic unit—clerics and the laity—and to be wholly separate from the monks' own discipline. All canons except the first four refer specifically to either clerics or laymen (as Bieler notes, *Irish Penitentials*, p. 4), and the first four probably do not belong to the original text (as Bieler again notes, p. 242, n. 1).

53. Bieler, *Irish Penitentials*, pp. 86–87, c. 33.

54. An example is the chapter concerning sexual offenses; clerical orders named there include the bishop, presbyter, deacon (the latter two may or may not have taken the monastic vow), and monks "of inferior status," including workers. *Ibid.*, pp. 112–117; see especially cc. 1–4, pp. 112–114.

confession).[55] These two penitentials represent the Irish handbook at its most complete, as both a guide to confession and an instrument for educating the confessor. In the range of social classes for which penance is prescribed, the penitentials reveal an ambitious plan to extend ecclesiastical discipline into the world surrounding the monastery.

This extension of monastic power must have taken place gradually. Among the forces resisting it was the powerful tradition of secular law to which all of Irish society was already subjected. Although the monasteries were obviously important in political and economic terms, their moral superiority was established with some difficulty. Both the native legal codes and the church's own canonical literature show that the laity was only slowly acclimated to the new Christian morality. Some of the resources, altered by the monks, attempt to conceal this resistance. The most notorious example is the prologue to a law tract known as *Senchas Már*, a somewhat fanciful version of the confrontation of Christian and native traditions in which the monks triumph with suspicious ease. The text claims that the sages of pre-Christian Ireland were, like the prophets, inspired by the Holy Spirit, so that when Ireland was converted only a small part of the native law handed down by these wise men had to be abrogated. Since the secular code governed much not discussed in scripture or Christian teaching, it necessarily had to be retained; it was, in any case, right in "all save the faith."[56] This vision of history defends the

55. E. J. Gwynn, ed., "An Irish Penitential"; a translation revised by D. A. Binchy appears in Bieler, *Irish Penitentials*, pp. 258–277. Binchy's introduction notes that "complete prose treatises on religious or ecclesiastical subjects do not seem to have been composed before the second half of the eighth century" in Ireland (p. 47). This would place the Old Irish text well after all the Latin penitentials except the *Bigotian*.

56. See D. A. Binchy, "The Pseudo-Historical Prologue to the *Senchas Már*"; the prologue is taken at face value by McNeill and Gamer, *Handbooks*, pp. 369–371. The Irish laws were first collected and edited as *Ancient Laws of Ireland*; see 1:1–60 for the text quoted above. This edition is notoriously defective, and diplomatic editions of all the Irish law tracts have now been published by Binchy in the *Corpus Iuris Hibernici*, an edition of use only to a few, for it contains no critical apparatus and no translation. I have cited only those tracts which have been re-edited and retranslated or to which other reliable guides are available. I cite *Ancient Laws* or other sources and not Binchy's edition; his introductory matter (see n. 10 above) includes a concordance to published tracts, pp. xxiii–xxv.

law texts against the inroads of the Christian system by denying the possibility of conflict between them. But early Irish canonical literature puts the confrontation of native and Christian traditions in a much different and more revealing light. The canons show a conflict between these two legal systems slowly resolved as limits to the church's power became clearly established. Although their contents overlap with some material also found in the penitentials, the canons concern church government in its most general terms, defining the responsibilities of its ministers and explaining their obligations. By comparing an early canonical text with one written as much as a century and a half later, we can observe the church's progress in adjusting to secular traditions.

The earliest canonical text is the *First Synod of St. Patrick*, written in the late sixth or early seventh century (and hence having nothing to do with St. Patrick or his followers).[57] Addressed to priests and lower grades of the clergy, the synod's decree forbids the acceptance of alms offered to the church by pagans, requires a cleric who gives surety for a pagan to assume the pagan's debt in case of default, and demands that a Christian who defaults on his own debt and so "acts like a pagan" be excommunicated.[58]

But the synod also insisted on strict separation of civil from ecclesiastical judicial processes. One who took a suit to the civil court, rather than to the church, was excommunicated, a high price to pay for ignoring the church's power to settle disputes.[59] Hence, while acknowledging native law, the church also sought a secure place for its own legislative machinery. Violations of church law were frequently punished by excommunication, although for theft one did penance for six months, and for murder or adultery for one year; at the end of this period, the sinner was, in the tradition of the public penitential system, formally absolved.[60] The comparison between the

---

57. Text in Bieler, *Irish Penitentials*, pp. 54–59; for commentary see Binchy, "St. Patrick's 'First Synod.'"

58. "Christianus qui fraudat debitum cuiuslibet ritu gentilium excommonis sit donec soluat debitum"; Bieler, *Irish Penitentials*, p. 56, c. 20.

59. "Christianus cui dereliquerit aliquis et prouocat eum in iudicium et non in ecclesiam ut ibi examinetur causa, qui sic fecerit alienus sit"; *ibid*, c. 21.

60. "Impleto cum testibus ueniat anno penitentiae et postea resoluetur a sacerdote"; *ibid*, c. 14.

early Irish church and the continental church in earlier centuries, suggested by this use of public reconciliation, is instructive: both struggled to establish themselves in hostile environments, and both reinforced their authority with public discipline.

The Irish church seen in the *First Synod of St. Patrick* was under episcopal jurisdiction; later ecclesiastical legislation reflects a church organized instead into families, or *paruchiae*, directed by abbots. This pattern emerged in spite of pressure to bring the Irish church into closer conformity with Rome. The efforts of Romanizing Irishmen (the "Romani") were offset by the Irish party, which was interested in bringing the church closer to native traditions.[61] Giving power to abbots, rather than to bishops, was one of the Irish party's aims; the abbot's *paruchia* was closely connected to the native tribal structure, usually through the patronage of the royal family which had endowed the monastery, and this was a link likely to promote the influence of secular power on the church. In the eighth century the church was "firmly ensconced in the pattern of tribal society"; it had, then, moved away from its earlier position of separation from pagan society, when its clerics were "not yet completely incorporated into the aristocracy," and its system of jurisdiction "not yet supported by secular law."[62]

The first text which reflects a coming together of ecclesiastical and secular law is the canonical collection known as the *Hibernensis*. Too little is now known about these canons to permit more than the most cautious interpretation of their significance.[63] But it is safe to say that the compilers of the *Hibernensis* either understood native law very well or worked with canonists who did. The *Hibernensis* uses native law extensively; it accepts the status given to monks in the secular codes and follows secular codes by assigning penalties to of-

61. The conflict between the reforms of the "Romani" and the "hard core of Celtic conservatism" is summarized by Hughes, *Early Christian Ireland*, pp. 75–78, and *The Church*, pp. 125–128.

62. Binchy, "Pseudo-Historical Prologue," p. 23; Hughes, *The Church*, p. 71.

63. Ed. F. W. H. Wasserschleben, *Die irische Kanonensammlung*. While we await a new edition, there is a good survey of the collection's manuscript tradition in Hubert Mordek, ed., *Kirchenrecht und Reform im Frankenreich*, pp. 255–259. For commentary, see Maurice Sheehy, "Influences of Ancient Irish Law on the *Collectio Canonum Hibernensis*," in *Proceedings of the Third International Congress of Medieval Canon Law*, Monumenta Iuris Canonici, vol. 4 (Salzburg, 1971), pp. 31–41.

fenses not censured by ecclesiastical canons elsewhere.[64] Whether we believe that the *Hibernensis* was the first such legal synthesis or hold with the more recent view that native and church jurists had cooperated long before it was compiled, it should be apparent that the church had, by the time this collection appeared—that is, by the seventh century—accommodated itself to native law in more than a cosmetic sense.[65] Before we evaluate this development, it is necessary to examine contemporary evidence from the penitentials, which do not offer a contrast similar to that between the Patrician synod and the *Hibernensis*. Finnian's penitential requires a layman who strikes another to give the injured party financial compensation and to undertake penance; a murderer exiled for ten years was upon his return required to "make satisfaction to the friends of him whom he slew, and compensate his father and mother, if they are still in the flesh, by filial piety and obedience."[66] Columbanus's handbook contains a similar though somewhat softened penance for murder and specifies that "capital sins" are punished "by the sanction of the law."[67] In the penitentials of both Columbanus and Cummean, one who injures another and prevents him from working must pay medical expenses, compensate the injured party's deformity, do his work while he recuperates, and perform penance for six months.[68] These secular legal obligations were incorporated into ecclesiastical penance in part to show the harmony between the two judicial systems, but also to at-

64. The *Hibernensis* takes up complex legal questions of suretyship, the giving of pledges, and legal evidence, not otherwise considered the church's business. Obviously the monks were increasingly concerned about protecting the church's property rights and legal status. See Hughes, *The Church*, pp. 126–128, for an excellent summary of these concerns.

65. The conventional view is that the *Hibernensis* reflects the process of synthesis, but Donncha Ó Corráin holds that the secular and ecclesiastical jurists had been cooperating long before the text was written. His paper "The Influence of Irish Law on the *Collectio Canonum Hibernensis*" was read at a symposium, "Ireland and Europe in the Middle Ages," on 29 May 1981 at University College, Dublin.

66. Text and translation in Bieler, *Irish Penitentials*, pp. 82–83, c. 23: "satis faciat amicis eius quem occiderat et uicem pietatis et oboedientie reddat patri et matri eius si adhuc in corpore sunt."

67. *Ibid.*, pp. 98–99: "legis animaduersione plectantur" (в-prologue).

68. *Ibid.*, p. 105, c. 21; for Cummean, see p. 121, 4. 9.

tach the force of native law to the penitential system, and so to strengthen it.[69]

Only *The Old-Irish Penitential* goes beyond this use of the native law and substitutes secular penalities for the church's own. For theft (of animals) this handbook assigns no other tariff than the compensation required by law: a stolen sheep was to be replaced by four sheep, a stolen horse by two horses, and so on. There were two alternatives: the thief could offer service in place of the animal, or, "if he offers it to God and does penance as his confessor prescribes, and does not possess anything that he can pay (as fine), he pays nothing to man, save only penance with a token of reconciliation."[70] The penances for murder in this handbook also show the influence of native law. The murderer's kinship to the victim determined the severity of his penance; outside the final degree of kinship (which extended to "the sons of the great-great-grandson, as far as the fingernail"), the homicide received a reduced penance. If the murderer paid fines to the kin of his victim, the penance was proportionately lessened.[71] It is difficult to know whether this penitential represents what had become a norm or whether its generous allowance for interaction with the native law was exceptional. Like *The Monastery of Tallaght, The Old-Irish Penitential* appears to be the product of a reform movement of the late eighth century; as a reaction to laxity and corruption, it may have been unusually severe. The penitential requires sinners to "publish" each other's offenses and to correct each other, practices more in the spirit of the monastic rule than the earlier, Latin handbooks.[72] The penitential constitutes the outer extreme of cooperation between civil and ecclesiastical legislation and contrasts with the evidence of the earlier texts; in them the interaction of penitential discipline and native law involves merely the in-

69. For a similar view, see Ludwig Bieler, "The Irish Penitentials: Their Religious and Social Background"; for additional comments on penance and secular law, see Leslie Hardinge, *The Celtic Church in Britain* (London, 1972), pp. 143–144.

70. See Bieler, *Irish Penitentials*, p. 266, 3. 4; and, for a similar provision in Cummean's penitential, p. 119, 3. 6.

71. *Ibid.*, p. 271, 5. 2; see p. 276, n. 26, on the degrees of kinship.

72. *Ibid.*, p. 268, 3. 21. One who did not "publish and correct" a capital sin "committed by his fellow" did the same penance as the sinner.

corporation of legal penalties into one's penance, an acknowledgment that grave crimes were punished by both church and state. This preserves the character of ecclesiastical discipline more clearly than the provisions of the vernacular text do, but even in them generally firm lines divide the ecclesiastical from the secular.

The accommodation of secular law in the penitentials appears to have been genuine and realistic. Evidence of the laws' concessions to the penitentials is much less creditable. Since the laws were not put into final form until after the law schools had become Christian, the church had an opportunity to stamp its influence on the laws' vocabulary. This accounts for Latin loan words in the Old Irish codes, "Christian colouring" layered over "a hard core of pre-Christian institutions."[73] Many references to ecclesiastical penance and penitentials were added to the tracts in this process. The *éric* fine (or compensation) assessed for civil offenses was supplemented by the requirement that ecclesiastical penance be performed before the crime was considered redressed.[74] This addition secured the authority of native law for the church's own legal system and in fact made satisfaction, in terms of the native code, dependent on the church. The laws also show that ecclesiastical authorities were brought into the social structure defined by the native code. Bishops were assigned an "honor price" equivalent to that of kings or princes; the clergy was given a set of rules for the archaic custom of "fasting in distraint"; and the church's penances were sometimes measured in the unit called the *cumal*.[75]

Two law tracts reveal an exceptional degree of interference from their Christian transcribers. *Cáin Lánamna* ("The Law of Married Couples") lists penance along with preaching, education, and the mass as part of the church's obligation to the *manaig*, its monastic

---

73. Binchy, "Linguistic and Historical Value," p. 218.

74. A common requirement in the *Senchas Már*; see *Ancient Laws*, 1:58, 62.

75. In the so-called *Book of Aicill*, injury to an ecclesiastic entails a fine of seven *cumala* of penance and seven *cumala* of *éric*. See Binchy's discussion, "Distraint in Irish Law," *Celtica* 10 (1973):22–71, and Oakley, "Cultural Affiliations of Early Ireland in the Penitentials," pp. 489–492. A *cumal* meant both a female slave and "the highest unit of value in ordinary reckoning, usually equivalent to a certain number of milch-cows"; see Gearóid Mac Niocaill, *Ireland before the Vikings*, pp. 159–160.

tenants. This requirement, stated in a gloss rather than in the body of the law, shows how the native codes were updated as social conditions changed.[76] A more elaborate manipulation of legal evidence appears in a later tract known as *Críth Gablach*, written in the early eighth century. Specifying how one's honor is to be cleansed after he violates a pledge, gives false testimony, or otherwise offends, the tract instructs that the dirt of dishonor should be removed from the face (punning here on *enech*, which means both "face" and "honor") with pumice, water, and a towel. Each item then acquires an allegorical interpretation derived from penitential practice. Pumice means "to begin with confession of the evil-doing before the person" and to promise not to offend again. This is not confession to the priest, but to the one offended, and its precedents are seen in the rules of Columbanus.[77] Water signifies repayment of anything damaged through the evil deed; the towel represents "penance according to the books," that is, the penitentials. This elegant exegesis transforms restitution under the law into an imitation of ecclesiastical penance. The fundamental nature of the law is unchanged, but its outward appearance is made to conform to Christian practices typical of monastic life. Mutual confession and the washing of visitors' feet were acts of cleansing which served as convenient figures for the removal of dishonor. *Críth Gablach* could have acquired this appearance only after the church's disciplinary system was well established and recognized as analogous to the native code.[78]

Such tinkering with the law tracts was an attempt to create harmony between the legal systems, and it should be understood as a defensive maneuver on the church's part. In fact, the penitentials and canons of the church were the new arrivals, and it is to be expected that the law's impact on them was much greater than their impact on

76. The *Cáin Lánamna* is edited, with a commentary and German translation, by Rudolf Thurneysen in *Studies in Early Irish Law*, ed. Thurneysen, Nancy Power, *et al.*, pp. 1–80. See pp. 8–9 concerning the *manaig*.

77. *Críth Gablach*, ed. D. A. Binchy, pp. 12–13, c. 21 (text), and p. 32 (commentary). For mutual confession in the *Communal Rule* of Columbanus, see Walker, *Opera*, p. 165; and in Cummean's penitential, see Bieler, *Irish Penitentials*, p. 121, 4. 16.

78. Binchy suggests that the tract is contemporary with the *Hibernensis* and the *Senchas Már* and hence early eighth to mid-eighth century.

the law. It is difficult to find examples of the law's capitulation to the church apart from the obviously fabricated evidence of the prologue to the *Senchas Már* or *Críth Gablach*. Where the church presented direct challenges to native institutions—for example, the laws which permitted divorce or polygamy or the laws governing the inheritance of property—the church appears to have lost the contest. The canonists were unable to replace long-standing tribal bonds with their own obligations; as Mac Niocaill has said, the church "could not breach the solidarity of the kin group."[79] The church's gains seem instead to have been made by approximating the structures of native society; with bishops, and later abbots, governing their *paruchiae* like so many princes governing their petty kingdoms, society was obviously encouraged to see the similarities between ecclesiastical and secular political organization. But the church remained separate from native society and maintained its own identity. It is difficult to disagree with the view that in Ireland Christianity "does not seem to have been more than a religion, whereas in the remainder of Christendom, both Latin and Orthodox, it became a whole social system."[80]

Especially in the early period—the seventh century, when the penitentials were taking shape—the church remained apart from the rest of society. This should lead us to question claims that native law exercised an important influence on the handbooks—an influence greater than the use of legal terms described above. The divisions and subdivisions used to structure tariffs in the handbooks have been compared to the schematic extremes of the law tracts. Some law tracts were overly schematic because they were purely theoretical. The degrees of social status defined in *Críth Gablach* present "a highly conventionalized order of society, a kind of ideal State" bearing "only a very limited relation to the realities of legal life in ancient Ireland."[81] In comparison, we find no apparent contradiction between the social classes named in the penitentials and those attested in other sources. The laws were also complicated by the addition of

79. Quoted from Gearóid Mac Niocaill, "Christian Influences in Early Irish Law," read at the symposium referred to in n. 65 above.

80. Kenneth Nicholls, *Gaelic and Gaelicised Ireland in the Middle Ages*, The Gill History of Ireland, vol. 4 (Dublin, 1972), p. 3.

81. Binchy, *Críth Gablach*, p. xix.

glosses to the primary text; as the codes became older, the institutions they described and even their language became increasingly obscure. As a result, witty and inventive glossators contrived explanations which suited the terms of the law to unprecedented conditions. Later scribes sometimes made no distinction between the glosses and the primary texts, with the result that the laws became encrusted with commentary, confused with commentary, and notoriously undecipherable.[82]

Compared with this farrago, the penitentials are structurally sound and simple, hardly reflective of the "notorious weakness" of the legal mind; much less are they "webs of casuistry" spun "in the monkish brain."[83] Their legendary fussiness has been much exaggerated. Not even the *Communal Rule* of Columbanus exhibits a fondness for gratuitous distinctions, although it analyzes behavior in greater detail than any handbook. The *Rule* does not multiply cases without cause, but instead seeks to specify the degrees of guilt possible within each offense:

> If any brother has been disobedient, let him spend two days
> on one loaf and water. If any says, I will not do it, three days
> on one loaf and water. If any murmurs, two days on one loaf
> and water. If any does not seek pardon or mentions an excuse,
> two days on one loaf and water.[84]

This penance makes no unreasonable distinctions, for it defines only two degrees of disobedience, one in which the monk made only a mild form of resistance to the command given, and another in which he refused the order.

Likewise, Cummean's penitential, although covering fewer minor infractions than a monastic rule, uses schematization only within clearly functional, rather than merely formal, limits:

82. The glossators' techniques are described by Binchy, "Linguistic and Historical Value," pp. 210–212.

83. The first quotation is from Bieler, "The Irish Penitentials," p. 339; the second from Nora K. Chadwick, *The Age of Saints in the Early Celtic Church* (London, 1961), p. 148.

84. Text and translation in Walker, *Opera*, pp. 158–159, c. x: "Si quis frater inoboediens fuerit, duos dies una paxmate et aqua. Si quis dicit, Non faciam, tres dies uno paxmatio et aqua. Si quis murmurat, duos dies uno paxmatio et aqua. Si quis veniam non petit aut dicit excusationem, duos dies uno paxmatio et aqua."

One who curses his brother in anger shall make satisfaction to
him whom he has cursed and live secluded for seven days on
bread and water. He who utters in anger harsh but not inju-
rious words shall make satisfaction to his brother and keep a
special fast. But if (he expresses his anger) with pallor or flush
or tremor, yet remains silent, he shall go for a day on bread
and water. He who merely feels incensed in his mind shall
make satisfaction to him who has incensed him. He, however,
who will not confess to him who has incensed him, that
pestilential person shall be cut off from the company of the
saints; if he repents, he shall do penance for as long as he was
recalcitrant.[85]

This passage hardly seems excessive in the distinctions it makes.
Harsh words are distinguished from a curse, a reasonable separation;
one so angry that he colored or trembled with rage obviously suc-
cumbed to his irritation more than one who merely spoke; in keeping with this gradation, one who merely thought he was angry paid
the smallest price. Only the hard-hearted one who refused to ask for
forgiveness was penalized severely. These distinctions may have been
reserved for monks, who were more likely than lay people to be
aware of sins of thought. On the other hand, devout laymen under
spiritual guidance—for example, those mentioned in *The Monastery
of Tallaght*—probably accepted these judgments as reasonable guides
to their conduct.

The distinctions observed in the penitentials were not introduced under the influence of native law. In fact, their textual traditions are, compared to those of the law tracts, simple and virtually
free of glosses.[86] Glosses were applied to texts used in the classroom

85. Text and translation in Bieler, *Irish Penitentials*, pp. 120–121, 4. 12–16: "Fratrem
cum furore maledicens ei cui maledixerit placat et .vii. diebus cum pane et aqua uiuat
remotus. Qui uerba aceruiora protulerit in furore, non tamen iniuriosa, satis faciens
fratri superponat. Si autem cum pallore uel rubore uel tremore tacuit tamen, .i. diem
cum pane et aqua sit. Qui mente tantum sentit commotionem, satis faciat ei qui illum
commouit. Qui uero non uult confitere ei qui se commotauit, abscedatur pestifer ille a
coetu sanctorum; si penitet, quanto tempore contradicit tanto peniteat."

86. Glossing a penance for fornication in *The Old-Irish Penitential* is the comment
"This is severe, O Penitentiary"; see Binchy's comments in Bieler, *Irish Penitentials*,
p. 275, n. 10.

as well as those whose provisions had become obscured with age. It is significant that the handbooks of penance belonged to neither of these categories. The lack of commentary on the handbooks should be understood as strong testimony to their practicality.

The only Irish penitential which can be properly described as excessive in its schematic design is the *Bigotian Penitential*, which is more than a handbook of penance. Unusually long, the text gathers dicta concerning penance from a variety of sources and interpolates this material—including an entire chapter of the Benedictine *Rule*—into the penitential tariffs.[87] Such a collection served as a *florilegium* of patristic opinions. It is doubtful that a collection so extensive and unwieldy could have been of much use to the confessor seeking a penance for a specific sin. The *Bigotian Penitential* is the exception which proves that the Irish handbooks were ruled by practical considerations.

If the penitentials borrowed any of the outstanding attributes from the laws, it may be the "fiction of uniformity and continuity" apparent in the secular codes.[88] Even though these tracts are not uniform, instead preserving customs peculiar to the various parts of Ireland in which the laws were compiled, they claim to be "the law of all Ireland." This fiction is equally evident in the penitentials. Cummean's claims the authority of the "ruling fathers before us"; *The Old-Irish Penitential*, much grander, begins, "The venerable of Ireland have drawn up from the rules of the Scriptures a penitential."[89] The legal fiction may be a manifestation of an Irish habit of mind or simply a natural expression of loyalty to earlier disciplinary codes. But the penitentials, like the laws, were local, preserving the standards of separate houses or monastic federations, not the whole of Ireland, and their claims to universality within Ireland may imitate claims made in the secular codes.

Comparison of the penitentials with the laws shows the handbooks to be largely independent of their influence, although deferential to their authority. Seen in another context also highly relevant to

87. The chapter concerns "the instruments of good works"; *ibid.*, pp. 210–212, c. 56.

88. Binchy, "Linguistic and Historical Value," p. 214.

89. For Cummean, see Bieler, *Irish Penitentials*, pp. 108–109, c. 1. For *The Old-Irish Penitential*, see p. 259.

their development, the monastic classroom, the penitentials again appear distinct in both form and content from literature which might be expected to have influenced them. Compiled by monks, and in one case by a great teacher, Finnian, the handbooks would have been susceptible to the stylistic devices employed in exegesis, catechisms, or other didactic texts. One such text is *The Alphabet of Piety*, a catechism listing, sometimes with the aid of alliteration, the four salvations of the soul (fear, penitence, love, and hope), the fifteen virtues of the soul, and much else potentially useful to the confessor.[90] Another text, *The Lambeth Commentary*, uses a question-and-answer format often seen in both exegesis and catechism.[91] Here the degrees of anger are analyzed in the same pattern Cummean used, from anger in thought to anger expressed in "reviling." But the matter seems purely academic; the *Commentary* emphasizes the distinctions themselves, not their practical consequences for offenders.

The only point at which the penitentials resemble these and similar pedagogical texts is in structure: like the catechisms, the penitentials were written to be read and possibly memorized. Cummean's handbook and *The Old-Irish Penitential*, both based on Cassian's list of the chief sins, could have been committed to memory, and the Old Irish handbook further simplifies its structure by dividing each chapter into two parts, dealing with a virtue and the vice opposed to it (linked by the theory of contraries).[92] Sins so divided and subdivided could be easily recalled; since confession was heard in impromptu

90. An eighth-century text, ed. and trans. Vernon Hull, "*Abgitar Chrábaid*: The Alphabet of Piety," p. 61, c. 8, and p. 69, c. 17.

91. Possibly early eighth century (725?), judging from its language; ed. Ludwig Bieler and James Carney, "The Lambeth Commentary"; see p. 8 for dating.

92. Gwynn notes that *The Monastery of Tallaght* requires the confessor to "read the penitential aloud" to the penitent. This took place at mealtime and was intended as a devotional exercise (see Gwynn, "Irish Penitential," p. 123, for his comment, and Gwynn and Purton, *Monastery*, p. 160, c. 78, for the text). "Reading" here could also mean "recitation" (Old Irish *legaid* means "to read" or "to recite"), and so the confessor may have recalled the text from memory. Passages likely to be recited or read were not lists of sins but lists of vices and virtues like those which form part of *The Old-Irish Penitential*. Given the cost of producing even simple, undecorated manuscripts, it is likely that more confessors memorized handbooks than actually owned them.

situations, such aids to memory were very useful if a penitential itself was not at hand. In fact, the Irish penitentials were probably oral literature at one time. Trained in memory, an important part of his education, the confessor could recall the schedule of tariffs more easily than he could consult a manuscript. It does not seem unreasonable to suppose that entire penitentials could have been memorized. None of the handbooks discussed here, with the exception of the *Bigotian Penitential*, is overly long or complex.

But the similarity between the handbooks and other monastic literature is not great. They were not treatises on the vices and virtues and so lack the numerical patterns of organization found in such literature. Nor did they explicate patristic wisdom or even expound upon it. They make no use of the stylistic devices—question and answer, parallel sentence structure, alliteration—found in discursive prose.[93] Even the *Bigotian Penitential* merely lists various opinions without attempting to reconcile their conflicting testimony. The penitentials came into existence in a literary climate of great richness and diversity, but they pay almost no homage to it. The authors of the handbooks knew about the traditions of Latin and vernacular Irish literature and presumably did not borrow from them because they were not relevant to the purpose at hand.

The ecclesiastical tradition most likely to have influenced the authors of the penitentials was public penance. This form of discipline was known in early Ireland but makes only a marginal appearance in the handbooks.[94] The *First Synod of St. Patrick* ruled that a murderer could be absolved only after the performance of his penance had been attested by witnesses; this would seem to presuppose a public ceremony. Certain particularly heinous sins, such as eating one's own scabs "or the vermin which are called lice," or eating or drinking excreta, required penance "with the imposition of hands of

93. See Bernhard Bischoff, "Turning-Points in the History of Latin Exegesis in the Early Middle Ages," trans. Colm O'Grady, pp. 84–86, for the main characteristics of discursive style.

94. Robert Cecil Mortimer argues that the Irish merely "adapted" public penitential methods to missionary purposes; see *The Origins of Private Penance in the Western Church*, p. 189.

his bishop," according to Cummean; and Columbanus required those who associated with heretics to be pardoned by the bishop.[95] Open or public confession formed part of a commutation in a canonical collection; presumably it was a greater mortification to confess sins openly to the people than to confess to the priest.[96]

Further evidence of public penance is found in the *Bobbio Missal*, written at a continental monastery under Irish influence; it contains references to an order of penitents and prayers for public reconciliation. The *Stowe Missal*, from Ireland, assigns the order of penitents a specific place in church.[97] Columbanus's penitential calls penitents the "lowest rank of Christians" and requires that sinners assigned to it be reconciled by the bishop.[98] Evidently public penance served the same purpose in early Ireland as it had elsewhere: it maintained the purity of the community and deterred the faithful from committing serious sins. The coexistence of public and private penance is apparently unknown before the early Irish period. The Irish monks not only invented the penitential for private confession and penance, but constructed a system in which both public and private forms of reconciliation were applied; they did not, however, formalize this dual system as the Carolingians were later to do.

The penitentials and liturgies describe the sacramental forms of reconciliation observed in early Ireland but do not tell us all we would like to know about the extent to which penance was observed by the laity. Narrative sources, especially the lives of the saints, are useful in supplementing the evidence of the administrative texts. Although penance is often mentioned in Irish saints' lives, it rarely

95. For the *Synod*, see Bieler, *Irish Penitentials*, p. 57, c. 14; for Cummean, *ibid.*, p. 129, 10. 18; for Columbanus, p. 107, c. 25. The prohibitions may derive from scriptural injunctions against unclean food.

96. Part of the *Canones Hibernensis*, ed. Bieler, *Irish Penitentials*, pp. 164–165; the commutation combines "confessionem peccatorum coram sacerdote et plebe" with a rigorous three-day period of prayer (c. 4).

97. See André Wilmart's comments in *The Bobbio Missal: Notes and Studies*, ed. E. A. Lowe *et al.*, p. 11, and the "Tract on the Mass" from the *Stowe Missal* in Stokes and Strachan, *Thesaurus*, 2:252–255.

98. Walker, *Opera*, pp. 178–179, c. xxv; a layman who communicated with heretics was ranked with catechumens for forty days and for eighty days was placed "in extremo christianorum ordine, id est inter paenitentes."

takes sacramental form, either public or private. Instead, the lives show the saints, women as well as men, hearing impromptu confessions and exhorting their followers to do penance. Although these stories concern the earliest Irish saints—Brigit, Finnian, Coemgen—the texts themselves may not be from the Old Irish period; but because their descriptions of penitential practice reveal nothing inconsistent with the administrative texts of that period, it seems acceptable to use the lives to complement them.[99]

The *Life of Brigit* in *The Book of Lismore* shows the saint hearing confession and assigning penance to a small boy who admitted to stealing a goat.[100] There is no monastic precedent for a woman's performing the confessor's office, and this story does not mean that women administered the sacrament. Rather, it shows the saint working as an intercessor. Brigit suspected this theft because she saw a goat's head in a chalice; when the boy performed penance, the head disappeared. For the purposes of hagiography, this comparatively small miracle overshadows the repentance of which it was a sign. In the *Life of Samthan*, the saint appears to a recalcitrant sinner (who would not allow Samthan's nuns to take his wood) in a dream, strikes him, and says, "Wretch, unless you do penance, you will quickly know your death." Stung—again, more by the blow and the apparition than by a guilty conscience—the man promptly gives up his wood and presumably guards his goods less jealously thereafter.[101] In this story "penance" and "confession" have a general, non-sacramental meaning and indicate merely a change of heart disposing the sinner toward good instead of evil. The *Life of Finnian*, also in the *Lismore* collection, reports that he upbraided gluttons and told them to weep and "do penance for their sin."[102] There is no confession, and no specific penance is assigned; this story describes only a general exhortation, and once again "penance" signifies a new moral orientation rather than a sacramental process.

99. There is a good introduction to the lives of the saints in Hughes, *Early Christian Ireland*, pp. 219–247.

100. Ed. Whitley Stokes, *Lives of the Saints from the Book of Lismore*, p. 196.

101. Ed. Plummer, *Vitae*, 2:258.

102. Ed. Stokes, *Lives*, p. 229.

Saints' lives are often thought to have much more specific evidential value for the study of Irish penitential traditions than the three lives cited reveal. Their extreme acts of asceticism are taken to be the epitome of penitential practice. The saints recited the psalms while standing neck-deep in icy water, or fasted so long that even angels tried to persuade them to stop. These feats established the saints' claims to piety and no doubt awed the audiences of the lives. But they are not connected to penitential practice: voluntary acts of asceticism were often the same as deeds assigned as penance—for example, the fast or the journey into exile—but did not support the penitential system itself. Irish penitential customs were, on the whole, far more moderate and practical than hagiography would lead us to believe. Although its severity cannot be denied, Irish penitential practice deserves to be exonerated; it was not "brutal," nor were its penalties uniformly "curious and extreme."[103] A passage frequently cited to show that the Irish employed exotic forms of discipline comes from *The Old-Irish Table of Commutations*, a schedule for substituting short, intense periods of penance for prolonged fasts. "Former lay men and women," now clerics and nuns, were permitted to commute a penance for manslaughter by spending the night with a dead body, or in water, or on nettles or nutshells. But those not guilty of manslaughter could commute a penance by spending the night in a cold church, praying "without respite."[104] This too is thought to be a text from the reform period in which *The Old-Irish Penitential* and *The Monastery of Tallaght* were written; it is pointless to take such evidence as typical of Irish penitential practice, for the penitentials themselves do not even remotely resemble the collection of commutations.

The existence of commutation tables does nonetheless raise important questions about the demands of penitential practice. All sorts of fasts and penances are commutable, according to *The Old-*

103. The first adjective is used by Kathleen Hughes and Ann Hamlin to describe Columbanus's penitential in *The Modern Traveller to the Early Irish Church* (London, 1977), p. 2; the others form the title of one section of the introduction by McNeill and Gamer to their *Handbooks*, pp. 30–35.

104. Bieler, *Irish Penitentials*, p. 279, c. 8; see also the commutations in the *Canones Hibernensis, ibid.*, pp. 162–167, for comparable exercises.

Irish Table of Commutations. A year's penance could be performed in twelve days of extremely rigorous mortification—eating only twelve morsels of bread with a little skim milk, performing ascetic acts, and "celebrating each canonical law." [105] A year's penance could also be commuted by chanting the *Beati* (Psalm 118) twelve times while standing with arms outstretched and never lowering them. Either penance must have been exceedingly difficult to undertake and complete. Other commutations involved two hundred deep genuflections; living seven months on bread and water, bound in fetters; or seven hundred genuflections accompanied by seven hundred blows "and a cross vigil after each hundred until the arms are weary." [106] It may be true that the practice of commutations eventually led to the corruption of the penitential system, but certainly it is difficult to detect laxity of any kind in the strict alternatives to regular fasting offered in this text. *The Old-Irish Table of Commutations* manages to make most penances assigned in the handbooks appear reasonable by comparison.

We should remember that penitential practice was not imposed by the monks on unwilling penitents. Rather, it seems that sinners confessed voluntarily and so were disposed to undertake a fairly strict penance as a requisite for absolution. The most demanding penances were reserved for the gravest sins, such as incest and murder, which led to exile.[107] The scale of fasts for other offenses was proportionate to their seriousness and may be interpreted, at least in a limited fashion, as an index to the priorities in the Irish church's plans for a Christian society. Sexual sins incurred severe penalties if they interfered with procreative functions. Hence, homosexuality and other non-reproductive forms of intercourse were given penances ranging from two to seven years of fasting; bestiality, apparently considered less perverse, required a penance of one year, the same as for fornica-

---

105. *Ibid.*, p. 280, c. 15A; presumably "celebrating" a law means "observing" it.

106. *Ibid.*, pp. 280–281, cc. 19, 23, and 27.

107. Finnian's penitential, c. 23, where a cleric who kills his neighbor is exiled for ten years (*ibid.*, p. 81); Cummean's penitential, 2. 7, where one who "defiles his mother shall do penance for three years, with perpetual exile" (*ibid.*, p. 115). As Bieler notes in another context, "strict" or "perpetual" exile probably meant spending one's life in a monastery; see p. 246, n. 9.

tion among lay people and masturbation.[108] Illicit sex which resulted in pregnancy was penalized more heavily than intercourse which did not; it was more serious to violate a virgin than a slave woman.[109] The logic behind these gradations is not always obvious; in fact, the very incompleteness of these lists of offenses, which omit some sins which we might expect to be covered, may tell us something about the origins of the handbooks. Such sins as drunkenness and gluttony entailed relatively light penances—one drunk on beer did penance for seven days (unless he was a cleric, in which case his penance lasted a year), and one who ate too much and suffered "excessive distention of the stomach" did penance for one day.[110] Avarice and false witness, like anger, were more heavily penalized because they had social consequences: they could lead to the misappropriation of property or to physical violence. Penances for these sins often involved both fasting and restitution of stolen property.[111] In Cummean's penitential the social valuation of sins extends even to mental ones; the "idler shall be taxed with extraordinary work," it says in the chapter "Of Languor," and a "wandering and unstable man shall be healed by permanent residence in one place and by application to work."[112]

If we analyze the lists themselves, it becomes apparent that the penitentials are collections of sins which had actually been confessed rather than catalogues of every kind of sin the monks remembered to write down. The sins of men far outnumber those of women; the sins of young boys are frequently cited, but those of young girls only rarely. Young men, of course, would have come to the monastery for schooling and perhaps for entry into orders; therefore they consti-

108. Cummean's penitential requires seven years for sodomy (2. 9), two for femoral intercourse (2. 10), and four for fellatio unless it was habitual, in which case seven (2. 8). For penalties for bestiality and masturbation (2. 6) and other sexual offenses, see *ibid.*, pp. 113–117.

109. *Ibid.*, p. 117, 2. 23–25.

110. *Ibid.*, pp. 111–113, 1. 1 and 1. 6.

111. *Ibid.*, p. 119, 3. 5. Theft required fourfold restitution, but if the sinner was unable to provide this, he did penance for one year.

112. *Ibid.*, pp. 120–121: "Otiosus opere extraordinario oneretur"; "Uagus instabilisque quis sanetur unius loci mansione operisque sedulitate" (6. 1–2).

tuted a higher percentage of the population, confessed more often, and were mentioned more frequently when early penitential decisions were recorded.[113] At some point the monks began to form their penitential standards into lists; as their decisions accumulated and as more of the faithful sought to undertake penance, it became necessary to establish uniformity and consistency at least within the monastic unit. We do not know how many different Irish penitentials there once were, but it is safe to conjecture that more than a handful of monks issued them. We can see in the differences in form and content between Finnian's handbook and that of Columbanus, or between Finnian's and Cummean's, a hint that each authority had his own ideas about which sins needed to be included and what penances were appropriate for them. If there had been such a thing as a complete inventory of sins applicable to most situations which the confessor was likely to encounter, it might well have become standard in many different monasteries. Instead, we can see that the lists of sins varied from monastery to monastery and that the penances too were altered. Perhaps each monastery had accumulated its own sets independently and incorporated only those parts of other lists which suited its needs. The origins of the penitential were therefore in private penance itself; surely it is more logical to see the literature growing out of the practice than to see the practice taking shape under the influence of a literary model. Our survey of Irish penitential literature shows that the handbooks are less a synthesis of existing traditions than an abrupt departure from them. Although they drew on canonical texts, homilies, and the monastic rule, the penitentials are not adaptations of these or other legislative texts. Nor are they Christianized versions of "Celtic" law codes. Handbooks did not gradually emerge from existing forms; no single form contains their principal features, and it is difficult to understand how a number of different genres could have contributed to the invention of a form which is substantially different from all of them. Penitentials did not exist until they were needed; when the practice of private penance had become sufficiently widespread, booklets in which penitential

113. Cummean's penitential devotes a chapter to "the decrees of our fathers before us on the (sinful) playing of boys"; *ibid.*, pp. 126–129.

decisions had been recorded became desirable. This reference work was easily enlarged to include instructions for the confessor in receiving the penitent and discovering the particular circumstances of his sins.

Unfortunately few penitentials survive as handbooks; most were copied into large codices containing several penitentials and often canonical texts as well. But there is fairly good evidence that small, hand-sized manuscripts were used for the penitentials. *The Old-Irish Penitential* was structured according to the eight chief sins, but one manuscript lacks both the general introduction to the text and the last one and one-half chapters. The text's first editor plausibly conjectured that the missing material was contained on the first and last folios of a small booklet whose outer pages "had been more or less damaged by use, as so often happens with MSS not protected by covers."[114] This manuscript would have contained only the penitential and would not have been covered or otherwise adorned, because it was not a service or liturgical book but a reference work subject to hard wear. It is the fate of portable works of reference to wear out; presumably the early handbooks, unglamorous manuscripts to begin with, were discarded when they had begun to deteriorate.

It is certainly a paradox that booklets about which so much has been written should themselves be so difficult to find. But this is not the only topic about which scholarship has been forced to conjecture; much of the literary history of penance in early Ireland has to be reconstructed in this admittedly hypothetical fashion and serves in the end to remind us how little we know about the Irish penitential tradition. Obviously much history remains to be investigated. What kind of laxity did the documents related to *The Old-Irish Penitential* seek to reform? Who made sure that the penitent actually performed the penitential deeds which he accepted in confession? If penitents could seek out their confessors, as *The Monastery of Tallaght* allowed, what was to stop them from confessing only to soul-friends who assigned light penances?

Answers to these and similar questions must await a more de-

114. Gwynn, "Irish Penitential," p. 123.

tailed investigation into early Irish penitential practice than has been possible here—an inquiry making full use of legal and historical documents as well as the vast and lamentably neglected body of religious poetry and prose in the vernacular. The Irish penitential tradition has too often been approached from the perspective of early English history, with the result that Irish penitential practice has been caricatured in a handful of commonplaces about extreme forms of mortification, abstruse handbooks of penance, and other exotic notions. Seen from a foreign perspective, Irish literary culture often appears bizarre, simply because it differs from that of Anglo-Saxon England. But much in that culture erroneously thought to be peculiar to the Irish was adopted by them from sources shared with other European Christian cultures.[115] Its penitential system, though new to the Irish, differed from earlier forms of reconciliation more in practice than in theory; we need not agree with Oakley's hypothesis in order to argue that penance among the Irish could reflect characteristics of the native culture without being heretical.

Suffice it to say that Irish culture is distinctive without being bizarre, original without being unorthodox, and traditional without being commonplace. And so too was its system of penance and penitential literature, which reflects much of what was best in that culture—a combination of imagination, practicality, fondness for detail, and reverence for traditions both native and new. How the elements of that system fared abroad is the subject to be addressed next. In England and on the continent, Irish penitential practice was strikingly new; to Irish missionaries, of course, it was merely another part of their tradition to be shared with those in need of preachers, teachers, and soul-friends. No Irishman would have understood the charge that his penitential system was heretical or even odd. When their customs were attacked as either new or unorthodox, the Irish responded confidently that it was they, and not their challengers, who maintained the more venerable tradition. Novel, in any case,

---

115. On the harmony between Irish exegesis and non-insular scripture study, see Robert E. McNally, "The Evangelists in the Hiberno-Latin Tradition," pp. 111–122. See also Clare Stancliffe, "Early 'Irish' Biblical Exegesis," *Studia Patristica* 12 (1975): 361–370.

would have been the last word an Irish monk would have used to describe the penitential code which ruled his life and the lives of those who confessed to him. Asked to explain its origin, he would, after Columbanus, have called it "a scheme . . . handed down by the holy fathers" and drawn no further distinctions among the canonical, legal, monastic, patristic, and scriptural strains which the penitential so firmly joined together.[116]

---

116. "Ordo a sanctis traditur patribus ut iuxta magnitudinem culparum etiam longitudo statuatur paenitentiarum"; from the A-version of the penitential of Columbanus, ed. Walker, *Opera*, p. 168, c. 1, and Bieler, *Irish Penitentials*, p. 96.

Chapter Three

Penance and Prayer
in Eighth-Century England

FOLLOWING in Bede's footsteps, English historians have often been of two minds about early Irish influence on the Anglo-Saxon church. United in praise of Irish piety, no less unanimously do they wish that the Irish had been more conventional in expressing it. Bede excused the method for dating Easter practiced by Columba and his followers at his monastery in Iona, which was established about 565, because the Irish "were so far away at the end of the earth" that no one could have brought them better information. Bede added, however, that "they diligently practised such works of religion and chastity as they were able to learn from the words of the prophets, the evangelists, and the apostles."[1] The Irish have been exonerated, at least in part, of charges that they observed Easter at a peculiar time.[2] But they continue to be thought of as unusual in other, more widely ranging matters wherein their influence on Anglo-Saxon England is apparent. When speaking of handwriting, manuscript illumination, exegetical principles, ascetic practices, or modes of prayer, to call a style "Celtic" is to call it odd and to imply that its origins lie somewhere "at the end of the earth," remote from the western, chiefly Roman, traditions at the heart of English ecclesiastical history.

Amid the lucidity of England's Roman heritage, and the sim-

---

1. *Bede's Ecclesiastical History of the English People*, ed. and trans. Bertram Colgrave and R. A. B. Mynors, 3. 4, p. 225.

2. See Kathleen Hughes, "Evidence for Contacts between the Churches of the Irish and English from the Synod of Whitby to the Viking Age," in *England before the Conquest*, ed. Peter Clemoes and Kathleen Hughes, pp. 51–52. By the eighth century most of Ireland was observing Easter in accordance with the Roman church.

plicity of its Germanic culture, the enigmatic and the recherché, we are invited to assume, is Irish. The racial assumptions behind such categorization may be "nonsense," an oversimplified division of English piety into "Roman" and "Celtic" strains.[3] But the implied tensions are useful in illuminating the process of adaptation through which Irish customs were assimilated by the English church. Private penitential practice was among these customs, and although foreign to the "Roman" tradition of public penance, it was rapidly established by Irish missionaries and, well before the end of the seventh century, embedded in the pastoral tradition of Anglo-Saxon England.

How the English adapted Irish habits of discipline and devotion is a process best studied on two levels. The first is administrative. English records of penitential practice include handbooks, ecclesiastical legislation, and secular laws. These reflect the potential of penance to establish order within the church and to integrate the church into the structure of secular power; hence, this literature applied broadly to Anglo-Saxon society, from slaves to kings, and shows the influence of penance at its deepest penetration into English life. The second level, individual rather than social, pertains only to the educated and literate, the higher clergy and the nobility, classes which were in England, as in Ireland, closely connected. For them, penitential practice supplied a vocabulary for self-expression, a language of prayer. Admittedly the penitentials shared their most characteristic language—for example, the metaphors drawn from medicine—with scriptural and patristic texts. But through private confession the handbooks applied this language to each penitent and in doing so encouraged him to think of himself in its terms not only when he confessed and did penance but also when he prayed.

An "English" as opposed to an "Irish" disciplinary system did not exist until Theodore of Tarsus arrived in Canterbury in 669 on assignment from Vitalian, the pope. Theodore began to centralize the monastic communities of Northumbria and Mercia under bishops in order to establish uniform standards among them.[4] One of his

3. This is the view of H. R. Loyn, *Anglo-Saxon England and the Norman Conquest*, pp. 272–273.
4. Especially good surveys of Theodore's work are Henry Mayr-Harting, *The Coming of Christianity to England*, pp. 129–147, and D. P. Kirby, *The Making of Early England*,

objectives was to contain the peripatetic habits of Irish missionaries, who were sometimes monks in orders under the jurisdiction of abbots. As bishops these men would have been confined to a specific territory, but as both monks and bishops responsible to an abbot, they were free to preach and baptize without regard to territorial limits. Bede's *Life* of the Irish bishop Cuthbert (d. 687) portrays the Irish missionary style at its finest. Arriving sometimes on foot, sometimes on horseback, Cuthbert deeply impressed dwellers in the villages he visited. They "made open confession of what they had done" to him because "they thought that these things could certainly never be hidden from him; and they cleansed themselves from the sins they had confessed by 'fruits worthy of repentance,' as he commanded."[5] Bede also praised the journeys of an earlier Irishman, Aidan, whose life "was in great contrast to our modern slothfulness."[6]

Although effective in reaching unbelievers in remote places, the wandering Irish missionaries hardly contributed to the consolidation of ecclesiastical authority which Theodore desired. Theodore's efforts to make Canterbury the dominant force in the English church led to much reshuffling of bishops favorable to those who supported him, and to the subdivision of large dioceses into smaller, more manageable units.[7] This restructuring and subdividing eventually reduced the influence of the large monasteries. The Synod of Hertford (672) marks a beginning; it restrained monks from wandering and confined bishops to a single area of administrative authority.[8]

As an instrument for setting and maintaining disciplinary standards, the penitential was inevitably involved in this movement toward centralization, but not until a handbook was issued under Theodore's name early in the eighth century. This penitential was written by a scribe known only as the "Discipulus Umbrensium," who recorded Theodore's judgments about penance as they had been

---

pp. 47–53. Mayr-Harting examines Theodore in the Gregorian tradition; Kirby focuses on the political consequences of his reforms.

5. Bede's *Life* is included in *Two Lives of St. Cuthbert*, ed. and trans. Bertram Colgrave, pp. 184–187.

6. *Bede's Ecclesiastical History*, 3. 5, p. 227.

7. Kirby, *Early England*, pp. 48–49.

8. Recounted in *Bede's Ecclesiastical History*, 4. 5, pp. 349–355; the second canon restricted bishops; the fourth confined monks to their own monasteries.

handed down by a subordinate known as Eoda.[9] For many reasons, Theodore's penitential is a landmark in the literary history of penance. It is the first known handbook to have originated outside an Irish monastery; the first English source to refer to the textual tradition of the penitential; and the first of the many non-Irish handbooks which significantly altered both the design and the purpose of the penitential.

Reflective of Theodore's interest in centralized administration and of his own training as an administrator, this penitential undertakes a full-scale reorganization of the materials available for administering private penance. The prologue attempts to order "confused" texts of the law already in circulation. These documents were early and disorganized collections of Theodore's judgments, of which several versions exist. In them tariffs for sins, the proper subject of the handbook, are mixed with canonical decisions not related to penance; for example, the procedure for ordination appears alongside the tariffs for homicide.[10] Such collections were not so much guides for the confessor as repositories of church law. A pragmatic combination of material of distinct purpose, they were obviously less useful to the confessor than a simple schedule of penitential tariffs. The Discipulus separates this material into two books, one a handbook, the other a collection of judgments non-penitential in nature.[11] The two-part compilation was then published as a penitential and introduced as "the booklet which Father Theodore, having been inquired of by different persons, prepared for the remedy of penance."[12]

Nowhere in the Irish penitentials is a handbook used to establish administrative order in this way. Where the Irish sources do not

9. Ed. Paul Willem Finsterwalder, *Die Canones Theodori Cantuariensis und ihre Überlieferungsformen.* Nothing is known about Eoda's identity; he is named only in the preface contained in two manuscripts; see pp. 140–146.

10. For these texts, see *ibid.*, pp. 1–10. The tradition of the penitential is discussed by John T. McNeill and Helena M. Gamer, *Medieval Handbooks of Penance,* pp. 179–182; they provide a complete translation on pp. 182–215.

11. The two books circulated separately, as Finsterwalder's survey of the manuscript tradition shows; *Canones,* p. 138. Although much in Book 2 relates to ecclesiastical discipline, these canons simply set forth rules and do not provide penances for their infraction; only Book 1 conforms to the definition of a tariff penitential.

12. *Ibid.*, p. 287.

maintain a clear distinction between penitential and canonical material—as, for example, when statements about ecclesiastical custom are introduced into the tariffs—the non-penitential matter appears to have been included for didactic reasons.[13] Theodore's earlier pronouncements, as well as the two-part compilation of the Discipulus, incorporate canonical information as well as penitential tariffs because they are handbooks of a new and more complete kind. Theodore's preface greets "all Catholics of the English, especially the physicians of souls."[14] So different from the claims to universality, or the "legal fiction," of the Irish penitentials, this phrase introduces a uniform penitential handbook for all English confessors—not so much *an* English penitential as *the* English penitential.

Theodore (or his followers) appears to have recognized the capacity of the penitential to enforce consistent standards of discipline and also to serve as a standardizing influence on ecclesiastical organization within each diocese. This was a significant development: created to serve a wandering, monastic, decentralized church, the handbook soon became a rulebook specifying that penance was properly the duty of the clergy and only a "liberty" or privilege of the monastery.[15] This is a statement with far-reaching implications. However widespread private penance in Ireland may have been, the handbooks strongly suggest that it was chiefly practiced by those living in close proximity to the monastery. Cummean's penitential, as we saw earlier, contains a chapter specifically devoted to the vices of small boys, probably those intended for monastic orders; it also contains a chapter of penances for those who mishandle the Eucharist or sacred vessels.[16] Moreover, Cummean's and other Irish handbooks list a number of offenses—for example, sloth, languor and vainglory—

13. An example in Finnian's penitential urges the redemption of captives, visitation of the sick, and other acts in obedience to the "commandments of Christ" (c. 33). See Ludwig Bieler, ed. and trans., *The Irish Penitentials*, pp. 86–87. These rather general exhortations are not really canons, but guides to more perfect Christian conduct.

14. "Discipulus umbrensium universis Anglorum catholicis propriae animarum medicis"; Finsterwalder, *Canones*, p. 287.

15. Book 2. 6. 16: "Nec non libertas monasterii est penitentiam secularibus iudicandam quia proprie clericorum est"; *ibid.*, p. 321.

16. See chapter 10. 1–21, concerning small boys (Bieler, *Irish Penitentials*, pp. 126–129), and chapter 11. 1–29, concerning the Eucharist (*ibid.*, pp. 130–133).

which may be categorized as sins of thought rather than word or deed and so presuppose a clientele capable of attending to fairly scrupulous examinations of conscience.[17] These sins may have been included because the structural plan of Cummean's handbook or *The Old-Irish Penitential* required them: both are based on the Cassianic list of the eight chief sins and therefore had to enumerate offenses in that list whether they were serious problems in the community or not. This no doubt is why the chapters on sloth and languor and vainglory are very short and those concerning the Eucharist, sexual offenses, and pride—this last category dealing with obedience—are so long.[18]

The world reflected in Theodore's penitential is very different from this. The English handbook devotes many chapters to sins not found in the Irish penitentials, among them the failure to observe Sunday, the worship of idols, the invalid reception of sacraments, and heresy, and under the last category takes clear aim at Irish paschal customs.[19] Among the sacraments discussed is penance; Theodore noted the absence of public reconciliation "in this province, for the reason that there is no public penance either."[20] The range of penitents is also widened in the English handbook, at least to the extent that many more offenses involving women are included. Where women are mentioned in the Irish handbooks, they are occasions of temptation or sin to men; for example, women are defiled, illicitly loved, or kissed, but they rarely commit sins of their own (there are of course exceptions, such as penance for a virgin who fornicates and a wife who deserts her husband).[21] In Theodore's penitential women are mentioned much more frequently: the penances

17. *Ibid.*, pp. 120–123, chapters 5–7.

18. Sloth, languor, and vainglory merit only two or three canons each; the other sins may have ten times that many, as do the sins mentioned in n. 16, above, for example.

19. Book 1. 5. 3 condemns those who keep Easter "with the Jews"; Finsterwalder, *Canones*, p. 295. Book 2. 9. 1 requires reconfirmation for those ordained by Irish or British bishops "who are not catholic" ("catholica non sunt") with regard to tonsure or the date of Easter; *ibid.*, p. 323.

20. Book 1. 13. 4: "Reconciliatio ideo in hac provincia publice statuta non est quia et publica penitentia non est"; *ibid.*, p. 306.

21. Cummean's penitential, 2. 17 (the virgin who fornicates), and 2. 29 (the wife who deserts her husband); Bieler, *Irish Penitentials*, pp. 115–117.

of widows are distinguished from those of girls; female homosexuality is penalized, as is masturbation; and women are linked with certain magical practices.[22] Here, for the first time, we have penance viewed through the eyes of a bishop rather than an abbot; penance is not the practice of a small segment of society living near a monastery, but a prescription for social observance intended for all devout Christians. Theodore's text unquestionably enlarged the role of penitential practice in church government and invited closer interaction between the church and secular authority.

The widening of the penitential's scope had an undesirable consequence for the structure of the text. The Irish penitentials clearly explain how penances are to be adjusted to the conditions of individual penitents and how the gravity of each offense is to be determined. Lying because of greed is distinguished from lying because of ignorance or lying deliberately; in this and other cases, intentionality was brought to bear on the penance assigned.[23] These degrees are not entirely absent in Theodore's handbook; desiring to sin sexually was judged differently from carrying out the desire.[24] But the confessor using the English penitential would not find his duty to discriminate among penitents and their sins made easy. A tariff for murder states, "If one slays a man in revenge for a brother, he shall do penance for three years. In another place it is said that he should do penance for ten years."[25] Fellatio was punished with seven years, or twelve, or "penance to the end of life." Fornication with one's mother required either fifteen years of penance or seven years with "perpetual pilgrimage."[26]

We see here not tolerance for diverse judgments but synthesis of

22. Book I. 2. 12–14 (homosexuality, masturbation, and widows distinguished from girls); Finsterwalder, *Canones*, p. 291. Magic was not exclusively associated with women, but see Book I. 15. 2, 4 (concerning superstitions and divinations); *ibid.*, pp. 310–311.

23. Cummean's penitential, 3. 16–18; Bieler, *Irish Penitentials*, p. 119.

24. Book I. 2. 10 (the penance for desiring to fornicate was twenty or forty days); Finsterwalder, *Canones*, p. 290.

25. Book I. 4. 2: "Qui occiderit hominem pro vindicta fratris III annos peniteat, in alio loco x annos penitere dicitur." See *ibid.*, p. 294; translated in *Handbooks*, p. 187.

26. Book I. 2. 15 (fellatio), 16 (incest); Finsterwalder, *Canones*, p. 291.

penances from several conflicting sources, made without any attempt to reconcile the inconsistencies which emerged. The failure to make the code standard may well have perpetuated the confusion of laws which the Discipulus hoped to overcome. But he may have gone no further in refining the tariffs because he did not intend his booklet to stand alone. Theodore's epilogue states that the collection is to be used in conjunction with a "booklet on penance" because the compiler is "still in doubt" about his own work.[27] Hence, he joined this booklet to his own, or so we are invited to suppose by the manuscript evidence. Several codices contain both Theodore's penitential and that of Cummean, along with the *Libellus Responsionem* of Gregory to Augustine of Canterbury, another highly valued collection of opinions about church government. Cummean's may well have been the "booklet of the Irish" named in the preface as one of Theodore's sources.[28] Such collections demonstrate the genre's conservatism: the new penitential not only builds on an older one but is put into circulation with it. In this way Cummean's handbook exercised double influence as one of Theodore's sources and as a complement or supplement to his penitential.

Theodore's penitential was itself a powerful influence both in Ireland and on the continent. It was quoted in the *Hibernensis* (in a chapter about clean foods) and in a continental collection of canons known as the *Vetus Gallica*.[29] Surer evidence of Theodore's influence on Irish penitential literature comes from *The Old-Irish Penitential*, which names him twice.[30] It is indeed curious that continental sources especially are our chief witnesses to the impact of Theodore's penitential and that evidence of his influence in England should be rather more difficult to produce. Without exception, early manuscripts of the text are from continental scriptoria, a fact which led

27. The epilogue is found in only two manuscripts and is complete in neither; it refers to "minor passages" in the booklet on penance ("libello penitentiae"). See *ibid.*, pp. 146–154.

28. The prologue contains material taken from an Irish booklet ("ex scottorum libello"); *ibid.*, p. 287.

29. See F. W. H. Wasserschleben, ed., *Die irische Kanonensammlung*, 54. 12, 14 (pp. 217–218); Hubert Mordek, ed., *Kirchenrecht und Reform im Frankenreich*, 46. 18–21 (pp. 536–537; see also p. 86).

30. Translated by D. A. Binchy in Bieler, *Irish Penitentials*, 1. 4 (p. 260), 2. 21 (p. 264).

one editor to argue that the text was written there, by a follower of Theodore, and not in England.[31] English manuscripts of any penitential, not only Theodore's, are unknown from the ninth century or earlier. This does not necessarily mean that the handbooks were less popular there than on the continent, where both eighth- and ninth-century codices are relatively plentiful. The evidently wide circulation of Theodore's penitential on the continent strongly suggests that the text was also used in England, since its chief exponents on the continent would have been English and Irish monks who acquired the handbook from monasteries at home.

The most decisive argument favoring the English origin of Theodore's penitential is that nothing in the handbook openly contradicts traditions or regulations attested by other and unquestionably English sources. Most of the handbook is based on Irish penitential literature; non-Irish customs cited are either Greek or Roman and were known to Theodore before he arrived in Canterbury. It is also possible that he knew of penitential literature belonging to his eastern heritage; the so-called penitential attributed to John the Faster, patriarch of Constantinople (d. 596), may be a sample of it.[32] But nothing in Theodore's penitential requires us to suppose that it was written outside England, even though the manuscript evidence suggests that it was.

We cannot, unfortunately, say the same for the two other handbooks traditionally assigned to the eighth-century English church, those attributed to Bede and Egbert of York. These penitentials raise large and complex issues which are still at some remove from resolution. Various handbooks have been assigned to each author, so that "the penitential of Bede" actually indicates four different handbooks, while "the penitential of Egbert" refers to three. Matters are only partially simplified by such designations as "pseudo-Bede" and "pseudo-Egbert," since they merely register the already obvious pos-

31. Finsterwalder's view, *Canones*, pp. 170–177, a position thoroughly demolished by Gabriel Le Bras, "Judicia Theodori."

32. *PG* 88: 1893–1896; translated by John Boswell, *Christianity, Social Tolerance, and Homosexuality*, pp. 363–365; the text may be considerably later than the sixth century, as Boswell notes (p. 365, n. 28). This text does not provide graded penances for sins and rather than a penitential is a set of instructions for the priest's use in interrogating penitents.

sibility that not all these texts are genuine. Egbert's texts are easily sorted out: two of the handbooks claimed for him are written in English of the tenth century and cannot possibly be genuine.[33] This leaves only a Latin penitential. The penitentials of Bede are more difficult to analyze, but again three of the four texts assigned to him show some influence of the penitential of Egbert, and this offers us at least a foothold on an otherwise slippery slope.[34]

Chronology will offer some guidelines as we attempt to determine which of these texts are, if not genuine, at least English and eighth century, and hence likely successors to the penitential of Theodore. Bede died in 735, and Egbert in 766; Bede was Egbert's teacher, and so we would expect the penitential of Egbert to be at least as heavily indebted to Bede's as to Theodore's.[35] However, if we accept as genuine for the moment the earliest version of a handbook assigned to either figure—Egbert's from a manuscript of the late eighth or early ninth century, Bede's from a manuscript of the early ninth—we find our expectations defeated.[36] There are few points of close resemblance between these penitentials: they use different chapter headings, include different sins, and make no references to each other.[37] Egbert's text twice names Theodore, while Bede's

---

33. These are discussed in chapter five; they are Josef Raith, ed., *Die altenglische Version des Halitgar'schen Bussbuches (sog. Poenitentiale Pseudo-Ecgberti)*, and Robert Spindler, ed., *Das altenglische Bussbuch (sog. Confessionale Pseudo-Egberti)*.

34. I have taken up the problem of the penitentials assigned to Bede and Egbert in "The Penitentials of Bede," forthcoming in *Speculum*. I offer here a condensed version of those arguments and a summary of evidence made fully available there.

35. Very little is known about Egbert, but Mayr-Harting sums up the outlines of his career in *The Coming*, pp. 241–243.

36. For Egbert's penitential, see F. W. H. Wasserschleben, ed., *Die Bussordnungen der abendländischen Kirche*, pp. 231–237; the earliest manuscript is Vatican, Palatinus Latinus 554, s. viii/ix. For Bede's penitential, see *ibid.*, pp. 220–230; the earliest manuscript is Vienna, Nationalbibliothek 2223. The Vatican manuscript is discussed more fully below, n. 47. The Vienna manuscript is dated s. ix^{1/3} by Bernhard Bischoff and Josef Hofmann, *Libri Sancti Kyliani: Die Würzburger Schreibschule und die Dombibliothek im VIII. und IX. Jahrhundert* (Würzburg, 1952), p. 53; it is from the region of the Main.

37. Compare the contents in Wasserschleben's edition: Egbert's chapters on divinations and auguries (7, 8) have no direct counterpart in Bede, while Bede's chapters concerning homicide (4) and the observance of Sunday (7) are not found in Egbert.

makes no reference to the archbishop; both, however, derive many canons from his and from Irish penitentials.[38]

The points at which the handbooks of Bede and Egbert do resemble each other argue even more persuasively for their independence. Chief among these is the similarity between Egbert's prologue, a long address about the priest's duties as confessor and pastor, and the second chapter of the Bedan text. It seems impossible that Egbert's prologue is an expansion of the scrappy and incoherent chapter in Bede, and very likely that the Bedan paragraph is only a hurried and inaccurate rendering of Egbert's address.[39] Other points of verbal correspondence are less decisive, but they too favor the possibility that the Bedan text derives in part from Egbert's penitential and that it cannot, therefore, have been written by Bede.[40]

If we strip away the chapters which show Egbert's influence, we are left with a Bedan penitential composed of a short preface and five (or in some manuscripts six) chapters.[41] This handbook, which might be called a pure Bedan text, has in fact been edited but never considered as the genuine penitential of Bede.[42] However, since it alone among the four handbooks ascribed to Bede is completely independent of Egbert's penitential, it appears to be the earliest Bedan handbook. No evidence has been found to link this short text—or, for that matter, any of the handbooks under discussion here—to Bede.[43] But such a text might well have been written in England as

38. Wasserschleben indicates sources or parallels for nearly every canon in both penitentials; not always strictly accurate, they are reliable for purposes of general comparison. Egbert cites Theodore in the prologue (Wasserschleben, *Bussordnungen*, p. 232) and 5. 11 (concerning the fornication of monks; p. 237).

39. Compare Bede 2 ("De sancta constitutione") and Egbert's prologue (*ibid.*, p. 221 and pp. 231–233); I set out parallel passages in "The Penitentials."

40. These include Bede 8. 4–6 (*ibid.*, p. 228) and Egbert 10. 3–4; and Bede 9 (p. 229) and Egbert 14 (pp. 245–246). At these points it is less clear that Egbert's is the fuller and more correct version of the material.

41. One may reconstruct this text by canceling chapters 2, 6, and 8–9 of the text printed by Wasserschleben (the text originally ended at 9, as Wasserschleben noted, *ibid.*, p. 229, n. 2). Some manuscripts of this short text do include chapter 6.

42. H. J. Schmitz, *Die Bussbücher und das kanonische Bussverfahren*, pp. 654–658. The manuscript is Vatican, Palatinus Latinus 294, s. xi.

43. The two sides of the debate about Bede's authorship are described in chapter one above, nn. 1–3.

well as on the continent; based on Theodore's handbook and various Irish penitentials, it contains nothing which clearly precludes the possibility that it originated in England in the eighth century.

The manuscript evidence of this short Bedan handbook will be set out in the next chapter, since it properly belongs to the Frankish rather than the English penitential tradition. For present purposes it is enough to note that the twelve-chapter version usually accepted as Bede's is, as are two other Bedan handbooks, compounded of the short text and Egbert's penitential. The twelve-chapter penitential takes only portions of Egbert's text, while the two others incorporate his penitential wholesale. In one, Egbert's penitential—usually without Egbert's name—is merely added on to the short text;[44] in another the two penitentials are completely reshuffled, and new material is added to create a handbook of a character very different from that of its component parts.[45] These revisions took place on the continent, not in England; our earliest evidence of them dates from the second quarter of the ninth century.[46]

Egbert's penitential is obviously helpful for deciphering the history of the various texts claimed for Bede. Earlier than any known manuscript containing a Bedan handbook is one which, in its original form, contained only Egbert's. This small booklet (approximately five inches by eight inches) was written either in England or at Lorsch, one of the most important Anglo-Saxon foundations on the continent.[47] Its size may be important evidence of its authenticity, for it appears to be just the kind of small text which would have served confessors as a handbook. Most of the *incipit* is missing from this

---

44. Ed. Bruno Albers, "Wann sind die Beda-Egbert'schen Bussbücher verfasst worden, und wer ist ihr Verfasser?" and partly translated by McNeill and Gamer, *Handbooks*, pp. 221–233. Egbert's prologue is transposed to follow Bede 1; Egbert's chapter 2 begins on p. 405 in Albers and on p. 226 in McNeill and Gamer.

45. Ed. Wasserschleben, *Bussordnungen*, pp. 248–282, as the penitential of "pseudo-Bede."

46. This is the date of a manuscript from Orléans now in Paris, Bibliothèque Nationale, Lat. 2341, s. ix²/⁴; dating and provenance given by Raymund Kottje, *Die Bussbücher Halitgars von Cambrai und des Hrabanus Maurus*, pp. 50–51.

47. Dating and provenance by Bernhard Bischoff, *Lorsch im Spiegel seiner Handschriften*, pp. 112–113; see also E. A. Lowe, ed., *Codices Latini Antiquiores*, 1:28 (no. 95). The manuscript is Vatican, Palatinus Latinus 554, s. VIII/IX.

manuscript, but Egbert's name is plainly visible, and the entire *incipit* probably once read as many manuscripts still do: "Excerpts from the canons of the holy fathers, or the penitential for the remedy of souls by Egbert, archbishop of York."[48] There are good reasons why Egbert's text may in fact be genuine, all of them more convincing than any which can be put forth to defend claims for Bede's authorship. As bishop and later archbishop, Egbert was in a position to issue such a document, just as Theodore was; Bede, on the other hand, had no pastoral authority. Moreover, the text of Egbert's penitential is consistent in a large number of manuscripts; its preface and fifteen chapters were not subjected to the alterations and revisions which complicate the history of the Bedan handbooks.[49] Finally, many manuscripts indicate that the text is Egbert's by means of the *incipit* quoted above. *Incipit*s for the various Bedan penitentials are not uniform or, since they appear at the head of so many different texts, trustworthy.[50] Up to this point, the case for Egbert's authorship is almost as strong as the case for Theodore's, and much stronger than the case for Bede's.

But the matter is not so simple, for certain chapters in Egbert's penitential appear to have been written outside England. Almost certainly of continental origin is material added at the end of the text allowing the commutation of penance.[51] This practice was de-

48. "Excarpsum de canonibus catholicorum patrum vel penitentiale ad remedium animarum domini [Egberti] archiepiscopi eburacae civitatis"; Wasserschleben, *Bussordnungen*, p. 231. Wasserschleben quotes Vienna 2223 for the *incipit*, which gives Egbert's name as "Eambercthi."

49. Even when Egbert's text was conflated with Bede's, its chapters remained intact; I give several examples in the appendix to "The Penitentials."

50. Each of the four Bedan penitentials described above claims to be his. The *incipit* in Vienna 2223 reads "Incipit exscrapsum domini Bedani presbyteri" (Wasserschleben, *Bussordnungen*, p. 220); the text of the short version in Munich, Bayerische Staatsbibliothek Clm 6311 (early ninth century, but probably later at this point) begins, "Incipit judicium bedani de remediis peccatorum capitula vi." It is worth noting that these titles do not give much information about Bede, except to call him a priest or an "English priest." The *incipit* naming Egbert, on the other hand, is specific about his rank and see.

51. Chapters 15–16 *ibid.*, pp. 246–247; only chapter 16 is found in the earliest manuscript (see n. 47). On the continental tradition of commutations, see Cyrille Vogel, "Composition légale et commutations dans le système de la pénitence tarifée."

nounced as a new one by the Council of Clovesho in 747—that is, during Egbert's lifetime. It is most unlikely that Egbert would have sanctioned a practice out of favor with his contemporaries.[52] Egbert's penitential also includes prohibitions aimed at certain superstitious practices, such as divination, in language which suggests continental origin. These practices were not unknown in England—in fact, Theodore's text refers to them—but most evidence of the church's struggle against them comes from the continent rather than from England.[53] There is also a list of books for the priest in Egbert's prologue which suggests the standards of continental churches in the ninth century rather than those of the English church a century before. The list includes "a psalter, a lectionary, an antiphonary, a missal, a baptismal, a martyrology for the cycle of the year for preaching with good works, and [a book of] computation with the cycle"; also included for him "who is ordained in this order according to the authority of the canons" is "his own penitential."[54] Such book lists appear most frequently in the conciliar texts of the ninth century and, again, do not suggest the English church of Egbert's time.[55]

Part of the problem in assessing the origins of this evidence is the relative paucity of documentation about the eighth-century English church. Had we more records of church councils at this time, and in particular more information about the episcopate of Egbert, we might be better able to determine what portions of this penitential are likely to have been written by him. Let us, in any event, allow for the possibility that certain portions of Egbert's penitential were

---

52. For the text (c. 26, "De eleemosynis"), see Arthur West Haddan and William Stubbs, eds., *Councils and Ecclesiastical Documents Relating to Great Britain and Ireland*, 3:371–372.

53. For Theodore on superstitions, see Book I. 15. 1–5; Finsterwalder, *Canones*, pp. 310–311. There is a good survey of condemnations of such practices in Jeffrey Burton Russell, *Witchcraft in the Middle Ages* (Ithaca, 1972), pp. 63–100; penitentials cited in the corresponding notes, pp. 306–307, are, with the exception of those assigned to Bede and Egbert, continental.

54. Wasserschleben, *Bussordnungen*, p. 232: "post autem suum penitentialem, qui hoc ordine secundum auctoritatem canonum ordinatur."

55. I give several examples in "The Penitentials." Schmitz seems to have been the first to argue that the book list suggested continental rather than English origins; see *Die Bussbücher und die Bussdisziplin der Kirche*, p. 568.

added to the text on the continent and that a core of genuine material exists in the text. We have reason to consider the earliest version as an expanded or augmented one, not only because of the canons about commutation, but because of the confused and contradictory nature of the first chapters. They are theological rather than practical, explanations of the chief sins "according to the canons" or "as St. Paul and Augustine and other saints listed them." The "major" sins in this opening statement are punished by penances ranging from four years (for laymen) to twelve (for bishops). But some of the same offenses appear in the next chapter as "minor" sins; it is difficult to see what might be considered as "minor" about theft, false testimony, sodomy, or the fornication of monks. A single mysterious penance for fratricide or patricide follows—mysterious because Egbert's penitential otherwise includes no chapter devoted to homicide.[56] These are not the only repetitions in Egbert's handbook, but they are the most serious and they invite the suspicion that the earliest manuscript of this handbook, like the earliest manuscript of a Bedan penitential, does not represent the first form of the text.

If we look at Egbert's penitential and at the brief Bedan penitential which shows no influence from Egbert, we should ask how either compares to Theodore's penitential. Both are shorter than the penitential of Theodore and would have been easier for a confessor to use; neither includes substantial canonical material, being generally limited to penitential tariffs. Egbert's prologue, which has no counterpart in the Bedan text except for a short introductory paragraph, goes far beyond anything which Theodore's penitential offers as instruction for the priest. Beyond these rather superficial, even "literary," points of comparison, more substantial differences can be found. These involve the interaction of the penitentials with secular law, a particularly valuable measuring stick, since it can show us the extent to which a given handbook accommodates secular judgments and, hence, the extent to which the practice of penance reflected in that text may actually describe social realities. The most important penances to be considered in this regard are those for homicide.

56. Wasserschleben, *Bussordnungen*, p. 234: "De parricidiis vel fratricidiis." The contradictions between major and minor sins were noticed by Schmitz, *Bussbücher und Bussdisziplin*, pp. 566–567.

Theodore's penitential groups slayings of various kinds into a single chapter and shows that secular authority was considered when penances for them were assigned. For example, one who murdered a bishop or a presbyter was judged by the king, not by an ecclesiastical official.[57] If a murderer did as secular law required and paid compensation to the victim's family, his penance was halved. If the murderer surrendered his arms after a premeditated killing, he again received a reduced penance.[58] These concessions to the native judicial system involved more than homicide; the king also decided on the disposition of money seized in a foreign province.[59] This deference to secular authority suggests that Theodore was "a cooperator, not a rebuker," anxious to establish the church's disciplinary authority by linking it to the king's.[60] We see here a state of affairs comparable to that seen in early Ireland; there too it was in the church's interest to cooperate with secular law rather than to attempt to contradict it.

The short handbook assigned to Bede follows closely the penances for homicide in Theodore's handbook. It includes a reduced penance for one who slew at his lord's command or killed in public warfare—both points having been raised by Theodore.[61] The Bedan handbook also requires compensation in addition to penance for one who wounded another.[62] The dependence of the Bedan text on Theodore's in these penances suggests that both belong to roughly the same milieu and stand together against Egbert's. His tariff for homicide involving the clergy depends on similar tariffs in Theodore's penitential but omits the possibility of reducing penance by paying compensation; nor is there a penance for killing in public warfare or at the command of one's lord.[63] Few crimes can have created more

57. Book 1. 4. 5; Finsterwalder, *Canones*, p. 294.

58. Book 1. 4. 1, 4 (*ibid.*); restitution of stolen goods also shortened the penance for theft: Book 1. 3. 3. (*ibid.*, p. 293).

59. Book 1. 7. 2; *ibid.*, p. 298.

60. See J. M. Wallace-Hadrill, *Early Germanic Kingship in England and on the Continent*, p. 69.

61. Bede 4. 6, 7; Wasserschleben, *Bussordnungen*, p. 225.

62. Bede 4. 11; *ibid.*

63. Egbert 4. 10 (*ibid.*, p. 235), but note that Egbert 4. 11 parallels Bede 4. 4–5. It is curious that Egbert takes no stand against blood-feud, a major problem for the church. See Wallace-Hadrill, *Early Germanic Kingship*, p. 69.

problems for either secular or ecclesiastical courts than murder, and it is difficult to know what to make of the brevity with which Egbert's penitential treats so vital and complex a topic.

We can conclude, however, that neither the Bedan nor the Egbertine penitential measures up to Theodore's in scope; both reflect limited—one might almost say local—concerns rather than the broad, "national" issues raised by Theodore. Only Theodore mentions matters which would require jurisdiction higher than the bishop's or archbishop's (that is, the king's).[64] If we were to speak of scale, the penitentials assigned to Bede and Egbert could be considered comparable and of a different, lesser order than Theodore's. In this they resemble the Irish handbooks, since they too are without the encompassing administrative ambitions of Theodore's penitential. Both are closer to the penitential of Theodore in the sins they include, but Bede's does contain an idiom which at least hints of Irish influence. The introductory paragraph claims that the text was written not with the authority "of a censor but rather the counsel of a fellow sufferer," a phrase which recalls an Old Irish homily wherein penance is defined as "fellow suffering." The word "counsel" too puts us in mind of the confessor's role in the Irish monastery.[65]

It is disturbing that the brave start represented by Theodore's penitential should appear to have no obvious consequences for his successors. It is tempting to accept at least the idea that Egbert wrote a penitential so that we can imagine a solid eighth-century English tradition of handbooks of penance. Egbert's authorship is certainly far more plausible than Bede's, and it is entirely possible that both the short Bedan text discussed above and some form of Egbert's penitential were in fact written in England in the eighth century. These two penitentials must be discussed again in the context of the Frankish reforms, which probably inspired attempts to conflate them into a single handbook. To the extent that both claim English authorship, they have had to be considered in the context of Theodore's peniten-

64. Bede 4. 1 is based on Theodore, Book 1. 4. 5, but omits penance for the murder of a bishop, which necessitated the king's participation. See Wasserschleben, *Bussordnungen*, p. 224, and Finsterwalder, *Canones*, p. 294.

65. "Non auctoritate censoris sed consilio potius conpatiens"; Wasserschleben, *Bussordnungen*, p. 220. For the *Cambrai Homily*, see chapter two, n. 24.

tial as well, even though they do not attest to the influence of that handbook with the vigor one would like.

Further evidence of the impact of penitential practice on eighth-century England must be sought from other sources. Among these the secular laws are most important and can be analyzed in tandem with ecclesiastical legislation which shows that penance was an established tradition at this time. Both kinds of legislative texts refer to penance as customary for the laity, and the church's canons required the clergy to administer penance as one of their chief responsibilities. Without the evidence of these laws, it would be difficult to claim that penitential practice had made much headway in English society. The penitentials had no compelling authority of their own. Nor did the sermons preached by the clergy. Society did not change simply because the church said it ought to; there was no automatic transfer of values from the church to the people the church governed. Episcopal decrees, backed by the secular laws, were necessary before a new and demanding form of discipline and the Christian life it prescribed could command both respect and obedience.

Because Anglo-Saxon laws were not subject to the "Christianizing" revision of monastic scribes, they offer more reliable evidence of penitential standards than the early Irish codes. English law was customary, based on precedent; the law codes record decisions actually arrived at by judges and are not mere theoretical constructs with little relevance to existing conditions.[66] Even before Theodore's arrival at Canterbury, the church cooperated closely with secular authority and based certain decisions on the desire for political unity. Such was the case at Whitby in 664, at a synod called to settle the conflict between the Irish and Roman methods of calculating Easter. The triumph of the Roman party was declared by the Northumbrian king, Oswiu, who feared the political disharmony likely to result from a failure to agree on one Easter, one form of baptism, and similar matters.[67]

As Theodore's penitential shows, royal opinions added the force

66. There is an excellent introduction to English law by Patrick Wormald, "*Lex Scripta* and *Verbum Regis*: Legislation and Germanic Kingship, from Euric to Cnut."

67. See Mayr-Harting, *The Coming*, pp. 104–107, for the political background to the synod.

of native law to certain of the church's prohibitions. In general the early law codes treat ecclesiastical penance as an addition to secular penalties. Although this attitude on the lawmaker's part helped to establish the church's authority, it does not signal a substantial Christian influence on native law, which retained a character completely different from ecclesiastical penance. The laws of Ethelbert, king of Kent (602–603 ?), do little more than specify a schedule for compensation of the church's property and officials; the "peace of a meeting" is also protected and a fine exacted for its disruption.[68] Later, the laws of Wihtred, also Kentish (695), not only protect the church's property but punish the violation of the Sunday observance and provide for a system of exculpation based on the relationship to the church of the parties involved. These laws also require the performance of ecclesiastical penance by those who live in illicit unions. After the laws were promulgated, anyone who entered into such a union "in spite of the command of the king and the bishop and the decree of the books" was heavily fined ("books" here could mean the penitentials as well as ecclesiastical canons). The laws of Ine, contemporary with those of Wihtred, refer to the church less frequently but require prompt baptism and the observance of Sunday and respect the sanctuary of the church for the condemned.[69]

The early law codes supported the penitentials but are not specifically indebted to them. Their relationship was complementary rather than closely cooperative because their objectives were distinct. The laws required compensation for crimes, while the handbooks served the nobler goal of restoring the soul to grace. Even when material compensation formed part of the sinner's penance, the sinner's cure involved spiritual atonement through fasting, almsgiving, or other penitential deeds.

The social classes reflected in the handbooks cut across those

---

68. The laws are edited by Felix Liebermann, *Die Gesetze der Angelsachsen*; for convenience I quote the translation in *English Historical Documents*, ed. and trans. Dorothy Whitelock and David C. Douglas (hereafter *EHD*). For an introduction to the laws, see *EHD*, pp. 357–389, and for Ethelbert 1, p. 391. In Liebermann, see 1: 3–8.

69. For Wihtred 5, see *EHD*, pp. 396–397, and n. 1; for Ine 1–3, 5, *ibid.*, pp. 399–400 (Ine 13 also penalizes one who bears false witness before the bishop). In Liebermann, *Gesetze*, see 1: 12–14 (Wihtred) and 88–123 (Ine).

established by the law codes. In the laws of Ethelbert, for example, the murder of a slave requires less compensation than the murder of a free man. No such distinction is made in the penitential of Theodore, although it assigns different penances for the murder of a cleric than for that of a layman, a distinction not made in the laws.[70] The penitentials also protected the rights of women, children, and the unborn more carefully than the laws. Ethelbert's code requires anyone having illicit relations with a female servant to pay compensation according to the status of her owner. Theodore's penitential takes a different approach, assessing a penance of six months to one who violated the slave but also giving her her freedom. If one violated a free woman, he did penance for one to three years.[71] These penances are based on the social status of the offended party rather than the offender. Their net effect is to raise the woman's worth, since it and not the status of the man who owned her determined the penance for those who violated her rights. The church distinguished between a free woman and a slave in this matter; the laws did not, but instead distinguished between the slave of a free man and that of a nobleman. It is generally agreed that women fared better in Anglo-Saxon times than in the later Middle Ages; they could inherit and manage property and, if they chose, divorce their husbands.[72] They were, of course, barred from holding ecclesiastical office; they were not allowed to enter church during the "time of impurity"; and they were more likely to be suspected of practicing magic than men.[73]

70. Book 1. 4. 5; the murderer of a cleric was required to relinquish his arms and "serve God" (meaning to enter orders) or to do penance for seven years; the murderer of a layman was not required to disarm; see Finsterwalder, *Canones*, p. 294.

71. Book 1. 14. 9–12; *ibid.*, p. 308. In Ethelbert 10–11, sex with the king's maiden was fined fifty shillings; with a nobleman's serving woman, twenty-five shillings; with a *ceorl*'s serving woman, only six (a *ceorl* was a free man of the lowest class). See *EHD*, pp. 391–392, and in Liebermann, *Gesetze*, 1: 3.

72. See Shiela C. Dietrich, "Women in Anglo-Saxon Society," and Marc A. Meyer, "Land Charters and the Legal Position of Anglo-Saxon Women," in *The Women of England from Anglo-Saxon Times to the Present*, ed. Barbara Kanner. Theodore's penitential offers some interesting evidence here: a woman whose husband was a thief or a fornicator was allowed, after one year, to remarry if she had not been married once already (Book 2. 12. 9); a legal marriage could be dissolved only with the consent of both parties (Book 2. 12. 7); Finsterwalder, *Canones*, p. 327.

73. Women's ministry in the church was delimited by Theodore (Book 2. 7. 1–4;

There is, therefore, no reason to be sanguine about their standing in Anglo-Saxon society, but it is necessary to observe that the church's influence was not strictly a negative or confining one where they were concerned.[74] It is doubtful that the penitentials would deliberately conflict with the accepted customs enforced by the secular laws, even if the church had traditionally assigned a higher place to women than the laws allowed. We should not look for evidence that the church used penance or other forms of ecclesiastical discipline to remake society.

Within the world of the church's own legislation, we find good evidence that penitential practice was an important part of eighth-century pastoral activity. The decrees of the Council of Clovesho required that bishops make sure, before conferring Holy Orders, that the candidates for priesthood know how to preach sound doctrine and discern suitable penances for sinners.[75] The same council urged frequent communion among the laity, which would have necessitated confession as part of the preparation for receiving the sacrament,[76] and required archbishops to take up those cases which bishops had been unable to decide—cases among which, we may suppose, penitential decisions were numbered.[77] As we have seen, the council was concerned about the laxity associated with commutations; it insisted that penance could not be performed vicariously, the option of those wealthy enough to hire (or force) others to undertake penances for them. Divine justice, the bishops warned, cannot

Finsterwalder, *Canones*, p. 322); they were kept from church during menstruation and were required to be purified after childbirth (Book 1. 14. 17–18); two canons concerning magic mention women as the instigators (Book 1. 15. 2, 4; *ibid.*, pp. 309–310).

74. For example, penances for women who committed abortion in effect protected the rights of the unborn (see Book 1. 14. 24, 27; *ibid.*, pp. 309–310). Additional canons protected the rights of children (cc. 25–26). For further discussion, see Thomas P. Oakley, *English Penitential Discipline and Anglo-Saxon Law in Their Joint Influence*, pp. 193–196.

75. Ed. Haddan and Stubbs, *Councils*, 3:364, c. 6: "qua namque potest ratione aliis integritatem fidei praedicare, sermonis scientiam conferre, peccantibus discretionem poenitentiae indicare."

76. *Ibid.*, p. 370, c. 23.

77. *Ibid.*, p. 371, c. 25.

be appeased by others: each man must stand alone before the tribunal of Christ.[78]

The church enforced penitential discipline as a part of habitual Christian observance not necessarily linked to the confession of sins. These ascetic acts included almsgiving and fasting. The laity would have undertaken these exercises during Advent and Lent, when confession and penance were urged on the faithful. Evidence for this practice is found in the *Dialogue* of Egbert, accepted as genuine and believed to have been written between 750 and 760. The *Dialogue* claims that the English are as accustomed to fasting, vigils, and almsgiving as if these customs were assigned by law, and that since the time of Theodore, not only clerics but also lay people "would approach their own confessors and would wash themselves of the fellowship of fleshly concupiscence by tears and by almsgiving," and so prepare themselves to receive communion on the feast of the Nativity. This too was done as if it were law.[79] Broadly interpreted, this may mean that confession and penance had become habitual among English Christians of the mid-eighth century. But it is well to remember that such practice formed part of the ideal of perfection which the church wished to set before the laity.[80] Interpreted more conservatively, the passage may say, in effect, "Clerics in the monasteries do penance at the appropriate times, and even lay people come to confess and give alms so that they may communicate at Christmas." The *Dialogue* leaves no doubt that a high standard was set, but

78. *Ibid.*, pp. 373–374, c. 27 (partly translated by McNeill and Gamer, *Handbooks*, p. 394).

79. Text in Haddan and Stubbs, *Councils* (Response 16), p. 413: "Nam haec, Deo gratias, a temporibus Vitaliani papae, et Theodori Dorobernensis Archiepiscopi inolevit in aecclesia Anglorum consuetudo, et quasi legitima tenebatur, ut non solum clerici in monasteriis, sed etiam laici cum conjugibus et familiis suis ad confessores suos pervenirent, et se fletibus et carnalis concupiscentiae consortio his duodecim diebus cum elemosinarum largitione mundarent, quatenus puriores Dominicae communionis perceptionem in Natale Domini perciperent." Translation based on McNeill and Gamer, *Handbooks*, p. 243.

80. The argument for habitual confession is made by Oscar D. Watkins, *A History of Penance*, 2:654–655; Mayr-Harting believes that the church, "galvanized" by "its low estimation of the married state," set a standard of perfection before the laity. His remarks on Egbert's *Dialogue* support Watkins's view that penitential practice was (as Mayr-Harting says) "deeply rooted in the life of the Anglo-Saxon church"; see *The Coming*, pp. 259–261.

as a text "suitable for the instruction of priests by a bishop, on matters of church discipline," it is obviously not to be given too much
weight as historical evidence.[81]

The *Dialogue* also states that anyone who had undergone public
penance was unable to take Holy Orders and requires public penance
for murder, fornication, worship of idols, and other serious sins.
Again it is not clear how far we should trust the evidence. The reg-
ulation about orders, for example, appears to be a transcription of a
canon from the early church.[82] Theodore observed that the public
reconciliation of penitents was not known to the English, and no
liturgical records of public penance date from his time or Egbert's.[83]
Penitents confessed openly to wandering monks, as Bede's *Life* of
Cuthbert shows, but such gatherings of the faithful around the confessor did not have a formal liturgical character and did not constitute public penance. Presumably the laity were instructed to confess
and do penance by the clergy who visited or those who lived in
villages and small settlements. In a letter written shortly before his
death, Bede urged Egbert to equip himself with a clergy able to baptize and preach to the "ignorant people," those "acquainted with no
language but their own." Bede also complained that those living in
less accessible areas had no bishops to visit them and supervise their
spiritual needs. Hence, it was particularly important for the clergy to
teach them to pray the Lord's Prayer and the Apostles' Creed "in
their own language" and by preaching to exhort and reprove them.[84]

The impact of penitential practice on literate classes is somewhat
easier to illustrate than the penitential habits of uneducated lay

81. McNeill and Gamer, *Handbooks*, p. 239.

82. Haddan and Stubbs, *Councils* (Response 15), p. 410; McNeill and Gamer, *Handbooks*, p. 240, n. 8, show the similarity between this provision and an early canonical
penance for the clergy.

83. Book I. 13. 4 (Finsterwalder, *Canones*, p. 306); Oakley argues for public penance in
England partly on the basis of the so-called *Pontifical* of Egbert, which contains a
ceremony for public reconciliation. But this is not an eighth-century liturgy, and it has
no association with Egbert except that it includes the prologue to his penitential; see
Penitential Discipline, pp. 74–77. On the correct dating of the *Pontifical*, see Max Förster, "Zur Liturgik der angelsächsischen Kirche," pp. 2–3.

84. *EHD*, p. 801; the letter is dated 5 November 734. On the location of village
churches, see Rosalind Hill, "Christianity and Geography in Early Northumbria,"
Studies in Church History 3 (1966): 126–139.

people. Only the laws and the penitentials, supported by synodical demands for preaching and penance, reflect the influence of penance on the lay population. Literate Englishmen left additional records which show that during the eighth century penance had become a part of their culture. One measure of this influence is the language of official documents. The Council of Clovesho, confirming the *Privilege* of Wihtred (742), recorded that the decree of Æthelbald, king of Mercia, was made "for the health of my soul, and for the stability of my kingdom." The *Privilege* of Æthelbald himself (749) was made "for love of the heavenly home and the remedy of my soul."[85] The charters offer additional examples of the medical metaphor, including the theory of contraries, in the legal language of early England.[86] These expressions may have been derived from sources common to the penitentials and to other forms, or from the handbooks themselves as the nobility knew about them through confession. By sharing ecclesiastical idiom in this way, their documents acquired the cast of devout expression.

One important literary form attests more strongly than any other to the impact of penance on the language of devotion in early England. This is private prayer. Once again the evidence reflects the thought and practice of the literate classes. Prayers recited by the laity include those listed by Bede and valued for their catechetical content. But in the eighth century far more elaborate private prayers were read and recited by monks and the nobility. The small books which contain them recall the handbooks of penance, and like the handbooks they may have been carried by the owner from place to place. Some of these prayers are fervent, intensely ascetic, and sophisticated in style; not surprisingly, they have long been seen as expressive of Irish influence because of both their verbal excesses and their apparent debt to penitential practice. The most famous such collection is *The Book of Cerne*; others include *The Book of Nunnaminster*, a Harleian manuscript known as the *Irish Libellus Precum*, and British

---

85. For the *Privilege* of Wihtred, see Haddan and Stubbs, *Councils*, 3:340–341; and for the *Privilege* of Æthelbald, pp. 386–387.

86. Evidence from the charters is noted by Margaret Deanesly, *The Pre-Conquest Church in England*, p. 127.

Library MS Royal 2 A. xx.[87] A famous description of these prayer collections distinguishes their "Celtic" and "Roman" styles. The Irish prayers were written "with all heart and much fluency with little mind," while those of Roman origin were composed with "all mind and . . . small heart."[88] What besides the excesses of such prayers brings the Irish church to mind? At first, it was only that the prayers employ the medical metaphor and apply it to the priest rather than to Christ as the doctor of souls, as the Mozarabic liturgy, an influence on Irish ritual, also does. In the Roman liturgy, the expression is applied only to Christ.[89] After this qualified beginning, claims of Irish influence on private prayer became much more sweeping. The lists of parts of the body in these prayers were traced to the penitentials; the prayers themselves were seen as examinations of the conscience but still related to "genuine confessions"; and some of the prayers were said to have been derived from Irish orders for private penance and adapted for private use.

An examination of the prayers for which so much Irish influence has been claimed will show that they acquired certain features from Irish sources, but probably not from the penitentials. The list of the parts of the body is an example. Popular in both Latin and vernacular texts in Ireland, the list appears in the "breastplate" poems, or *loricæ*, in charms, and in the liturgy for baptism and exorcism.[90] Nowhere was the list used as part of a confession of sins, however, and this is precisely its most interesting use, though not its only one, in the

---

87. The early English and Irish prayer collections are surveyed by James F. Kenney, *The Sources for the Early History of Ireland*, pp. 723–732. For editions see: *The Prayer Book of Aedelauld the Bishop Commonly Called the Book of Cerne*, ed. A. B. Kuypers; Walter de Gray Birch, ed., *An Ancient Manuscript of the Eighth or Ninth Century; Formerly Belonging to St. Mary's Abbey, or Nunnaminster, Winchester*. Kuypers prints the Royal manuscript on pp. 201–225 and compares the contents of *Cerne*, the Royal manuscript, and Harley 7653 on pp. 232–233.

88. Edmund Bishop, *Liturgica Historica*, p. 385.

89. See Bishop's "Liturgical Note" to the *Cerne* collection, p. 246 in Kuypers's edition.

90. The *lorica* is a prayer to be recited in time of danger (hence as a "breastplate"); the English evidence is surveyed by Kathleen Hughes, "Some Aspects of Irish Influence on Early English Private Prayer." See also Thomas D. Hill, "Invocation of the Trinity and the Tradition of the *Lorica* in Old English Poetry," *Speculum* 56 (1981): 259–267.

early English prayers. Some of these prayers ask God to take custody of the senses, thus paralleling the *lorica*, which was recited to gain protection for the parts of the body. Such prayers give the *lorica* a "completely ethical and non-physical content" by attaching an action to each part of the body (theft to the hands, for example) and asking that each part be protected from the weakness to which it inclines.[91] The sixth prayer in the *Cerne* collection is an example: the sinner prays that his mouth will be protected against secular stories and cursing and used only to praise the Lord; his eyes are to be kept from seeing and desiring women; and so forth, a progression of the anatomical catalogue which works from head to foot, as does the *lorica*.[92] This and similar prayers are not extensive catalogues; they name only those parts of the body normally associated with serious sin.

The confessional prayers, in contrast, are outstanding because they name a great many parts of the body, and do so in a disorderly fashion. The eighth *Cerne* prayer, a "confessio sancti penitentis," is a rather extreme example; the tenth, an "alma confessio," is more restrained. In the former, a long list of sins is followed by an exhaustive list of body parts, including kidneys, hair, mouth, tongue, hands, and feet; the speaker adds the phrase "everything wet or dry, inside or out" to show that he wishes no part to be omitted.[93] The tenth prayer begins with a long prayer of praise and then enumerates sins and lists a few parts of the body; the choices seem to have been made for euphonic reasons: "peccavi in naribus et in audibus, peccavi in manibus et in pedibus, peccavi in lingua et guttore, peccavi in collo et in pectore."[94] Such confessions have been called the "corollary" to the penitentials, especially since both the prayers and the penitentials list more sins than one person could possibly commit.[95] This is a superficial similarity at best. Certainly the handbook was not, in its most ambitious Irish incarnation, intended as imaginative literature, nor were its sins supposed to have been committed by a single per-

91. Hughes, "Aspects," p. 55.

92. A list of parts and an analysis of their order in Isidore of Seville's *Etymologies*, one of the *loricae*, and the seventh-century Irish *Antiphony of Bangor* is given by Patrick Sims-Williams, "Thought, Words, and Deed: An Irish Triad," p. 92.

93. Kuypers, *Cerne*, pp. 91–94.

94. *Ibid.*, pp. 95–99.

95. Hughes, "Aspects," p. 55.

son. Its completeness is functional, not formulaic: it was supposed to provide penances for all the sins which the confessor's congregation might have committed.

The second link between these prayers and the penitentials is the medical metaphor, but this supposed similarity is no more convincing than the first. The prayers do not extend or exploit the metaphor; rather, they use only one of its many facets, the identification of the priest with a physician, and neglect other possibilities which belong to the metaphor, such as the theory of contraries and references to wounds or cures. Whatever the Irish background to the confessional prayers in *The Book of Cerne* is, it is not to be seen in the Irish penitentials' use of the medical metaphor. Nor are there Irish "orders" of penance from which such prayers might have been adapted—at least none pertaining to the ceremony of private confession. Where the *Cerne* prayers suggest a liturgical context—as, for example, the fourteenth, the "Reconcilio Penitentium"—we see remnants of the public rather than the private rite. Since public reconciliation was known in Ireland, this prayer may have been derived from an Irish order of public penance; but since this particular prayer does not contain a list of parts of the body, it seems unnecessary to look for its antecedent in Irish rather than continental penitential practice.[96]

It is difficult to connect the confessional prayers to confession and private penance as governed by the handbooks, but easy to see them in another context, that of devotional confession. In addition to confession to the priest, Irish penitents confessed to each other, and to God alone. One of the "twelve remissions of sin" in the preface to Cummean's penitential testifies to this kind of non-sacramental confession: "I will confess against myself my injustice to the Lord, and you have forgiven the iniquity of my sin."[97] Finnian endorsed this method of confession; his penitential considers sins of thought forgiven if the sinner "shall beat his breast and seek pardon from God and make satisfaction."[98] Private prayers in which the sinner claims to have committed many sins, and then asks for absolution, are the devotional counterpart to confession of this kind. They ob-

96. Sims-Williams, "Thought," p. 104, says that "formulae" for private confession "clearly underlie many prayers in these books," and cites *Cerne* no. 14 as an example.

97. Bieler, *Irish Penitentials*, p. 109. For the tradition of confession to God alone, see Cyrille Vogel, *Les "Libri Paenitentiales*," pp. 55–57.

98. Bieler, *Irish Penitentials*, p. 75.

tain forgiveness without the intercession of the confessor. They also have a more specific devotional function which explains their exaggerated style: their multiple accusations against the sinner emphasize his utter unworthiness in order to exalt the greatness of God's mercy.[99]

How the confessional prayers would have worked as part of a private confession is difficult to imagine. The purpose of that encounter was to uncover the sinner's guilt and assign expiation for his offenses. A long recitation of imagined offenses would not facilitate that process. But in a ceremony not concluded by the assigning of penance—such as the public reconciliation of penitents—and in private prayer, long confessions served an obvious purpose. They were a way to ensure that the penitent had confessed completely; and they were sure to impress on the sinner his weakness and his need to guard against it.[100]

The vast majority of confessional prayers in English manuscripts avoid lengthy enumerative catalogues, either of sins or of parts of the body. The most extreme example, the eighth prayer in the *Cerne* collection, appears in no other manuscript yet known; the tenth, which circulated widely both in England and on the continent, contains only abbreviated forms of either list.[101] The remainder of the prayers are, by comparison, moderate in style and quite unlike either of these. The *Cerne* collection suggests a toning down of possible excesses, an avoidance of extremes also seen in the English penitentials. The strictly formal pattern of organization used in Cummean's penitential—the eight chief sins—and the complex system of tariffs seen in other Irish penitentials were abandoned by the English. Likewise the English modified the private prayers which incorporated the confession of sins with a list of parts of the body. In addition to the

99. Mayr-Harting, *The Coming*, p. 183; quoting *Cerne* no. 10, Mayr-Harting calls it "a prayer to be gone through slowly by one who would carefully consider the implications of his own thoughts and actions under each item." The proximity of such prayers to incantations does not suggest that they were necessarily recited thoughtfully; in any case, the "implications" of certain items—for example, the sins of the hair—would seem rather far-fetched.

100. See *Le Pontifical Romano-Germanique du dixième siècle*, ed. Cyrille Vogel and Reinhard Elze, 2: 16–17.

101. See Sims-Williams, "Thought," p. 108, n. 179, for a list of early manuscripts containing *Cerne* no. 10.

Cerne manuscript, evidence of this transformation appears in continental prayer collections. These are the *libelli precum*, written in the first half of the ninth century (some manuscripts are from the early part of the century); some appear to have been compiled under the supervision of Alcuin, the Northumbrian who became Charlemagne's teacher.[102]

Several of these prayerbooks contain a prayer believed to be Alcuin's and employing both kinds of lists. In it the sinner confesses that his feet raced after pleasure but were slow in obeying the Lord's commands, that his knees bent more gladly in fornicating than in worship, that his stomach swelled with gluttony and drunkenness.[103] Much in the prayer suggests the synthesis of a creative mind working to reshape the materials of a rather primitive motif. The prayer moves from the foot up, using a selective, carefully ordered arrangement and at the same time inverting the head-to-foot progression found in the *lorica* and the English prayer collections. Sins are not only assigned to specific parts of the body but animated: the feet run, the stomach swells. Nothing confessed here is extravagant. The sinner's hands are said to be bathed in blood, but even this detail may be appropriate, for the prayer is thought to have been written for Charlemagne, whose actions as emperor inevitably had their cost in human life.[104] The prayer also uses the medical metaphor in a way apparently new to such confessions. Sins are compared to wounds, and the confessor is said to cure them. Commonplace in other sources, these expressions do not appear in the English prayers before Alcuin. Although the prayer clearly goes beyond its predecessors, it remains very much like them: it lists some twenty-three parts of the body, a list shorter than the *lorica*'s (over one hundred) but longer by far than that found in any other confessional prayer.[105] Alcuin knew collec-

102. For a general introduction, see André Wilmart, "Manuscrits de Tours copiés et décorés vers le temps d'Alcuin," *RB* 42 (1930): 46–54.

103. Text in *PL* 101:1404–1405; identified as Alcuin's by Wilmart, "Le manuel de prières de saint Jean Gualbert," p. 282, n. 5.

104. Wilmart, *Precum Libelli Quattor Aevi Karolini*, p. 21, cites a manuscript claiming that Alcuin wrote the prayer for Charlemagne.

105. Isidore lists 86 parts, and an Irish *lorica* over 120; see Michael Herren, "The Authorship, Date of Composition, and Provenance of the So-Called *Lorica Gildae*," *Ériu* 24 (1973): 46.

tions like *The Book of Cerne* and included some of their contents in his own *libelli*.[106] But he reworked the tradition of protective and confessional prayers, eliminating excesses and emphasizing those qualities which made the prayer a vivid and moving confession.

Alcuin's restraint, if not his imagination, finds a counterpart in the *Cerne* collection. Many of the *Cerne* prayers are confessions, but only the eighth and the tenth employ the anatomical catalogues and the list of sins. The ninth is a "sancta confessio" which includes neither catalogue; the seventeenth, though not a confession, uses the anatomical motif to describe Christ's body and to contrast his physical sufferings to man's sins. The twenty-third, twenty-fourth, and twenty-fifth prayers are confessions, but again none uses either list. Prayers in another section of the manuscript, written slightly later than the first, make use of some of the earlier entries, but with important changes. For example, the forty-ninth prayer is a revision of the seventeenth which drastically reduces the anatomical catalogue, transforming its "pious abandon" with "sobriety and restraint."[107]

"Sobriety and restraint" might well be said to characterize English adaptations of both disciplinary and devotional materials from the Irish tradition. Because the Irish penitentials and prayers have been seen as more exotic than they really are, their differences from English disciplinary and devotional materials are easily exaggerated. But it would be difficult to deny that these differences exist. Some of the characteristics of Irish religious literature not found in the English evidence would seem to reflect ancient Irish traditions much older than Irish Christian culture. The confessional prayers are an example. They retain the flavor of an oral literature; like litanies, they were meant to be recited, to be chanted; part of their beauty lies in the pleasure they give the ear.

Reading the confessional prayers, one thinks of the Irish fondness for the psalms and the hagiographic motif in which the saint chants the *Beati* for protection during a journey. "The path I walk, Christ walks it," says one prayer; "may the land in which I am be

106. *Cerne* no. 15 and no. 21 both occur in the *libelli*; Sims-Williams, "Thought," pp. 99–103, notes several examples of prayers from the early English collections which appear in later continental manuscripts.

107. Kuypers, *Cerne*, p. xix.

without sorrow."[108] Equally characteristic of the early Irish imagination is a simple, literal vision. One famous poem, possibly ninth century, draws a comparison between a hooded monk and a singing
bird, also "dressed" in gray, and encourages no further analysis of
this straightforward juxtaposition.[109] A bird in an Anglo-Saxon lyric
would never get off so lightly: it would be made to represent either
the soul or the mind; its literal properties alone would not justify its
appearance in the text.[110]

Inviting though such contrasts are, they are also admittedly superficial. Nonetheless, they offer a useful if limited way to gain
a perspective on "English" as opposed to "Irish" qualities in both
prayers and penitentials. English texts are less varied and colorful
than the Irish for several reasons. It may be that the English were,
after all, soberer and more restrained. But it is also obvious that they
were working with materials foreign to their own culture and seeking to adapt them to administrative purposes and pastoral conditions
which, if not entirely new, were at least substantially different from
those of the early Irish mission.

Evidence of the first stage of the English penitential tradition is
admittedly weak, not only in comparison to the Irish period which
preceded it, but also in comparison to the continental traditions contemporary with it and subsequent to it. England's reception and
modification of the Irish handbooks find close counterparts in the
continental churches of the eighth and ninth centuries. Those
churches were nourished by English as well as Irish missionaries, and
their disciplinary and devotional materials alike display this twin in-

108. Text edited by James Carney, "Three Old Irish Accentual Poems," *Ériu* 22
(1971): 28. On the tradition of reciting the *Beati* (Psalm 118) for protection, see Charles
Plummer, ed., *Vitae Sanctorum Hiberniae*, 1: clxxix (with many references to the lives
of Irish saints).

109. "The Scribe in the Woods": "A hedge of trees overlooks me; a blackbird's lay
sings to me (an announcement which I shall not conceal); above my lined book the
birds' chanting sings to me. A clear-voiced cuckoo sings to me (goodly utterance) in a
grey cloak from bush fortresses. The Lord is indeed good to me: well do I write
beneath a forest of woodland." Ed. and trans. Gerard Murphy, *Early Irish Lyrics*, p. 5.

110. Indeed, whole articles are written about this topic; see Margaret Goldsmith, "*The
Seafarer* and the Birds," *RES* 5 (1954): 225–235; the bird's figurative meaning is dis-
cussed by Neal Hultin, "The External Soul in 'The Seafarer' and 'The Wanderer,'"
Folklore 88 (1977): 39–45.

sular heritage. It is one of the paradoxes of the history of penance that the English mission to the continent survives more fully in the manuscripts than the Irish. More continental manuscripts of penitentials cite the authority of Theodore, Bede, and Egbert than of any Irishman; the only possible exception is Cummean, whose penitential, interpolated with non-Irish material, was exceptionally popular.[111] There are many reasons for this, but one is certainly a suspicion, voiced on the continent already in the eighth century, that Irish intellectual traditions were arcane and that certain authorities cited by Irish penitentials (among them Gregory and Augustine) had not written the books which the Irish claimed for them. The English do not seem to have suffered from similar prejudices; indeed, the long and vigorous tradition assigning a penitential and many other texts to Bede, on no authority whatsoever, would seem to suggest that his authority, like Theodore's and Egbert's, was preferred.

On the continent the penitential was, for the first time, a subject of controversy. The English church of the eighth century experienced no similar uprising against the handbook, no doubt because Theodore's penitential subsumed the text into an administrative corpus of "national" scope; although recognized as foreign, the handbook was not seen as intrusive or disruptive. This early and wholehearted acceptance of the Irish system of private penance was to have far-reaching consequences for English history. It set a precedent followed by reformers two centuries later, when Theodore's text was known in several versions, Egbert's was well known, and Egbert himself was credited with translating a handbook into Anglo-Saxon. In the later period the eighth-century English church, and not the Frankish, was seen as the source of the English disciplinary and devotional tradition. Given the demonstrable discontinuities of the handbooks, whose tenth-century form differed greatly from that of the eighth, this was a remarkable assumption.

In the Frankish church, the penitential gained fresh form and expanded function, partly as a result of Frankish bishops' efforts to regulate and reform private confession and penance, and partly as a result of the influence of the public penitential rite. Neither of these

111. See Kenney, *Sources*, p. 243.

forces was at work in the early English church. The English seem to have known little more about penance and confession than the Irish had taught them; for this reason the English subjected the private penitential system to only minor modification. The Franks were in a much stronger position. Unable to reject the Irish system—an ambition which has unconvincingly been imputed to them—they changed it substantially, hoping to bring private confession and penance into closer alignment with the canonical traditions of the early church. The Franks also attempted to construct a theology to support private confession and penance, and so to integrate the practices fully into received tradition.

Flexible texts whose generic identity depended on their utility rather than on specific content, the penitentials did not lose their most important attributes in this process of revision and reform. As long as the text served the priest in hearing confession, and as long as it attached graduated penalties to the sins listed, it was a penitential. The Franks reshaped it to accomplish more, but in so doing they demonstrated the text's capacity for expansion rather than its inherent limits. It might seem that the penitential, after its minor transformation at English hands and its major overhaul on the continent, had ceased to be Irish in a meaningful sense.[112] But the English and Frankish authorities who issued penitentials worked from Irish handbooks, selected some of their provisions, kept faithfully to their formulae, and so continually renewed the tradition on which the text was based. They did not do so out of reverence for the Irish themselves, but out of a strong administrative sense that the handbook, whatever its antecedents and however great its capacity to generate legislative chaos, was a splendidly practical tool for establishing discipline and fostering devotion. These were the dual purposes of the church's mission, the pastoral equivalents of the counsel and correction first dispensed by Irish monks.

112. For this view, see G. S. M. Walker, ed., *Sancti Columbani Opera*, p. xxxiii: "there is scarcely one European penitential which does not show some trace of Irish influence." But this is to forget that the penitential, as a form, was Irish.

Chapter Four

Irish, Anglo-Saxon, and Frankish
Penitentials in the Ninth Century

O N the continent in the ninth century, the handbook of penance was for the first time the subject of a clearly focused
controversy. Frankish bishops attacked inconsistent standards represented by penitentials introduced in earlier centuries by
Irish and Anglo-Saxon missionaries; they questioned the authority
which the handbooks invested in the priest and ultimately doubted
the efficacy of private confession and penance. Their misgivings led
them to bring the penitentials into conformity with older, canonical
standards of discipline and to ensure that the ritual of confession
engaged both priest and penitent in a conscientious effort to acknowledge and atone for sins. The concerns of the bishops were
theoretical as well as practical; while the handbooks were being revised and made more systematic, theological arguments were advanced to establish the orthodoxy of the private penitential system.

The ninth-century reformers sought to eradicate weaknesses to
which the handbooks were prone—for example, inconsistencies in
the severity of penances or too great a dependence on the priest's
judgment—and which had become pronounced during the two centuries of the handbooks' use on the continent. The penitential was
introduced to continental churches by Irish missionaries. The most
famous of them, Columbanus, wrote his penitential in northern Italy
near the end of the sixth century.[1] Although the handbook must have
been among the features which distinguished the Irish monks from
their continental counterparts, it is not mentioned by Columbanus

1. Ed. G. S. M. Walker, *Sancti Columbani Opera*, pp. 168–181; on the date see
pp. lii–lv.

in a defensive context. His letters assert the superiority of those customs attacked as heretical (the dating of Easter, the style of tonsure), but about church discipline they say only that standards of Irish austerity were far stricter than those observed by the holy men of Gaul.[2] Understandably enough, Columbanus's greatest success was not among the clergy whom he challenged, but among the laity. "Women, especially, were seduced by the rigors of Columban's teaching," Riché writes, and they evidently flocked to convents in Gaul to share in a renewed female monasticism.[3] It is doubtful that anyone could be "seduced" by asceticism unless he or she had already been fully committed to the Christian life. Perhaps the teachings of Columbanus injected new life into the Christianity of the laity who met him; but perhaps the difference he made in their lives was one of kind rather than degree. In either case we may surmise that he was effective among small groups of the very pious, who were, of course, also the nobility with the learning and the leisure to pursue religion as an occupation. It was from that social level that private penitential practice descended into the mainstream of continental Christian life.

A second current carrying penitential discipline reached the continent shortly after the Columbanian mission. This came from the Anglo-Saxon church, which had become involved in political life in Frisia in the seventh century. This contact began during the episcopate at York of Wilfrid (d. 709), who had lived in Gaul, and it flourished under another Northumbrian, Willibrord (d. 739), who was "to England what Columbanus had been to Ireland."[4] Following Willibrord was the best known of the English missionaries,

2. See the letter to Gregory the Great, *ibid.*, pp. 9–11; Columbanus was referring to bishops who ordained "for hire" and to monks who left the place of their first profession. His authorities were Finnian and Gildas.

3. Pierre Riché, *Education and Culture in the Barbarian West*, trans. John J. Contreni, p. 329. Riché cites the penitential as evidence of the demands Columbanus placed on his lay followers; it would be especially interesting to know what they meant for his women followers. Most topics in the handbook pertain specifically to men and rarely mention women (e.g., male homosexuality, bestiality, brawling, and intoxication are covered; women are mentioned specifically only in the matter of the death of infants). Riché cites canon 26 of the penitential (see his n. 129, p. 329), but this is singularly inappropriate to his argument, this part of the handbook being devoted to "the minor ordinances of monks" (Walker, *Opera*, p. 178).

4. See Wilhelm Levison, *England and the Continent in the Eighth Century*, pp. 45–69, and p. 60 for the quotation.

Boniface (d. 754), a West Saxon. The success of the Englishmen was no less closely linked to the interests of the continental nobility than was that of the Irish. When reading about these missions to the continent, one is too inclined to think of unstructured, even covert, activity—a romantic vision of missionary life—instead of the highly organized, bureaucratic process which established English influence abroad, especially in the German churches. Boniface was under the protection of Charles Martel; he organized a system of dioceses which created the foundations of the Frankish church. Essential to his success was the interest of territorial politicians in a well-organized and well-disciplined church.[5] The linking of ecclesiastical to secular power had important consequences for the foreign missions and for their concern with penitential discipline.

The extensive penetration of the Irish and Anglo-Saxon monks, attested by records from the many houses they established, eventually was checked by a combination of ecclesiastical and political interests on the part of native authorities.[6] This was to be expected, since the missionaries' success went hand in hand with their usefulness to the governments which ruled the territories where the monks proselytized. In the north especially, local authorities sought to entrust ecclesiastical power to their own, rather than to foreign, bishops. The first great reformer among the Franks was Chrodegang, bishop of Metz (742–766, hence contemporary with Boniface and Egbert of York). More than any other eighth-century Frank, Chrodegang enjoyed a combination of ecclesiastical power and political influence. His greatest achievement was a reform of the clergy, whose weaknesses had been deplored by Boniface. Under Chrodegang's *Rule* the clergy were required to live communally, under a bishop (that is, as canons), at least where this was possible. Part of the discipline thus imposed on them was a system of confession and penance clearly monastic in outline, requiring them to confess to

5. *Ibid.*, pp. 70–93; see also J. M. Wallace-Hadrill, "A Background to St. Boniface's Mission," in *England before the Conquest*, ed. Peter Clemoes and Kathleen Hughes, pp. 35–48.

6. The conflict between the wandering Irish and the increasingly centralized continental churches is analyzed by Kathleen Hughes, "The Changing Theory and Practice of Irish Pilgrimage"; on the identification of Irish and Anglo-Saxon centers, see Friedrich Prinz, *Frühes Mönchtum im Frankenreich* and "Monastische Zentren im Frankenreich."

their bishop as monks did to the prior.[7] This is an isolated instance, but an important one; here we see private confession serving as an instrument of clerical discipline and, by implication at least, setting a standard for the laity as well.

In England private penance made rapid headway because other forms of reconciliation were apparently unknown. But this was not true on the continent, where the tradition of public penance had been established in the early Christian era, in the Gallican church especially. Had this ritual been in full force in the sixth and seventh centuries, the handbooks would have gained ground less quickly. Certainly public penance had not disappeared. Our first continental reference to the penitentials, in fact, comes from a synod at Toledo, which in 589 declared objection to a method of private reconciliation of sinners recently introduced into churches in the region; the bishops stated that ancient, canonical methods of public reconciliation were to be preferred. A scant half-century later, councils at Chalon-sur-Saone (644–656) endorsed private penance, and for the next hundred years the penitentials were to figure in controversies between public and private penance.[8] When the penitentials first appeared, the public system was in decline. In his homilies, Caesarius, bishop of Arles (d. 542), lamented that public penance was not widely or carefully observed. We should not expect a homilist to be optimistic in such matters, but it seems reasonable to conclude that the public tradition had weakened in many parts of Western Europe by the seventh century.[9] Its decline naturally facilitated the introduction of a new method of ecclesiastical discipline.

But public penance re-emerged powerfully in the reforms of Charlemagne. In a series of councils held in 813, he sought to revital-

7. See Wallace-Hadrill, "Background," pp. 41–43. The *Rule* of Chrodegang is edited by Carlo de Clercq, *La législation religieuse franque de Clovis à Charlemagne*, 1:145–155; for background see Eugen Ewig, "Saint Chrodegang et la réforme de l'église franque."

8. See the summary by Cyrille Vogel, *Les "Libri Paenitentiales,"* pp. 35–36. For the Toledo synod, see Giovanni Domenico Mansi, ed., *Sacrorum Conciliorum*, 9:995 (c. 11); for the Council of Chalon, see *MGH Conc* 1:210 (c. 8).

9. On the decline of public penance, see Cyrille Vogel, *La discipline pénitentielle en Gaule des origines à la fin du VIIe siècle*; Caesarius's concern for public penance is discussed by H. G. J. Beck, *The Pastoral Care of Souls in South-East France during the Sixth Century*. A good many of Caesarius's homilies are surveyed by O. D. Watkins, *A History of Penance*, 2:506–514 and 550–562.

ize the church by defining the duties of bishops and priests and especially by improving the quality of the clergy's training.[10] The council
meeting at Chalon issued a much-quoted denunciation of the "texts
called penitentials, whose errors are certain and whose authors are
uncertain."[11] The reform was to some extent a revival; the bishops
looked back to the early church for precedents in penitential discipline and consequently were made suspicious of the handbooks,
whose vintage was so much more recent. The bishops mistrusted the
penitentials because their authorities were not only unknown (at
least compared to Gregory and Augustine) but multiple, and because
private penance itself invested too much authority in the priest. The
Chalon council was the only meeting which actually denounced the
handbooks; the council at Tours called instead for bishops to specify
"whose penitential book, of those written by the men of old, is pref-
erably to be followed."[12] The bishops endorsed three authorities
as acceptable guides for penances: canons, the Bible, and accepted
custom.[13]

In theory, of course, these guides were all that was needed, but
in practice they had notable shortcomings. Accepted customs were
the most useful, since they constituted local precedent and so had the
best chance of being enforced. The Bible cannot have been nearly so
useful, although it too could be seen as a collection of case histories
and precepts. The guide about which we know the most is canon
law, to which the bishops were presumably referring. Obviously they
did not include the handbooks among the "canons," possibly reserv-
ing that term for the large collections of ecclesiastical law circulating
widely in the eighth and ninth centuries.[14] These collections made

10. The objectives of the reform are analyzed by Rosamond McKitterick, *The Frankish Church and the Carolingian Reforms, 789–895*, pp. 12–15.

11. "Quos paenitentiales vocant, quorum sunt certi errores, incerti auctores"; *MGH Conc* 2. 1:281 (c. 38).

12. "Cuius antiquorum liber paenitentialis potissimum sit sequendus"; *ibid.*, p. 289 (c. 22).

13. "Quod in canonibus sacris invenerit, aut quod illi secundum sanctarum scriptu-rarum auctoritatem et eclesiasticam consuetudinem"; *ibid.*, p. 280 (Council of Chalon, c. 34).

14. See Hubert Mordek, "Kanonistische Aktivität in Gallen in der ersten Hälfte des 8. Jahrhunderts"; for background see A. van Hove, *Prolegomena ad Codicem Iuris Can-onici*, 2d ed. (Mechlin-Rome, 1945); Rudolf Buchner, ed., *Deutschlands Geschichts-*

little allowance for private penance, although two of them noticed in the last chapter—the *Hibernensis* and the *Vetus Gallica*—used Theodore's penitential as a source. The canons were compiled from earlier synodical decisions, patristic sources, and papal decretals.[15] They did not assign penances, and of course they were not intended to be used by the confessor, but to aid bishops and archbishops in maintaining ecclesiastical discipline on a broader scale.

The reform councils therefore made no specific allowance for the handbooks of penance, but neither did they attack them or seek to eradicate them. The Chalon council's position was exceptional and, as we shall shortly see, bears out the influence of a most important bishop, Theodulf of Orléans, with his own ideas about confession and penance. A later council, at Paris in 829, issued an even more florid denunciation of the handbooks, but it reveals the source of the bishops' discontent. They objected especially to the abuses which naive clergymen had introduced into the system of private confession. Partly through carelessness and partly through ignorance, priests were ignoring canonical authority in favor of the penitentials. In so doing they were catering to sins rather than curing them. Thus, it seemed salutary "that each bishop seek out these erroneous booklets in his own diocese and consign those he finds to the flames so that ignorant priests may no longer deceive men through them."[16] Clearly the bishops were concerned with raising the disciplinary standards of their dioceses; they believed that the penitentials allowed confessors too many opportunities for poor judgment.

The bishops did believe in private confession and penance. The Paris synod required bishops to instruct priests how to inquire discreetly about the penitent's sins and determine a penance conform-

quellen im Mittelalter: Die Rechtsquellen (Weimar, 1953); and H. E. Feine, *Kirchliche Rechtsgeschichte*, 5th ed. (Cologne-Vienna, 1972).

15. See chapter three, n. 29, and Hubert Mordek, *Kirchenrecht und Reform im Frankenreich*, pp. 255–259 (on the *Hibernensis*), and pp. 1–61 (on the *Vetus Gallica*). Other collections treating the same subjects as the penitentials are the *Collectio Dacheriana* and the *Collectio Vaticana*, the former being perhaps the most influential of the canons (it is discussed by Mordek on pp. 259–263). See also H. J. Schmitz, *Die Bussbücher und die Bussdisziplin der Kirche*, pp. 712–719.

16. "Ut unusquisque episcoporum in sua parroechia eosdem erroneos codicellos diligenter perquirat et inventos igni tradat, ne per eos ulterius sacerdotes imperiti homines decipiant"; *MGH Conc* 2. 2:633 (c. 32).

ing to canonical authority. The Chalon council of 813 instructed the priest to hear confession according to the eight chief sins (this was the method suggested by Theodulf) and to inquire carefully about the penitent's wrongdoing.[17] Most of the councils were more specific about the need for public penance, citing this as the approved ancient method, but noting that some sins could be expiated through private penance instead.[18] Their reservations against the penitentials were, therefore, not based on misgivings about private penance itself, and their support for public penance was not an attempt to reassert the older method at the expense of the newer. We must understand these points if we are to understand the subsequent history of the continental penitentials, for after the councils they continued to flourish. In the mid-ninth century, Rodulf, archbishop of Bourges (d. 866), denounced the penitentials in the language of the 813 Council of Chalon, and he too recommended public penance for public offenses as the ancient canons required it. A council in Mainz in 852 permitted secret confession and penance for secret sins.[19] Thus it defined the role of private penance in the dichotomous penitential system of the ninth-century continental churches.

There were good reasons for the bishops' reservations about the handbooks and their preference for the authority of the canons. But their reservations seem limited when compared with their strongly worded and widely applied statutes requiring priests to own and use the handbooks. Charlemagne's *Capitula a Sacerdotibus Proposita* and *Interrogationes Examinationis* (802–803) instruct bishops to make sure that their priests know how to hear confession and how to use the penitential.[20] Statutes issued by Gerbald and Waltcaud, bishops of Liège (787–810 and 810–813, respectively), and Haito of Basel (bishop from 806 to 823), and statutes from Freising and Vesoul (both issued in the early ninth century), specify that the priest must

17. *Ibid.*, 2. 1: 279 (Council of Chalon, c. 32).

18. See the Council of Chalon, c. 25 (*ibid.*, p. 278); the Council of Rheims, c. 31 (*ibid.*, p. 256); the Council of Arles, c. 26 (*ibid.*, p. 253).

19. See Rodulf's *Capitula*, prologue (*PL* 119: 703), and the Council of Mainz, c. 10 (*MGH Cap* 2. 189).

20. *MGH Cap* 1. 110 (c. 4) and *ibid.*, p. 234 (c. 3). See also the statute "Quae a Presbyteris Discenda Sint," *ibid.*, p. 235 (c. 7).

understand the penitential.[21] A collection of laws made by the monk Ansegius in 827 stipulates that the priest must ask which penitential he is to use[22]—a requirement similar to that of the 813 council at Tours.

This concern about which penitential is to be authorized appears to have been well founded, for the texts of the handbooks had, in many cases, become corrupted and confused. Some penitentials were written on the continent, but most were brought from England and Ireland and were recopied at continental scriptoria. As they were recopied, they were also revised. Our earliest manuscripts contain versions of the penitentials of Cummean and Theodore rather than their genuine penitentials; one copy of the revised text of Cummean dates from the first half of the eighth century.[23] These augmented editions of the genuine handbooks did not in themselves lead to difficulties. So long as a penitential claimed the authority of Cummean or Theodore, it was acceptable. But early in the ninth century we find the first of a series of protests against the penitentials, and the chief objection seems to have been their anonymity. Amid penitentials attributed to English and Irish ecclesiastics, we find those of unknown authorship. Some of these handbooks are short works based on the penitential of Columbanus; *The Bobbio Penitential* (identified in the manuscript only as "iudicius penitentialis") is an example.[24] But most continental penitentials of the late eighth and ninth centuries are not compact handbooks, but instead sprawling,

21. For background and full references to these texts, see Jean Gaudemet, "Les statuts épiscopaux de la première décade du IXe siècle," pp. 320–331, and McKitterick, *Frankish Church*, pp. 49–52 and 70–72.

22. Made for Louis the Pious and, according to McKitterick, cited by him in 829 (see *Frankish Church*, p. 21). The text is in *MGH Cap* 1:382–450.

23. Copenhagen, Kongelige Bibliothek, Ny. Kgl. S. 58. 8, s. viii^in (it contains excerpts from the *Hibernensis* as well as the *Libellus Responsionum*); Cologne, Dombibliothek 91, s. viii/ix, contains the *Vetus Gallica*, part of the penitential of Theodore, and letters of Gregory I as well as pseudo-Cummean's penitential; for other early manuscripts containing these and related texts, and for additional information about the manuscripts listed here, see Franz Bernd Asbach, *Das Poenitentiale Remense und der sogen. Excarpsus Cummeani*, pp. 23–24 and 47–55.

24. This and other short penitentials are described by Vogel, *Les "Libri,"* pp. 74–76; I cite Vogel as a guide to editions and some secondary works, not as a guide to dating, a point on which his work is not reliable.

confused, and contradictory syntheses of tariffs from the penitentials of Cummean, Theodore, and Columbanus.[25] It is difficult to find a systematic plan to these compilations; it is impossible to believe that they were intended as guides for confessors, for they would have been useless in a practical situation. A confessor would not have known which part of the text to consult and might have found conflicting advice if he consulted one text in two places.[26]

We might expect such conditions to lead to the composition of new penitentials as well as to complaints about the old ones. Indeed, the Franks did introduce innovations into the texts which eventually became standard features. If the earlier handbooks were planless, those designed by the Franks were in comparison highly structured and formal. The penitential proposed by Theodulf of Orléans was, in fact, pure structure. His ideas were set forth in the first of his capitularies, issued about 800.[27]

Although he endorsed private confession and penance, Theodulf did not accept the penitential. His recommendation—followed by the 813 Council of Chalon—was that the priest should ask the penitent about the occasion of his sins and assign penance according to the penitent's guilt. This interrogation was to be guided not by the handbook, but by the list of the eight chief sins—gluttony, fornication, sloth (or languor), avarice, vainglory, envy, anger, and pride. The priest determined the degree of the penitent's guilt by

25. *Ibid.*, pp. 76–79.

26. The same might be said of the pseudo-Cummean penitential itself, which is earlier than the so-called tripartite handbooks ("tripartite" because composed of tariffs from Cummean, Theodore, and earlier canons). One of the most extensive and confused of the ninth-century penitentials is that known as the *Poenitentiale Martenianum*, which Vogel describes as "remarkably incoherent" (*ibid.*, p. 78). It is edited by F. W. H. Wasserschleben, *Die Bussordnungen der abendländischen Kirche*, pp. 282–300, and mixes tariffs from Cummean, Theodore, Columbanus, Bede, Egbert, the *Hibernensis*, and various synods.

27. Theodulf issued two collections, the first about 800, the second about 813; for the first, see *PL* 105: 191–208, and for the second, de Clercq, *La législation*, 1: 323–351. My discussion is concerned with the first; the second has been said to resemble a penitential, but this is open to question. See Peter Brommer, "Die Rezeption der bischöflichen Kapitularien Theodulfs von Orléans," p. 114; Brommer later altered his opinion: see "Capitula episcoporum: Bemerkungen zu den bischöflichen Kapitularien," p. 212. Also of the opinion that the second capitulary is comparable to a penitential is Gaudemet, "Les statuts," pp. 326–327.

asking him about each sin.[28] Although Theodulf required the priest to tailor the list to each penitent, he offered the confessor the minimum of information necessary to that process. Excluded from Theodulf's system because it was not canonical, the penitential was not replaced by a more reliable or thorough tool; indeed, the list of eight sins was, if anything, inadequate to the task Theodulf set for it. The principle behind the use of the chief sins to guide the priest's inquiry was, so far as we know, first applied to confession by Cummean; Theodulf adopts the method without the benefit of detailed tariffs for the sins, in this and in his list of the "seven remissions" of sin imitating Irish precedent rather than improving on it.[29]

The penitential teachings of Theodulf show that the intellectual climate of the early Frankish church was highly favorable to private penance, if not expressly to the penitential. Theodulf's reasons for rejecting the handbook can only be guessed at, but they may have been based on his celebrated contempt for the Irish scholars in Charlemagne's court.[30] It does not seem impossible that he saw the penitential as an arcane form of obscure origin, utterly "un-Roman" (which it was) and hence unworthy of his endorsement. Whatever its causes, Theodulf's contempt for the penitential seems highly idiosyncratic, out of step with the attitudes of other bishops and the general tenor of ecclesiastical legislation in the early eighth century.

Though it was not typical either, the response of Halitgar, bishop of Cambrai, was far more important to the subsequent history of both penance and penitentials. Halitgar may have had a hand in some legislation concerning the penitentials; his own handbook was written at the request of Archbishop Ebbo of Rheims, probably in 830, the year before Halitgar's death.[31] Halitgar's penitential was an attempt to accommodate the handbook to the objections of the

28. "Quando ergo quis ad confessionem venit, diligenter debet inquiri quomodo aut qua occasione peccatum perpetraverit, quod peregisse se confitetur, et juxta modum facti debet ei poenitentia indicari"; *PL* 105: 201 (c. 31).

29. *Ibid.*, p. 203 (c. 36).

30. Discussed by M. L. W. Laistner, *Thought and Letters in Western Europe, A.D. 500–900*, pp. 339–341.

31. See Raymund Kottje, *Die Bussbücher Halitgars von Cambrai und des Hrabanus Maurus*, pp. 13–84, for an analysis of the text and its tradition.

reformers. It is the ultimate, and the only, genuinely Frankish penitential, for it responds to all of the reformers' concerns: it supplies a procedure to guide the administration of confession, the *ordo confessionis*; it provides for confession to God alone and to the priest, as well as for public penance; and it brings the handbook's tariffs into alignment with canon law. No previous—or subsequent—handbook was its equal in meeting both the theoretical and the practical demands of private penance.

Halitgar called his six-book compilation "a penitential in one volume," compiled from the canons of the ancient fathers; the preface, "On the usefulness of penance," shows that he intended to provide a practical guide for confessors faced with conflicting authorities and at the same time to supply a theoretical justification for penance itself.[32] The first two books are a treatise on the vices and virtues; the third, fourth, and fifth treat canonical guidelines for administering penance, canonical penances for lay people, and canonical penances for the clergy. Up to this point, Halitgar's compilation is in strict and exclusive accordance with canon law. The sixth book is a different matter. Halitgar called it a "Roman penitential" and claimed that it had been taken from a "book repository of the Roman church," although he denied knowledge of its compiler.[33] This vagueness drew a convenient veil of Roman respectability over Halitgar's efforts to synthesize canons with the penitentials of Columbanus, Cummean, and Theodore, the chief sources for his sixth book.[34] After Halitgar it became possible to see the penitential as a text accepted in Rome and elsewhere as a standard guide to private confession and penance. In fact, the penitential penetrated more slowly into Rome than anywhere else, although in the mid-ninth century Pope Nicholas knew and recommended it as useful.[35]

32. For the text, see H. J. Schmitz, *Die Bussbücher und das kanonische Bussverfahren*, pp. 252–300.

33. The claim, which only Schmitz took seriously, is discussed by McNeill and Gamer, *Medieval Handbooks of Penance*, pp. 295–296. They translate the sixth book, pp. 297–314.

34. These were established by Paul Fournier, "Le livre VI du Pénitentiel d'Halitgar," in "Etudes sur les pénitentiels," pp. 529–553.

35. In his letter to the Bulgars, written in 866; see Vogel, *Les "Libri,"* p. 31.

In addition to its dependence on canonical regulations concerning penance, mixed with tariffs from the handbooks, Halitgar's penitential established two precedents which eventually helped to redefine the penitential's purpose. The first was its acknowledgment of the public penitential rite. The preface to the six-book collection distinguishes between public and private satisfaction, apparently recommending the former for serious offenses but also allowing these to be confessed privately. The instructions to the priest included in the sixth book, the "Roman penitential," include the imposition of hands and reconciliation for penitents on Holy Thursday.[36] Neither formula would have been useful to the priest in receiving penitents individually; Halitgar's reasons for including them may be seen in the nature of his penitential as a synthesis of accepted practices and in his understanding of the *ordo's* purpose.

Closely related to Halitgar's concern for public penance is the second development which was to become standard after his time: the incorporation of the *ordo confessionis* into the handbook. Halitgar's was not the first penitential to contain a ceremony for receiving the penitent; the anonymous handbooks based on the penitential of Columbanus, written in the early eighth century, contain similar orders, though less elaborate than Halitgar's.[37] The *ordo* advises the priest how to receive the penitent and specifies which prayers were to be recited before the penitent confessed. Although this procedure is referred to in the Irish penitentials, neither they nor the handbooks of Theodore or Egbert included an *ordo*. The ceremony was derived from the public rite of reconciliation found in many early liturgies, including the *Bobbio Missal* and the *Gelasian Sacramentary*, which was in use in Francia in the mid-eighth century.[38]

The *ordo* served two purposes. The first was to bring private penance closer to the public ritual by dictating a standard liturgy for the reception of the penitent, his confession, and the granting of

36. Schmitz, *Bussverfahren*, p. 293: "Incipit reconciliatio penitentem v feria Pasche."

37. See the *Poenitentiale Floriacense* and the *Poenitentiale Sangallense*, in Wasserschleben, *Bussordnungen*, pp. 422–426.

38. Orders for public penance in the liturgy are described by Antoine Chavasse, *Le sacramentaire gélasien* (Tournai, 1958), pp. 145–149; for background, see Josef A. Jungmann, *Die lateinischen Bussriten in ihrer geschichtlichen Entwicklung*, pp. 156–157.

absolution. The second, equally important to the objectives of the Frankish reform, was to provide stricter guidance for the confessor in the use of the handbook and the exercise of his own judgment. The *ordo* yields insight into the strategies employed to induce the penitent's candor and the techniques used by the bishops to make reasonably certain that confessors acted discreetly and responsibly. The *ordo* brings to mind Egbert's letter to his clergy, which prefaced his penitential: both remind the priest that his own salvation could not be separated from that of those who confessed to him.[39] Halitgar's *ordo* was severe in enforcing this link. It commanded the priest to accept penance himself each time he required penance of another.[40] The *ordo* posed the priest as a model for the penitent. When the sinner came to confession, he was to find the priest "sad and weeping for his (the penitent's) evil deeds"; thus, the penitent, "being himself the more moved by the fear of God, will be the more grieved and abhor his sins."[41] This recommendation took the pedagogical techniques employed in confession a considerable distance beyond anything even hinted at in the Irish or English penitentials: Halitgar wished the priest to teach by example as well as precept, not merely to live as a good Christian ought to, but to demonstrate, through his own emotional responses, the misery caused by sin.

Halitgar's penitential exerted only limited influence on contemporary handbooks, such as those of Hrabanus Maurus,[42] and it did not curb the influence of either the anonymous Frankish penitentials or those of Irish or English origin. Most of the handbooks to be found in manuscripts after the first third of the ninth century fall short of the high standards set by Halitgar's compilation: they are without the *ordo*; they take no notice of public penance; they consist

39. Ed. Wasserschleben, *Bussordnungen*, pp. 230–233.

40. Schmitz, *Bussverfahren*, pp. 290–291: "Quotiescunque Christiani ad penitentiam accedunt, jejunia damus et nos communicare cum eis debemus jejunio unam aut duas septimanas aut quantum possumus."

41. *Ibid.*, pp. 291–292: "Videns autem ille, qui ad paenitentiam venit, Sacerdotem tristem et lacrymantem pro suis facinoribus, magis ipse timore Dei perculsus, amplius tristatur et exhorrescet peccata sua."

42. See Kottje, *Die Bussbücher*, pp. 198–199; the penitentials of Hrabanus, addressed to Otgar (written in 842) and to Heribald (written ca. 853) consist chiefly of excerpts from canonical and patristic collections; they are not tariff penitentials. See also Vogel, *Les "Libri,"* p. 83.

almost entirely of tariffs drawn from penitentials and make little or no use of canon law. Nothing better illustrates the limitations of Halitgar's influence than the manuscript tradition of the handbooks attributed to Bede and Egbert. Nominally they belong to the English penitential tradition of the eighth century, but their common as opposed to individual textual history forces us to consider them as part of the Frankish tradition of a century later. The attempt to combine these two penitentials into a single handbook, which was briefly outlined in the last chapter, was Frankish; yet it was also outside the immediate influence of the Frankish reform and in some ways at odds with its objectives. The joint history of the handbooks of Bede and Egbert exposes the diversity and inconsistency tolerated at a time when reformers were seeking to establish uniformity and conformity among the penitentials.[43]

I argued in chapter three that the earliest penitential of the four assigned to Bede is not the twelve-chapter text of the earliest manuscript, widely accepted as genuine, but a short text of five or six chapters which shows no evidence of influence from Egbert's penitential. The twelve-chapter text acquired credibility because it is found in an early (first third of the ninth century) manuscript from the Main-Frankish region, which was heavily influenced by the English mission; this manuscript also contains the penitentials of Theodore and Egbert as well as the *Libellus Responsionum* of Gregory to Augustine of Canterbury.[44] But is the authority of this manuscript clearly greater than that of a Lorsch codex half a century later (that is, written before 875), which also contains the penitentials of Cummean, Theodore, and Egbert? This manuscript's Bedan penitential is the short or "pure" version; it may well be a copy of an earlier codex, and the manuscript's contents significantly older than the manuscript itself.[45] The Lorsch manuscript actually contains two versions of Eg-

43. This is not to suggest that the Frankish reforms could have achieved uniformity of standards on an actual, as opposed to a theoretical, level; see Raymund Kottje, "Einheit und Vielfalt des kirchlichen Lebens in der Karolingerzeit."

44. Vienna, Nationalbibliothek 2223; see chapter three, n. 36, and, for a partial list of contents, McNeill and Gamer, *Handbooks*, p. 450.

45. Vatican, Palatinus Latinus 485; dated by Bernhard Bischoff, *Lorsch im Spiegel seiner Handschriften*, pp. 44–46, 112–113. For contents, see Kottje, *Die Bussbücher*, p. 121, n. 132. Kottje assumes that the Bedan text in this manuscript is the same as that in

bert's penitential, one free-standing, the other conflated with the Bedan text.[46] This information too suggests that the codex represents a gathering of materials which span many years.

If we begin with the "pure" Bedan text and Egbert's as independent penitentials, we can see three stages of their conflation. The first, the twelve-chapter version, was described in the preceding chapter; it is not necessarily earlier than the second or third. The second actually comprises two sub-stages. In the earlier of these, the "seam" between the two handbooks is clear: Egbert's text follows the short Bedan text in these manuscripts, and Egbert is named as its author.[47] In the later stage, found in most of the manuscripts I have seen, the seam is concealed: Egbert is not named, and the entire compound text is attributed to Bede.[48] This version, widely attested, appears in a German manuscript of the second quarter of the ninth century, a codex of the first half of that century from the Lake Constance region, and a Breton manuscript of the tenth century, to name a few examples.[49]

This compound penitential was clearly the result of a deliberate attempt to form a new text from two less complete ones and not an accident; we know this because Egbert's prologue was transposed to form an introduction following the short preface to the Bedan text. But the attempt was not a success. The five or six chapters of the Bedan handbook were copied after Egbert's prologue; they concern sexual offenses, homicide, perjury, and unclean food. Then the text awkwardly begins anew with the words of Egbert's first chapter:

Vienna 2223, but it is not, although both have twelve chapters. See Kottje, *Die Bussbücher*, p. 121, n. 132.

46. The free-standing version is on fols. 73r–80v; another, much shortened, is found on fols. 98v–101r, immediately following the Bedan penitential.

47. As in Vienna, Nationalbibliothek 2171, s. ix$^{3/4}$, possibly from Alsace; fols. 46r–47r and (Egbert's penitential) 47r–51r; see Kottje, *Die Bussbücher*, p. 121, n. 133.

48. An example is Paris, Bibliothèque Nationale, Lat. 2341, s. ix$^{2/4}$, fols. 233rb–234vb. See *ibid.*, p. 121, n. 134.

49. St. Gall, Stiftsbibliothek 682, s. ix$^{2/4}$, pp. 334–393; on dating and provenance, see Raymund Kottje, "Kirchenrechtliche Interessen im Bodenseeraum vom 9. bis 12. Jahrhundert," p. 34. Karlsruhe, Badische Landesbibliothek, Aug. CCLV, s. ix^1, fols. 95v–106v; see Kottje, *Die Bussbücher*, p. 121, n. 135. London, British Library, Royal 5 E. xiii, s. x; see G. F. Warner and J. P. Gilson, *Catalogue of Western Manuscripts in the Old Royal and Kings Collection*, 4 vols. (London, 1916): 1:116.

"Now I shall explain the capital sins according to the canons."[50] This statement was not a bad way to begin Egbert's handbook, but in the joint penitential it interrupts the tariff penitential already in progress. Much repetition ensues, Egbert's text taking up sexual sins, sins involving oaths, and other matters already covered by the early, Bedan portion of the text. The inadequacies of this synthesis prompted another compiler, later in the ninth century, to undertake yet another reorganization of the material, the third (and last) to be examined here. He produced the so-called *Double Penitential*, a reshuffling of the canons of the last-mentioned document with an *ordo confessionis* added.[51] This text too was assigned to Bede, as its predecessor had been; it is of special interest because in several codices it replaces the sixth book of Halitgar's penitential. Where Halitgar announced the "Roman" penitential, these manuscripts announce "the penitential of Bede."[52]

The development of the joint Bede-Egbert penitentials was carried out under Frankish authority. It may reflect efforts to consolidate and perhaps to update older handbooks of penance. By synthesizing the two under Bede's name, the Franks would have attacked the problem of multiple authorities and capitalized on the great literary reputation of Bede, swelled in the ninth century by the attribution of anonymous works to him.[53] The various Bedan penitentials appear in manuscripts of very good authority. The Lorsch manuscript containing penitentials of Egbert, Theodore, and Cummean and a Bedan handbook also contains the *Capitula* of Theodulf.[54] Halitgar's sixth book occurs in a manuscript with a joint Bede-Egbert penitential and the *Collectio Dacheriana*.[55] A manuscript

---

50. "Nunc igitur capitalia crimina secundum canones explicabo." Quoted from Bruno Albers, "Wann sind die Beda-Egbert'schen Bussbücher verfasst worden, und wer ist ihr Verfasser?" p. 405.

51. Ed. Wasserschleben, *Bussordnungen*, pp. 248–282.

52. This appears to have been noticed first by Wasserschleben; *ibid.*, p. 47.

53. See C. W. Jones, *Bedae Pseudepigrapha* (Ithaca, 1939), and M. L. W. Laistner, *A Hand-List of Bede Manuscripts* (Ithaca, 1943), pp. 16–18.

54. See n. 45 above; the *Capitula* is on fols. 80v–91r.

55. See n. 48 above; the sixth book occurs on fols. 231rb–233rb, and the *Collectio Dacheriana* on fols. 204r–231ra.

from Vesoul contains this penitential and episcopal statutes requiring the priest to understand how penitentials are to be used.[56]

The reforms did not circumscribe the penitentials, much less discard them.[57] Indeed, the reformers seem to have relied as heavily on the early Irish and English collections as on the penitentials of Halitgar and Hrabanus. The older handbooks—Cummean's, Theodore's, and those attributed to Bede and Egbert—survived for various reasons, but chiefly because they were part of a well-established tradition. Included in "collection books," anthologies from which authorized texts were copied for small libraries, they continued to be issued throughout the reform period. Such collections are now far more numerous than separate texts copied from them. Manuscripts which were "handbooks" by virtue of size and relative cheapness have all but disappeared. An exception is the earliest manuscript of Egbert's penitential, which has already been discussed, and a St. Gall manuscript which contains the pseudo-Cummean penitential. It appears that this handbook was joined to a manuscript of saints' lives and other non-legislative texts; hastily written, on parchment of poor quality, the penitential may at one time have been a separate book, later attached to the manuscript so that it would not be lost or destroyed.[58]

Among the places where the handbooks would have been stored was the parish library. Church inventories of three Bavarian "parish" churches in the mid-ninth century include penitentials among other canonical and liturgical texts. Similar records from east Frankish churches, including churches in Prüm and Lorsch, also attest to the existence of penitentials outside the large episcopal libraries which would have housed the "collection books." These small libraries were doubtless poor and rarely replenished; it is easy to understand why a

56. Vesoul, Bibliothèque de la ville, 73, s. x/xi(?); also included are fragments of Theodore's penitential and part of the *Libellus Responsionum*. See Asbach, *Das Poenitentiale*, pp. 35–36 (for dating), and McKitterick, *Frankish Church*, p. 70.

57. For arguments that the reforms did take effect against the penitentials, see Rosamond Pierce (now McKitterick), "The 'Frankish' Penitentials," and my reply, "The Significance of the Frankish Penitentials."

58. St. Gall, Stiftsbibliothek 550, described by Gustav Scherrer, *Verzeichnis der Handschriften der Stiftsbibliothek von St. Gallen* (Halle, 1875), pp. 169–170; this is a small octavo volume, s. ix[ex].

penitential placed in such a library was likely to remain there. This may explain why the Frankish reformers found it difficult to bring the handbooks into conformity. Reforms might be decreed, and perhaps they were easily carried out at the highest levels of church and society; but local churches would have offered resistance to change and continued to use material which could not be easily or readily replaced.[59]

The synods which met throughout the ninth century were uniform in their insistence on public penance and recommended that it be performed with private penance on certain occasions. The most important cases which came before the bishops involved penance to be performed by nobles and those who fought their wars. Earlier the penitential system had been used by the secular government to bring unwilling peoples into submission. The most extreme example is the *Capitula* of Paderborn, issued in 785: for refusing baptism or violating the Lenten fast, one was liable to be put to death; tithing requirements imposed on the Saxons were so stiff that Alcuin protested.[60] In the ninth century, the church found penance a useful means of extending its influence over secular government. Imposing penance for "misgovernment," the bishops forced Louis the Pious to give up his arms, and in effect to cease to rule. This penance was pronounced by Hincmar, outstanding among the ecclesiastics of his time for his political activity.[61] Although penance was required for the soul of the individual, it had great consequences when the soul was the king's.

Frankish bishops also exercised the prerogative of penance after the wars in which Louis's sons struggled for his kingdom. After Louis and Charles defeated Lothair at Fontenoy in 841, they asked

59. The church inventories are surveyed by Carl I. Hammer, Jr., "Country Churches, Clerical Inventories, and the Carolingian Renaissance in Bavaria." The "collection books" are discussed by D. A. Bullough, "Roman Books and Carolingian Renovatio." Bullough calls the original manuscripts, from which copies were made, "authentica."

60. For a discussion of the Paderborn *Capitula* and Alcuin's protest, see H. R. Loyn and John Perceval, *The Reign of Charlemagne* (London, 1975), pp. 6, 51–54. The church's use of penitential discipline to punish participation in warfare has been analyzed by G. I. A. D. Draper, "Penitential Discipline and Public Wars in the Middle Ages," *International Review of the Red Cross* 1 (1961): 4–18 and 63–78.

61. Hincmar's role in the penance of Louis is analyzed by Janet Nelson, "Kingship, Law and Liturgy in the Political Thought of Hincmar of Reims," *EHR* 92 (1977): 241–279.

the bishops how they might atone for the slaughter of the long campaign. Recorded by Nithard, the answer was twofold: since the war against Lothair was God's will, those who had obediently participated in it had acted only as the instruments of divine plan. But those whose behavior was not faultless—those who had "either counseled or committed anything on this campaign from wrath or hatred or vainglory or any other passion"—were to undertake penance. Each was to "confess secretly his secret sin and be judged according to the measure of his guilt."[62] The regular penance for participation in public warfare was a fast of forty days, but the imposition of such penance sometimes created diplomatic or political complications, raising questions about just war and bringing the church actively into debates about secular claims to power.

The intersection of penance with public affairs attests only indirectly the observance of the disciplinary aspects of penance among the laity, much less the devotional ones. We do not know the number of penitents who sought out confessors, or how often they might have done so, although Theodulf recommended Lenten confessions, and among devout laymen this may have been the custom.[63] Because the reform stressed pastoral work among the laity and encouraged praying and preaching in the vernacular, it is likely that penance too found a place in the spiritual program designed for laymen. Vernacular versions of baptismal formulae and confessional prayers are found in ninth-century manuscripts; the latter are comparatively common.[64] Decrees requiring preaching in the vernacular are not supported by a manuscript tradition of such homilies in surviving collections, as are decrees which demand that the priest use the penitential. Nonetheless, it seems reasonable to conclude that both penance and

62. Nithard's *History* is translated by Bernhard Walter Scholtz, *Carolingian Chronicles* (Ann Arbor, 1972), pp. 129–174; see pp. 155–156 for the imposition of penance, and Nelson, "Kingship," pp. 243–244.

63. In his first *Capitula*, c. 36 (*PL* 105:203).

64. Vernacular confessional prayers are edited by Elias von Steinmeyer, *Die kleineren althochdeutschen Sprachdenkmäler*, pp. 306–336; see also Wilhelm Braune, *Althochdeutsches Lesebuch*, ed. Ernst Ebbinghaus (Tübingen, 1968). McKitterick lists royal and episcopal legislation requiring the laity to memorize prayers; see *Frankish Church*, p. 187.

preaching were conducted in the vernacular in ninth-century Frankish kingdoms.[65]

The vernacular confessional prayers are strong evidence of this vernacular tradition in pastoral literature. The *ordo* for public penance in liturgical books requires penitents to confess in their own language; the prayers which were taught to them include catalogues of sin similar to those found in *The Book of Cerne* and other early English prayer collections, although the Old High German texts may have been directly derived from the homilies of Caesarius.[66] In the manuscripts, these prayers are usually the only texts written in any language but Latin. The Lorsch manuscript of the penitentials by Bede and Egbert and the *Capitula* of Theodulf inserts a vernacular confession into an *ordo*.[67] Although these prayers functioned in the public rather than the private penitential ritual, they accustomed the laity to confessing and hence reinforced the private system.

In England in the following century, both prayers and penitentials were translated into the vernacular. It may be that the vernacular tradition was stronger in England than on the continent, although England too lagged behind Ireland in acquiring penitential literature in the vernacular. *The Old-Irish Penitential, The Old-Irish Table of Commutations, The Monastery of Tallaght*, and other literature of the "Céli-Dé" reform would appear to be the first texts in Western Europe to give both practical and theoretical penitential literature in the native tongue. The Irish also had a tradition of vernacular preaching at least as early as the eighth century, although the extent and nature of this tradition remains imperfectly known.[68] As for England in the

65. The preaching tradition is examined by Milton McC. Gatch, *Preaching and Theology in Anglo-Saxon England: Ælfric and Wulfstan*, pp. 27–39; for a survey of vernacular catechetical texts, see McKitterick, *Frankish Church*, pp. 184–205.

66. See Franz Hautkappe, *Über die altdeutschen Beichten und ihre Beziehungen zu Cäsarius von Arles*. Prayers of confession "rusticis verbis" are required by the public *ordo* in the *Pontifical Romano-Germanique du dixième siècle* (mid-tenth century), ed. Cyrille Vogel and Reinhard Elze, 2:16–17.

67. Vatican, Palatinus Latinus 485, fol. 2v: "Confessio omnium peccatorum." For the text see Steinmeyer, *Sprachdenkmäler*, pp. 323–326.

68. For the view that the Irish homiletic tradition was limited, see Milton McC. Gatch, "The Achievement of Ælfric and His Colleagues in European Perspective," in *The Old*

eighth century, we should remember that Bede's letter to Egbert expressed contempt for clergy weak in Latin and strongly recommended teaching in the vernacular for them.[69] Bede restricted his comments to prayers of a catechetical nature; there is no evidence, however, that England possessed penitentials in the vernacular at this time.

The expansion and development of penitential handbooks during and after the Frankish reforms have no close parallels in devotional sources. But the writings of Alcuin are an indispensable supplement to the administrative penitential texts of the Franks. Alcuin is an important source for the theology of penance in the early ninth century, especially valuable because, as a Northumbrian, he reflected the standards of eighth-century England and of the Carolingian centers in which he taught.[70]

Alcuin's interest in penance and confession took its most characteristic form in the collections of private prayer generally associated with Tours scriptoria, possibly St. Martin's, where Alcuin was abbot after 801. These collections, the *libelli precum*, contain several confessional prayers.[71] As devotional exercises for the nobility, such prayers were recited with the psalms; the model for this program of prayer was the psalter, which included both verses from scripture and private prayers. These confessions were made to God, not to acknowledge specific faults, but to obtain general absolution; their rationale, probably derived by Alcuin and Theodulf from a common source, is simple: what man remembers, God forgets.[72] The belief that small

---

English Homily and Its Background, ed. Paul. E. Szarmach and Bernard F. Huppé, pp. 51–54. But Patrick O'Neill argues that the early Irish were "well acquainted with the art of homiletics in the vernacular"; see "The Background to the *Cambrai Homily*."

69. The letter is edited by Arthur West Haddan and William Stubbs, *Councils and Ecclesiastical Documents Relating to Great Britain and Ireland*, 3 : 314–325.

70. For background see Luitpold Wallach, *Alcuin and Charlemagne*; Arthur Kleinclausz, *Alcuin*; and H. B. Meyer, "Alkuin zwischen Antike und Mittelalter."

71. Four important prayer collections are edited by André Wilmart, *Precum Libelli Quattor Aevi Karolini*; and Pierre Salmon, "Libelli Precum du VIIIe au XIIe siècle," *Analecta Liturgica*, Studi e Testi, vol. 273 (Vatican City, 1974), a continuation of Wilmart's work, pp. 121–194.

72. Alcuin, *Liber de Virtutibus et Vitiis*, PL 101 : 624; for the concept in Theodulf's first *Capitula*, c. 30, see PL 105 : 200.

sins could be forgiven by confession to God alone was held by Caesarius and by the Irish and was generally accepted as part of penitential theory.[73] Like other means of obtaining the remission of punishment due to sin, it generated its own literature. Among the Carolingians, as among the English, the confessional prayers can be used to describe confession and penance among the educated and elite only. The nobility, educated in monastic schools, acquired habits of piety based on monastic models; confessional prayers, and the confession of small sins, were among those customs.[74]

But Alcuin did not believe that confession to God alone was sufficient, and in his correspondence he reacted against excessive reliance on this practice. A confession made privately to God was not a substitute for auricular confession made to the priest, even though that confession might result in the penitent's embarrassment.[75] In his treatise on the virtues and vices, the most substantial theological discussion of penance in this period, Alcuin recommended confession to the priest and to God. He stressed the penitent's interior disposition—the sincerity of his contrition and his willingness to accept penance—as conditions necessary for the forgiveness of sins. Scornful of those who performed penance without the intent to repent, he likens them to the devil, who also fasts (being a spirit, he does not need food) while doing evil. Alcuin's fundamental assertion was that true repentance was not measured by the number of years one fasted, but by the sincerity with which he turned from sin.[76]

This idea seems to imply that Alcuin thought confession more

73. This tradition is represented in the penitentials as well as in the councils of the Frankish bishops; for a partial list of sources see Cyrille Vogel, "Composition légale et commutations dans le système de la pénitence tarifée."

74. The monastic schools are studied in detail by Riché, *Education and Culture*; see especially pp. 421–446 for the situation in Gaul and Germany in the eighth century. See also André Wilmart, "Le manuel de prières de saint Jean Gualbert," and Franz Xaver Haimerl, "Mittelalterliche Frömmigkeit im Spiegel der Gebetbuchliteratur Süddeutschlands," pp. 5–20.

75. See Alcuin, *Epistola 112* ("Ad fratres in provincia Gothorum"), MGH Epp 2: 216–218, which urges confession to the priest so that he can serve as a witness to the sinner's repentance and reconcile him.

76. *Liber de Virtutibus et Vitiis*, "De poenitentiae," PL 101: 622–623. "Poenitentia vera non annorum numero censetur, sed amaritudine animi. . . . Non enim longitudinem temporis tantum requirit Deus, quantum affectum sinceritatis (poenitentis) pensat."

important than penance: the validity of the sacrament seems to depend on the penitent's contrition rather than the priest's power of absolution.[77] But Alcuin was not Abelard. Though he emphasized the inner reality of penance, its interior or individual aspect, he did not dismiss acts of penance: he only required that they, like confession, be undertaken sincerely. Alcuin speaks of confession and penance together, laments that the Goths do not observe them, and in his correspondence frequently exhorts his patrons, friends, and brothers to do penance.[78]

Alcuin's attention to the spiritual anxieties of his patrons seems quite remote from the efforts of Frankish bishops to catechize the laity and teach them to pray. But there is one important thread in Alcuin's prayers and penitential writing which was to become a predominant concern later in the ninth century. That was his insistence on sincerity in confession and repentance. Hrabanus Maurus, writing in mid-century, echoed Alcuin's belief that unless confession began with compunction—humbleness of mind, tears, and the fear of judgment—forgiveness was impossible.[79] This theory is itself so important for the history of penance and penitential literature that it will be examined more fully later. Its place in the intellectual background to ninth-century penitential practice is prominent because before the end of the century it found expression in the *ordo confessionis*. Confessors had always been encouraged to investigate the sincerity of their penitents' contrition, but during the Frankish reform this investigation took new and explicit shape. Halitgar's wish that the priest weep with the penitent for his sins expresses the desire for sincerity as graphically as possible. But confessors were also given more systematic, and probably more reliable, methods for ensuring that the penitent was sincerely sorry for his sins.

77. See Gerald Ellard, *Master Alcuin, Liturgist*, p. 209, and Ludwig Eisenhofer and Joseph Lechner, *The Liturgy of the Roman Rite*, trans. A. J. and E. F. Peeler, pp. 376–377, for the view that beginning with Theodulf the church believed that confession alone effected the forgiveness of sins.

78. See especially Alcuin's "De Confessione Peccatorum ad Pueros Sancti Martini," in which the performance of penance is mentioned as often as confession; *PL* 101: 649–656.

79. *Ibid.*, col. 620; Hrabanus Maurus, *De Ecclesiastica Disciplina, PL* 112: 1257.

The first, observed in the Irish and English as well as the Frankish penitentials, was to inquire into the circumstances of the sin and to weigh the penitent's social status against his wrongdoing before determining his guilt.[80] In the Council of Worms, held in 868, this inquiry received its most concise and efficient form: the confessor was to discern the time and place of each offense and the other persons involved in it before determining the penitent's guilt.[81] Long before the Fourth Lateran Council (1215), the church approximated the "classical" theory of circumstances in hearing confession.[82]

Even in the ninth century, this inquiry was not a departure from previous practice, much less indicative of a new concern with the interior or personal, as opposed to the exterior or social, aspects of penance.[83] What was new in the Frankish era, and evident in the Worms council and in the decree of the Synod of Tribur in 895, was the formulation of that concern into a procedure for the confessor.[84] Orders for private confession written in the second half of the century introduce a second means of establishing the penitent's sincerity: an interrogation concerning his faith, followed by an affirmation of his integrity. This procedure first appears in the *ordo confessionis* attached to the *Double Penitential*. This *ordo* is composed of that pro-

80. Cummean's penitential asks the priest to determine "with what intensity of weeping" the penitent is afflicted ("qua uidetur adfligi lacrimabilitate"); see *The Irish Penitentials*, ed. Ludwig Bieler, pp. 132–133, c. 1. The prologue to the penitential attributed to Egbert tells the priest to measure the sinner's degree of compunction in making amends for his wrongdoing ("quale conpugnatione emendat"); ed. Wasserschleben, *Bussordnungen*, p. 232.

81. Ed. Giovanni Domenico Mansi, *Sacrorum Conciliorum*, 15:873. For background, see Wilfried Hartmann, *Das Konzil von Worms 868*; confessors were told to give attention to "the qualities of times and persons, of places and ages," to attend to "the character of the crimes and to the contrition of each offender" ("temporum etiam et personarum, locorum quoque et aetatum qualitates inspicere, ut etiam pro consideratione locorum, aetatum vel temporum").

82. D. W. Robertson, "A Note on the Classical Origin of 'Circumstances' in the Medieval Confessional," argues that after this council the penitentials were abandoned because the list of circumstances provided a briefer and better guide for the confessor.

83. This is the view of Hartmann (*Konzil*, p. 88), who sees the council as opposing the external discipline of the handbooks.

84. For the Synod of Tribur, see *MGH Cap* 2:196–247. Its "ethical imputations" are discussed briefly by Josef Raith, *Die altenglische Version des Halitgar'schen Bussbuch*, p. xxxvii.

vided by Halitgar, with an additional, quite lengthy interrogation to follow. The penitent was asked if he believed in the Trinity, in the resurrection of the flesh, and in the eternal consequences of his sins and good works. He was also asked to forgive those who had offended him, so that his sins could be forgiven. Up to this point, the interrogation parallels the *ordo* in two anonymous eighth-century handbooks.[85] But then a new requirement appears. The priest must ask the penitent if he is *incestuosus*; if the sinner will not discontinue his sinful liaison, he is to be refused penance and, evidently, dismissed without absolution.[86] This procedure is also required in an *ordo confessionis* inserted into the *Enlarged Rule* of Chrodegang, in which, after the penitent confesses his sins, he is asked if he wishes to turn from them; if he will not, the priest is unable to absolve him.[87] Two important tenth-century sources, the *Ecclesiastical Discipline* written by Regino, archbishop of Prüm, and the *Pontifical Romano-Germanique*, model their *ordines* on the version found in the *Double Penitential*.[88]

It would be tempting to see in these methods for ensuring the penitent's sincerity early manifestations of the concern with the individual conscience which, in the twelfth century, became an important part of confession. Certainly the *ordo* is a sign of increasing sophistication in penitential practice, requiring greater discretion on the priest's part and the consent and cooperation of the penitent. But nowhere in either the theoretical writing about penance or the handbooks themselves does conscience or confession predominate over the acceptance and performance of penitential deeds. Alcuin could write, and others repeat after him, that true repentance depended on the sinner's contrition rather than on acts of penance. To some extent

85. See the *Poenitentiale Floriacense* and the *Poenitentiale Sangallense* in Wasserschleben, *Bussordnungen*, pp. 422–423 and 425–426.

86. The *ordo* accompanies the *Double Penitential, ibid.*, pp. 248–256; this penitential quotes the Synod of Tribur on pp. 281–282.

87. A late ninth-century expansion of the *Rule* of Chrodegang; see Albert Wermminghoff, "Die Beschlüsse Aachener Concils im Jahre 816," *Neues Archiv* 27 (1902): 605–651. The text is in *PL* 89:1057–1095.

88. The *ordo* is edited by F. W. H. Wasserschleben, *Reginonis Abbatis Prumiensis, Libri Duo de Synodalibus Causis et Disciplinis Ecclesiasticis*, p. 136; for the *ordo* in the Pontifical, see Vogel and Elze, *Pontifical Romano-Germanique*, 2:234–245.

the handbooks reflect that belief in bolstering the means available to the confessor for testing sincerity and in refusing penance to those who were insufficiently sorry for their sins and unwilling to forsake them. But the test of sincerity was not an anticipation of later developments in the theory of confession. It merely established a procedure for measuring the penitent's disposition; earlier handbooks assume what the Frankish texts make explicit. The test was not prompted by a new interest in the individual personality, but by the need to catechize penitents: the test of sincerity was also a test of faith. It ensured that no one received penance who did not believe in the power of the priest to forgive sins. It was also a concession to the stricter standards of public penance. In the early church one could accept penance only once; to permit penance many times was dangerously close to tolerating recidivism. Hence, the Frankish *ordo confessionis* warned the sinner that unless he rejected his sins, he could not be forgiven. Halitgar made this point by asking the sinner to fast even after his assigned penance had been completed; the author of the *ordo* substituted a rule for a request.[89]

Although continental penitential texts of the tenth century continued to refine and expand on ninth-century tradition, the ninth-century texts are, from the English perspective, the culmination of a phase. That phase was ratified in the work of Regino, whose book on church discipline drew from the *Double Penitential* and required priests to use the handbook.[90] By the end of the ninth century, the Frankish penitential reforms had taken final shape. The history of both penance and penitentials in tenth-century Anglo-Saxon England can be understood only in the context of the many changes which the Franks had wrought. In penitential practice, the chief accomplishment of the Frankish reform was to revive public penance and, by incorporating confessional prayers in the vernacular into the public rite of reconciliation, to link that ceremony with the tradition of confession to God alone.

---

89. "Si enim egerit ea quae illi Sacerdos praeceperit, peccata eius remittentur: si vero postea ex sua voluntate jejunaverit, mercedem sibi adquiret et regnum coelorum"; in Schmitz, *Bussverfahren*, p. 292.

90. See Kottje, *Die Bussbücher*, pp. 128–131, for manuscripts of the *Double Penitential* and their possible connection to Regino.

Building on Carolingian precedent, the Franks introduced confessional prayers in the vernacular. This too was a significant development, for it shows the influence of monastic spiritual habits outside
the circle of the educated nobility. Prayer and catechesis were the
Franks' chief means of educating the laity; penitential practice, both
public and private, offered an excellent opportunity for instruction
and correction. In this way the Franks joined discipline with devotion and demonstrated the efficiency of penance in introducing and
reinforcing Christian ideas and habits.

The Frankish reforms were less successful in accommodating
the penitential to their purposes. Penitentials newly issued in the
ninth century refurbished older and less complete handbooks. Earlier penitentials sometimes supplied material for inclusion in *florilegia*; such excerpts did not serve as guides to the priest, but as
isolated bits of information, enumerating, for example, the chief
sins.[91] The fragments of penitentials, collected with didactic materials, thus circulated more widely than strictly legislative texts would
have. Such collections remind us that the penitentials served more
than judicial aims. But the Franks' most remarkable achievement was
not breaking down the handbook into smaller parts; rather, the
ninth century should be remembered as a time when the penitential
grew to staggering proportions. Already apparent in Halitgar's sixth
book, which appeared in the first quarter of the century, this ten-
dency to add to the handbook rather than to limit or redefine it
continued unchecked. Its extreme manifestations are the combined
forms of the handbooks attributed to Bede and Egbert; that version
known as the *Double Penitential* is easily the most unusual, containing the prologues to both penitentials, Halitgar's *ordo*, the procedure
for testing the penitent's sincerity, a detailed interrogation into many
serious sins, and only then the tariffs of penance.[92] So elaborate a
procedure was a challenge as formidable to the confessor as to the
sinner. However one views this expansion of the handbook, it cannot be seen as a great leap forward. It reduced the flexibility of the

91. For a survey of the *florilegium* tradition, see McKitterick, *Frankish Church*, pp.
155–183.

92. Ed. Wasserschleben, *Bussordnungen*, pp. 248–257.

handbook and put great strain on the confessor's ability; it is impossible to imagine that the document describes a procedure which the priest actually followed.

In both theory and practice, the Anglo-Saxons of the tenth century modeled their penitential tradition on that of the Frankish reformers. Often this modeling was a simple matter of translating such texts as Theodulf's *Capitula* and the *Enlarged Rule* of Chrodegang into Old English. But it also involved a more complex process of synthesizing and adapting Frankish texts, including the penitentials and prayers, as well as translating them. In doing so, the English were really only reclaiming what had been theirs to start with: Alcuin's prayers and treatises and the penitentials of Theodore and Egbert. But genuinely English penitentials had ceased to exist in the ninth century, the victims of invasions, collapsing monastic discipline, and the consequent decline in the promulgation of either secular or ecclesiastical legislation. The revival of penitential practice in England was in both its broadest objectives and its means of reaching those objectives a reflex of the Frankish reforms. And because the English approached penitential discipline as a custom handed down from an earlier and more prosperous era, they succeeded far better than the Franks in producing a synthesis of practices and a body of penitential texts unique to their own culture.

Chapter Five

The Penitential Tradition
in Tenth-Century England

IN the tenth century, as in the eighth, penitentials and penance were new to the English and were again accepted without protest or controversy. In the later period the penitential tradition was successfully reconstructed at least in part because it was seen as a revival of earlier practice. In fact, both the theory and the practice of penance in the late Anglo-Saxon period were derived from continental texts of the ninth century. But the Anglo-Saxons believed that some of these texts had been handed down from Theodore, Egbert, and Bede—a belief not without some justification—and they endorsed penitential practice as a return to the customs of a better time.

The usual starting point for studies of Anglo-Saxon contact with continental centers is the so-called Benedictine Reform, a movement without an official beginning but traditionally connected with the reign of Edmund (which began in 939) and his support of St. Dunstan and the monastery Dunstan governed at Glastonbury.[1] In 956 Dunstan was exiled by Eadwig and took refuge in St. Peter's, a monastery at Ghent; but under Edgar he returned to England and became one of the three pillars of the subsequent reform of English monasticism; by 963 Edgar had appointed Dunstan to Canterbury, Æthelwold to Winchester, and Oswald to Worcester. So positioned,

---

1. For a comprehensive sketch of the reform, with full references, see P. A. Stafford, "Church and Society in the Age of Ælfric," in *The Old English Homily and Its Backgrounds*, ed. Paul E. Szarmach and Bernard F. Huppé. The fullest discussion of the reform in its historical context is David M. Knowles, *The Monastic Order in England*.

the three abbots "coloured the whole ecclesiastical history of England in the last century of the Old English state."[2]

Studies of the literature produced by the reformers rarely focus on materials of the reform itself; instead, they concentrate on a group of manuscripts from the eleventh century, known as "commonplace books," which preserve many of the homilies, ecclesiastical laws, and handbooks of penance along with some prayers and catechetical texts written in the vernacular.[3] These texts do not represent the work of Dunstan, Æthelwold, and Oswald, but that of their successors, Ælfric, abbot of Eynsham (near Oxford), and Wulfstan, bishop of Worcester and archbishop of York.[4] It was they and their contemporaries who synthesized and translated continental source materials into the vernacuar texts which were to become the reform's literary achievement.

There are two difficulties in studying the reform through the commonplace collections. They are themselves a corpus of evidence more diverse in scope and purpose than many have realized and hence lend themselves badly to generalization. Moreover, they constitute only a late stage of the material they bring together: they are neither its first nor its final version. The commonplace books telescope evidence in a way which conceals much Anglo-Saxon history; they do not show the origins of their content, the adaptation of continental sources to the needs of the English church, or the ultimate form which was intended for either the separate texts or the collections themselves. Since the commonplace books contain much,

2. See Frank M. Stenton, *Anglo-Saxon England*, p. 449. Stenton (p. 445) and others credit Dunstan with the central role in initiating the reform; the political implications of his interest in monasticism must be considered in estimating his achievement, as D. P. Kirby points out, *The Making of Early England*, pp. 108–112.

3. The term "commonplace" is ill-advised in this context, since it describes material which appears to have been far from commonplace in the late Anglo-Saxon period. Important early essays about the commonplace books are Mary Bateson, "A Worcester Cathedral Book of Ecclesiastical Collections Made ca. 1000 A.D.," and Dorothy Bethurum, "Archbishop Wulfstan's Commonplace Book."

4. Kirby, *Early England*, p. 107; for a controversial and stimulating argument de-emphasizing Dunstan's importance and suggesting a "reforming conscience" as early as Ælfheah, bishop of Winchester 934–951, see Eric John, "The Sources of the English Monastic Reformation," pp. 197–199.

though not all, of the vernacular literature pertaining to the tenth-century penitential tradition, it is necessary to circumvent the false perspective which they impart in order to see that tradition as a development, not an accomplishment. The vernacular materials were rooted in a Latin tradition older than the reform. That tradition, like the reform itself, was based on continental sources, though not those most evident in the reform. The period most important to our understanding of the vernacular literature about penance which the commonplace books contain is the early rather than the mid-tenth century.

To begin with the early tenth century is really to begin with the reign of Alfred, king of Wessex (d. 899), who was the first figure of literary importance in England after the death of Bede in 734. Alfred's attempts to reinvigorate ecclesiastical culture have left few visible traces in the records of English monasticism. But pastoral literature was immensely enriched by his translations, especially of Gregory's *Pastoral Care*, and his efforts to educate his clergy.[5] Although the evidence is meager, it is at least highly likely that Alfred's England possessed a private penitential tradition of some kind and that the penitential system represented in the commonplace books was a continuation, expansion, and refinement of this small and probably primitive beginning. For the purposes of this discussion, the commonplace books with their homilies and penitentials will be examined after the materials of the Latin tradition, some of which may have been known and used in Alfred's time.

When Alfred became king, England had barely begun to recover from the devastation of the invasions. Although he may have "heavily overpainted the depression of English learning" brought about during the ninth century, the limited success of his educational and pastoral programs suggests that he did not have an adequate supply of either books or learned men to use them.[6] At the same time, Al-

5. A good introduction to Alfred and his achievement is Eleanor Shipley Duckett, *Alfred the Great*; a recent bibliography of Alfred's writing and of secondary sources is provided by Thomas A. Carnicelli, ed., *King Alfred's Version of St. Augustine's "Soliloquies"* (Cambridge, Mass., 1969), pp. 40–43. *King Alfred's West-Saxon Version of Gregory's Pastoral Care* is edited by Henry Sweet.

6. Stenton, *Anglo-Saxon England*, p. 270. For a different view, see Margaret Deanesly, *The Pre-Conquest Church in England*, p. 259. Alfred discussed the state of learning as

fred's laws show that penitential discipline had not altogether disappeared, and in a period from which no handbooks can with certainty be claimed for the English church, such evidence must be given special weight.

Alfred's laws themselves show some familiarity with Frankish legal codes. He is believed to have made the collection of earlier laws and combined them with his own judgments in imitation of Frankish example.[7] Alfred's code refers to ecclesiastical penance in three cases, two concerning the keeping of oaths and pledges. One who did not fulfill a pledge was required to entrust his arms to his friends, to be imprisoned for forty days on the king's estate, and there to perform "what penance the bishop prescribes for him." One guilty of a breach of surety was to pay for the corresponding breach of pledge "as his confessor prescribes for him." Alfred also provided that one born deaf and dumb, who could not "deny sins or confess them," was to have his misdeeds compensated by his father.[8] Laws promulgated at Grately some thirty years after Alfred's death by Athelstan, one of his successors, resemble the first of Alfred's references to penance: the bishop was required to witness that an oathbreaker had done penance as the confessor had assigned it, but to do so only after the confessor certified that the penance had been performed. The treaty between Guthrum and Edward, Alfred's successor (d.924), established a secular compensation for both Christ and the king, so that one who refused ecclesiastical penance was punished by the state. This was one way of coping with those who, in the words of the treaty, "would not otherwise subject themselves to religious penances, as they should do."[9]

---

he found it—few priests who could understand the liturgy in English or translate Latin—in the preface to the *Pastoral Care*, ed. Sweet, I. 2–9.

7. Alfred's work is called a "vigorous archaism" by J. M. Wallace-Hadrill, "The Franks and the English in the Ninth Century," in *Early Medieval History*, an excellent analysis of Alfred in the continental context.

8. I quote the laws in translation from *EHD*; see pp. 407–416 for Alfred's laws, and for laws quoted above, I. 3 and I. 8 (p. 409) and 14 (p. 411). There is a good discussion of the laws by William A. Chaney, *The Cult of Kingship in Anglo-Saxon England*. They are edited by Felix Liebermann, *Die Gesetze der Angelsachsen*; see I: 48, 58 for passages discussed here.

9. For Athelstan's code see *EHD*, pp. 417–422, especially 26 and 26.I, (p. 422); in

The laws of Alfred may not accurately mirror either the secular or the ecclesiastical law of his time. It has been suggested that his code, which makes no distinction between received customs and newer practices, was compiled in order to provide the king with a written legal text, an "image" of the law. If this were so, the code would not have been intended for the use of judges settling disputes and there would be no certain historical value to Alfred's references to confession and penance.[10] But his laws make fuller use of ecclesiastical penance than any earlier English collection, and this would seem to reflect his wish that the church play a more substantial role in the law's proscriptions, especially those against perjury; even without the ecclesiastical administrative organization necessary to carry out his plan, his laws hint at a desire for a cooperation between native law and the penitential system new to English government.[11]

The penitential system referred to in Alfred's code may have been a vestige of the eighth-century church, but it is highly unlikely that the machinery of private penance would have fared well during the ninth century invasions. Its dual underpinnings—a well-organized ecclesiastical administration and monastic centers able to produce the penitentials—were badly weakened. Even in those sees, such as York, where the succession of bishops was not broken, it must have been difficult to maintain penitential discipline in an age so plagued with the Danish disaster as to be itself a penance.[12] Al-

---

Liebermann, *Gesetze*, see 1:164 for Athelstan and 1:128 (Prol. 2) for the treaty of Edward and Guthrum. These laws are discussed by Thomas P. Oakley, *English Penitential Discipline and Anglo-Saxon Law in Their Joint Influence*, pp. 136–166.

10. See Patrick Wormald, "*Lex Scripta* and *Verbum Regis*," pp. 115–116, 120–123, and 136. Wormald argues that English laws were spoken rather than quoted from written documents and that the documents may have served as an "image" of the law issued for political purposes. Compare Chaney, *The Cult*, pp. 201–203.

11. Alfred's laws seem to be the first to make ecclesiastical penance a part of secular punishment; earlier codes, such as Ine's (688–694), assess heavy fines for false witness given in the bishop's presence but do not mention penance for this; see *EHD*, p. 400 (no. 13), and Liebermann, *Gesetze*, 1:94.

12. "There can be no question that the Danish invasions of the ninth century shattered the organization of the English church, destroyed monastic life in eastern England, and elsewhere caused distress and anxiety which made the pursuit of learning almost impossible": Stenton, *Anglo-Saxon England*, p. 433. York may have fared better than other dioceses, as Stenton observes, p. 436.

fred's laws were the first to be compiled since the eighth century (or at least the first to survive). It is equally plausible that he or the scholars he gathered around him had to make a fresh beginning with penance and penitentials as well. Well acquainted with the Frankish court and the traditions of the Frankish church, Alfred may well have shaped both secular and ecclesiastical laws under the "full force of Frankish example."[13] He would have learned about the penitential tradition of the Frankish church from one of its most important authorities, Archbishop Fulk of Rheims.

Before Alfred's reign, Rheims was one of the most active of the monastic and episcopal centers in northern Germany. During the long pontificate of Hincmar (d. 882), Rheims had become a principal center for the production of canonical texts. Hincmar's support for private penance—and hence for penitentials—is well known.[14] This was the tradition which Fulk, Hincmar's successor, inherited and which he continued to improve upon until his death in 900. He restored schools at Auxerre and St. Amand as well as at Rheims and took a keen interest in the education of the clergy.[15] His correspondence with Alfred gave the English king the benefit of Fulk's extensive pastoral and administrative experience. Alfred asked for more than advice from Fulk: he also requested priests and scholars. In a famous reply, Fulk promised to send the priest Grimbald from the abbey of Saint-Bertin (in northern France) to instruct the English in canonical and other matters.[16] Grimbald arrived in England in 887. It seems entirely possible that the Frankish penitential tradition would, in some form, have arrived with him, if it had not already been introduced through Alfred's earlier contacts with the Frankish court and church.[17]

13. Wallace-Hadrill, "The Franks," p. 209.

14. For Hincmar's use of public and private penance, see Jean Devisse, *Hincmar, archevêque de Reims*, 1:339, 547–548 (private), and 1:548 and 2:881 (public). As Devisse notes, Hincmar did respect contemporary reservations about the handbooks (3:1431).

15. See John J. Contreni, *The Cathedral School of Laon from 850 to 930*, pp. 42–43 and 142–144.

16. The letter is translated in *EHD*, pp. 883–887.

17. Summarized by Wallace-Hadrill, "The Franks," pp. 111–113. These contacts began in the generation prior to Alfred's; for additional information, see G. C. Dunning,

Such contacts were one possible source for a penitential tradition in England well before the Benedictine revival. Another is the contact between England and Brittany which is evident in various early tenth-century sources. The Northmen were also raiding Brittany in the late ninth century; the *Nantes Chronicle* reports Breton refugees fleeing to Wareham in 931, a pattern which may well be older than this date. Subsequent Breton influence on various English documents, including charters and the liturgies, was the product of the Breton immigration. Winchester liturgical texts were heavily influenced by Brittany in the tenth century, and a reaction to the foreigners' influence can be seen in an Old English poem known as *The Seasons for Fasting.*[18]

Brittany, like Rheims, was a source rich in both canonical and penitential literature, and several Breton manuscripts known to have been in England in the tenth century explain the influence of Breton legislative traditions on subsequent English texts. A number of manuscripts contain the *Hibernensis*, the Irish canon law code which was especially popular in Brittany, where it acquired a distinctive manuscript tradition.[19] It is instructive to study the use the English made of this material as a possible model for their adaptation of penitential texts. The *Hibernensis*, written for the early Irish church, was reflective of traditions and institutions of little or no relevance to either Frankish or English ecclesiastical legislation. For this reason, the collection was often known in the form of excerpts; canons concerning marriage and the grades of the clergy were among those most often

---

"Trade Relations between England and the Continent in the Late Anglo-Saxon Period," and D. J. V. Fisher, "The Church in England between the Death of Bede and the Danish Invasions."

18. The *Nantes Chronicle* is quoted in translation in *EHD*, pp. 345–346. The importance of Brittany as a source for English ecclesiastical texts was the subject of David N. Dumville's O'Donnell lectures (Oxford, in press). Breton influence on the liturgy is noted by F. A. Gasquet and Edmund Bishop, eds., *The Bosworth Psalter*, pp. 54–56, and Thomas Symons, ed., *Regularis Concordia*, pp. x–xi. On the charters, see Donald A. Bullough, "The Educational Tradition in England from Alfred to Ælfric," pp. 474–476. The reference to Bretons in *The Seasons for Fasting* was first noticed by Kenneth Sisam, *Studies in the History of Old English Literature*, pp. 55–56.

19. Discussed by Henry Bradshaw, *The Early Collection of Canons Known as the Hibernensis*; see also Ludwig Bieler, ed., *The Irish Penitentials*, pp. 20–24. A catalogue of Breton manuscripts is being compiled by David N. Dumville.

selected for separate circulation.[20] Where we find the *Hibernensis* quoted in English canons of the late tenth century, the *Pseudo-Egbert Excerptiones* chief among them, we find only fragments.[21] The English identified those sections of the imported texts most useful for their own purposes and selected them for inclusion in new canonical compilations.

Brittany and Rheims have been singled out here as two likely sources of ecclesiastical texts for the English church of the pre-reform period. Neither figures among the centers usually named when the sources of the reform itself are discussed. However, contact with the great reformed houses of Europe, such as Fleury, became a strong influence only when the reformers' programs were underway. Æthelwold sent his monk Osgar to Fleury to observe customs there sometime after 956, and such forms of direct contact, which speeded the reformation of English houses, are unknown much before the mid-century.[22] But the development we are concerned with here is not exclusively monastic, and its sources are independent of those which inform us about English monastic revivals in the tenth century. Ultimately the reinvigoration of penitential practice in England depended on the educational resources available only where monasteries were functional. Yet we have to assume that intellectual and religious life existed in England before the reform period. Hard evidence to back up this assumption is not necessarily abundant, but it exists in continental manuscripts which appear to have reached England before the reform began. We are confronted by a gap between the evidence from Alfred's reign and the commonplace books. Fortunately there are manuscripts containing penitentials to help us fill it, and to suggest, if not to prove, that church discipline had begun to re-establish itself before the middle of the tenth century.[23]

20. See Roger E. Reynolds, "The *De Officiis* VII *Graduum*: Its Origins and Early Medieval Development," *MS* 34 (1972): 113–151.

21. Ed. Robin Ann Aronstam, "The Latin Canonical Tradition in Late Anglo-Saxon England"; see pp. 2–3.

22. According to Stenton, "the work of monastic reformers in Lorraine and the Low Countries had made no effectual impression on English churchmen" before this time; *Anglo-Saxon England*, p. 448.

23. The analysis which follows has appeared in my essay, "The Tradition of Penitentials in Anglo-Saxon England," pp. 37–41. Some of the materials discussed below are also

The preceding chapter outlined three distinct families of continental penitentials: those based on early Irish handbooks; those derived from Irish and English penitentials (including those assigned to Bede and Egbert as well as Theodore's); and what might be called genuine Frankish penitentials, such as that of Halitgar. In the tenth century, English authorities had access to all three continental families; some continental manuscripts brought to England in the tenth century still survive, and many others written in England at this time are clearly, at least in part, copies of continental exemplars. An example of such a continental manuscript is Oxford, Bodleian Library, Bodley 311 (tenth-century, with a gloss in Old English written in the tenth or eleventh century, possibly at Exeter).[24] It contains the genuine penitential of Cummean, the *Canones Gregorii* (Theodoran), an anonymous handbook of the tripartite family, and a canonical collection.[25] The manuscript is unusual in that it was systematically rubricated and corrected throughout as a single collection; it is easy to believe that such a manuscript of primarily penitential texts was compiled in a continental center for purposes of export. Another continental manuscript, written in Brittany in the ninth century, is London, British Library, Royal 5 E. xiii; it too was in England (Worcester) in the tenth century, as a gloss indicates.[26] The manuscript contains apocryphal and pseudo-Cyprian texts, a version of Bede's penitential incorporating all of Egbert's handbook, and the *Hibernensis*.[27] We may safely suppose that this manuscript entered England amid the "*furore* in Bretonism" so marked in the history of this period.[28] An additional continental manuscript may belong to

---

discussed in Helmut Gneuss, "A Preliminary List of Manuscripts Written or Owned in England up to 1100," *ASE* 9 (1981): 1–60, and F. A. Rella, "Continental Manuscripts Acquired for English Centers in the Tenth and Early Eleventh Centuries," *Anglia* 98 (1980): 107–116.

24. For dating and provenance, see N. R. Ker, *Catalogue of Manuscripts Containing Anglo-Saxon*, p. 360.

25. See F. Madan and H. H. E. Craster, *A Summary Catalogue of Western Manuscripts in the Bodleian Library at Oxford*, 7 vols. (Oxford, 1895–1953), 2: 1. 220.

26. See G. F. Warner and J. P. Gilson, *Catalogue of Western Manuscripts in the Old Royal and King's Collection*, 4 vols. (London, 1921), 1:116; on the date see Reynolds, "*De Officiis*," p. 132.

27. See the discussion in chapter four, especially n. 49.

28. Quoted from Gasquet and Bishop, *Bosworth Psalter*, p. 56.

this list, although the date of its arrival in England is uncertain; Oxford, Bodleian Library, Bodley 516, written in northern Italy in the third quarter of the ninth century, contains the entire six-part penitential of Halitgar and theological texts.[29]

The extent of continental influence on English penitentials in the tenth century is more easily seen in manuscripts written in England but based on continental exemplars. A most important example is Cambridge, Corpus Christi College 320, a manuscript from the second half of the tenth century, with additions in Old English made in the tenth or eleventh century.[30] The older portion of the manuscript contains the two-book penitential of Theodore, which, with a Latin epigram, may have survived in England from the earlier period. But also included is the *Poenitentiale Sangermanense*, which is composed in part of the shortest of the Bedan penitentials and preceded by an *ordo* for confession based on Halitgar's.[31] At least at this point, the manuscript is a copy of a continental handbook.

Also based on a continental exemplar is Oxford, Bodleian Library, Bodley 718, written in the tenth century at Exeter and believed to have been at Worcester before Wulfstan arrived there.[32] It is in a hand identical or very similar to that of Paris, Bibliothèque Nationale, Lat. 943, the *Sherborne Pontifical*, written after 960.[33] In both manuscripts the prologue to Egbert's penitential is followed by Frankish statutes; the Bodleian manuscript then contains the remainder of the penitential, two orders for confession, and a canonical collection.[34] Continental origins are obviously necessary to explain the presence of both the statutes and the orders for confession.

To this list of manuscripts many others could be added. Dif-

29. See Madan and Craster, *Catalogue*, 2: 1. 430–431.

30. Dating and provenance by Ker, *Catalogue*, pp. 105–106.

31. See M. R. James, *A Descriptive Catalogue of the Manuscripts in the Library of Corpus Christi College, Cambridge*, 2 vols. (Cambridge, 1911–1912), 2:133.

32. See Bethurum, "Commonplace Book," p. 928.

33. See Ker, *Catalogue*, pp. 437–438.

34. One *ordo* is numbered as chapter 19 of Egbert's penitential, fols. 14v–15v; the second *ordo* is longer and includes a litany, fols. 15v–21v. The canonical collection has been edited by Franz Josef Kerff, "Der Quadripartitus: Überlieferung, Quellen und Bedeutung" (Ph.D. diss., Rheinisch-Westfälische Technische Hochschule, 1979; publication is planned).

ferent from those already cited is London, British Library, Cotton Vespasian D. xx, a hand-sized book written in large letters, with fifteen lines to the page. The manuscript does not contain a tariff penitential, but it includes a series of Latin confessional prayers and an *ordo* for confession derived from Halitgar's. This appears to be a manual used strictly for devotional rather than judicial or disciplinary purposes; because both the priest and the penitent are mentioned in the *ordo* for confession, the manuscript was probably not used solely for private devotion.[35] A long Latin confessional prayer somewhat similar to the prayers in this manuscript is found in Cotton Vespasian D. xv, which also contains a version of Theodore's handbook similar to the *Collectio Dacheriana*.[36]

When we turn to the so-called commonplace books, written at the end of the tenth century and in the eleventh century, we find a more extensive collection of penitentials—a sign, no doubt, that as the tenth century progressed, access to continental centers improved. The commonplace books indicate the range of English penitentials at its widest, since in addition to vernacular handbooks, whole or in part, they include a variety of Latin penitentials. Egbert's penitential is contained in Cambridge, Corpus Christi College 265, a Worcester manuscript written in the mid-eleventh century, and also in the twelfth-century Oxford manuscript, Bodleian Library, Barlow 37.[37] A long Latin penitential attributed to Theodore but in fact composed of parts of his two-book penitential, Halitgar's penitential, and the handbooks of Bede, Egbert, and Cummean, is found in Cambridge, Corpus Christi College 190, from the first half of the eleventh century, written at Exeter and containing Leofric's "scriftboc on english" willed to Exeter in 1072.[38] This pseudo-Theodoran penitential

35. Dated by Ker to the mid-tenth century; *Catalogue*, p. 278. The prayer has been edited by Henri Logeman, "Anglo-Saxon Minora," pp. 97–100. The *ordo* begins on fol. 4r and continues for almost forty sides; the imposition of hands is at fol. 51r; other evidence of liturgy: "Tunc dicit sacerdos," fol. 42r, and on fol. 63r a reference to confession made before the priest.

36. Dated by Ker to the mid-tenth century; *Catalogue*, pp. 277–278.

37. *Ibid.*, pp. 92–94, for the dating and provenance of CCCC 265; and for Barlow 37, see Madan and Craster, *Catalogue*, 2: 2. 1057. These manuscripts have recently been analyzed by Hans Sauer, "Zur Überlieferung und Anlage von Erzbischof Wulfstans 'Handbuch.'"

38. Dating and provenance given by Ker, *Catalogue*, pp. 70–73.

also appears in Brussels, Bibliothèque Royale 8558-63, tenth-century at this point.[39] These manuscripts also contain some fragments of Latin penitentials, including Halitgar's, and CCCC 265 at one point quotes the penitential of Bede and cites him by name.[40]

The vernacular handbooks form a sharp contrast to this group of Latin penitentials. There are three texts which may be classified as vernacular penitentials, but they do not form a homogeneous group. Two are closely associated and are found exclusively in the same manuscripts; they are normally referred to as the "Confessional" and the "Penitential." The third, "A Late Old English Handbook for the Use of a Confessor" (which will hereafter be simply the "Handbook") has an independent manuscript tradition and should be considered separately. The variations in the form and function of these three texts suggest that the Anglo-Saxons modified and adapted the penitential and did not merely translate or transcribe material from continental centers. These variations are worth close scrutiny; they reveal how well the Anglo-Saxons grasped the penitential as a form and how successful they were in bringing their own changes to it.

The "Confessional" and the "Penitential" are found in CCCC 190 and two Oxford manuscripts, Bodleian Library, Junius 121, written at Worcester in the third quarter of the eleventh century, and Laud Miscellaneous 482, from the mid-eleventh century and also possibly written at Worcester.[41] Previous editions and discussions refer to both texts as "pseudo-Egbertian," creating the impression that the manuscripts claim Egbert as their author. But this is not the case. The link to Egbert rests solely on the *incipit* in CCCC 190, which says, "Here begin the chapters of the book we call 'scrift boc'; Egbert, archbishop of York, translated these chapters from Latin into English so that the unlearned might understand them more easily."[42] The

---

39. *Ibid.*, pp. 8–10.

40. Bede is named on fol. 51r of CCCC 265, following a passage which corresponds to chapter 11 of the Bedan penitential printed by Wasserschleben, *Die Bussordnungen der abendländischen Kirche*, p. 230.

41. See Ker, *Catalogue*, pp. 412–418 for the Junius manuscript, and pp. 418–422 for the Laud manuscript.

42. Printed by Josef Raith, *Die altenglische Version des Halitgar'schen Bussbuches*, p. xii: "Her onginnaþ þisse boce capitulas þe we hata∂ scriftboc. Þas capitulas Ecgbyrht Arcebisceop on Eoforwic awende of ledene on englisc þaet þa ungelæredan hit mihton þe e∂ understandan."

text which immediately follows is the "Confessional," followed in turn by the "Penitential," "exhortations to penance" for the priest's use, and translated parts of Theodore's penitential.[43] The question is whether the *incipit* refers to both texts or to the "Confessional" alone; what exactly is being claimed for Egbert here, and on what authority? An examination of the rubrication suggests that only the "Confessional" is referred to in the *incipit*, for the chapters which follow it are for the "Confessional" alone (the "Penitential" is divided into four books, all but the last having their own headings). Moreover, the *incipit* refers to "this book" rather than to "these books," supporting the view that the "scrift boc" is the "Confessional" alone and not the entire collection of texts which accompany it.[44] We can take this reasoning a step farther if we remember that neither the "Confessional" nor the "Penitential" is given a specific title apart from the *incipit* in this manuscript. "Confessional" is merely Thorpe's translation of "scrift boc," and "Penitential" was chosen as a title because this text depends in large part on the penitential of Halitgar.[45] "Penitential" is a generic term which suits this text, but "confessional" is not a generic term—there is no criterion for saying that a given text is a confessional rather than a penitential—and so should be abandoned in favor of "Scrift boc," which is a generic term in the vernacular used by the scribe of CCCC 190, probably on the authority of his exemplar. We should prefer his language to Thorpe's.

The claim that Egbert translated the "Scrift boc" must be considered spurious. The language of the text is in the main late West Saxon; although some Mercian forms are present, no research has yet established that they were retained from a copy of the "Scrift boc" written earlier than the tenth century.[46] But are there reasons

43. *Ibid.*, and see also Ker, *Catalogue*, pp. 71–72.

44. "þisse boce capitulas": that is, "the chapters of this book."

45. Benjamin Thorpe, ed. and trans., *Ancient Laws and Institutes of England*, 2: 128–169.

46. The "Scrift boc" is edited by R. Spindler, *Das altenglishe Bussbuch*; his analysis of language, pp. 112–125, argues that the earliest form of the text was East Mercian. His linguistic criteria should be reviewed, a project I hope to undertake as part of a new edition of the text. It is not immediately obvious from Spindler's edition that the "Scrift boc" takes three different forms in three different manuscripts, one of them

for thinking that the "Scrift boc" is, if not prior to the tenth century, at least earlier than the "Penitential"? Any sound criteria for establishing the priority of either text over the other would be very welcome, for it would suggest a chronological sequence now concealed by the codices which contain these handbooks. If we could show that the "Scrift boc" is the earlier text—which seems at least very probable—we could begin to see how handbooks of penance developed in the course of the tenth century. One sign that it is earlier is that it follows its sources closely, whereas the "Penitential" translates portions of Halitgar's text freely, with many additions.[47]

This difference in style of translation points to another and more substantial difference. Both modern editions of these texts include a four-part introduction, but one editor of the "Scrift boc" was able to show that the introduction was not original with his text and that it was closer in its language to the "Penitential" (if not necessarily written by the translator of that text).[48] The introduction consists of directions telling the priest how to interrogate penitents, distinguish their social grades and degrees of culpability, and shorten periods of penance; it concludes with a list of the twelve remissions of sin.[49] The last three parts have parallels in handbooks written before Halitgar's; the first part was partly derived from an *ordo* later than Halitgar's.[50] Material of this sort is not characteristic of eighth-century insular penitentials or those written on the continent before Halitgar's. Had the translator of the "Scrift boc" had access to an

---

(that in Junius 121) being nearly half again as long as another (that in CCCC 190). His tables, pp. 6–8, compare the contents of each version (his edition follows the exact order of none of them).

47. *Ibid.*, pp. 14–16, where Spindler says about the translator of the "Scrift boc": "Im allgemeinen übersetzt er streng wörtlich." The translator of the "Penitential," Raith says, had a Latin original, "das er schlecht und recht übersetzt" (*Die altenglische Version*, p. xxix).

48. Spindler, *Bussbuch*, pp. 165–169.

49. For the text, see *ibid.*, pp. 170–175, and Raith, *Die altenglische Version*, pp. xli–xlvi.

50. The Latin text suggested by both Raith and Spindler as the source for part of the vernacular introduction is the *ordo* found with the latest of the Bedan penitentials; hence, both editors call the source "pseudo-Bede." Other possible sources are the *Rule* of Chrodegang and the first *Capitula* of Theodulf of Orléans; see Spindler, *Bussbuch*, pp. 140–147.

ordo confessionis, it seems likely that he would have used it. Instead, it appears that another editor modernized the "Scrift boc" by inserting the introduction at a later time, when such material was available in England.[51]

The most convincing arguments for the priority of the "Scrift boc" are based on its sources and its structure. The sources of this text may all be older than Halitgar's penitential; none is necessarily more recent than that handbook, written about 830. The "Scrift boc" is drawn from both books of Theodore's penitential, Egbert's penitential, some form of a handbook assigned to Bede, and the penitential of Cummean (or pseudo-Cummean). No fewer than eleven handbooks have been listed among the vernacular penitential's sources, but this may be excessive, especially if we remember that the Bede-Egbert material could have been taken from one rather than two penitentials (that is, a version which conflated them).[52] Whether his sources were many or few, the compiler of the "Scrift boc" did not imitate any of them closely. His arrangement of tariffs and his chapter headings have no exact counterparts in known Latin penitentials. His departures from his sources in these respects are troubling because he translated the tariffs themselves literally. He could certainly have translated any one of his sources and created a more orderly and inclusive handbook; his patchwork suggests that he was working not from a set of individual handbooks but from a single exemplar in which many penitentials had already been rather awkwardly combined. Such an examplar may well have been continental, of course, since the tradition of such "mixed" handbooks was very strong there in the ninth century.[53] The disorder of the "Scrift boc" is extreme. Penances for homicide are spread over several chapters, as are offenses against the Eucharist; there is no separation of the sins of

---

51. As I show in "The Tradition," the four parts of the introduction appear together only once, with the "Scrift boc" in CCCC 190; it is therefore far from certain that they should be considered as a fixed group. For an overview of the distribution of the parts of the introduction, see Raith, *Die altenglische Version*, pp. xx–xxi.

52. Spindler proposes eleven separate handbooks as sources (*Bussbuch*, pp. 22–23), but all the content of the various Bedan handbooks and Egbert's could have been derived from a single text attributed to Bede, making eight a more plausible number.

53. See texts referred to in chapter four, n. 26.

the clergy and the laity, and the final chapter is an arbitrary grouping of tariffs for unclean food, theft, and the mistreatment of slaves and rules for the fasts of the sick, among other items.[54] Such an amalgam can have had but little practical value for the confessor.

The compiler of the "Penitential" applied better methods to a more specific purpose. His text combines the third, fourth, and fifth books of Halitgar's penitential with a collection of tariffs drawn from various sources, including the "Scrift boc," Halitgar's sixth book (the so-called Roman penitential), and the penitential of Cummean or pseudo-Cummean. The tradition of adapting Halitgar's handbook in this way originated on the continent in the late ninth century.[55] The resulting four-book penitential is comprehensive in both theory and practice: the first book explains different occasions when penance is necessary (they include public penance, deathbed penance, and others); the second is a collection of tariffs for the laity; the third is a collection of tariffs for the clergy; and the fourth book is a supplement which refers to cases not already mentioned. The "Penitential" is therefore not only more strictly about confession and penance than the "Scrift boc," but also much better organized.

The strongest link between the "Scrift boc" and the "Penitential" is that the latter's fourth book draws in part on several tariffs from the "Scrift boc."[56] This suggests that the "Penitential" superseded the "Scrift boc" and that it is therefore the younger handbook. The Junius manuscript which contains both these texts shows that at some point there was an attempt to conflate them: the fourth book of the "Penitential" was abbreviated and the entire "Scrift boc" substituted. This was not the original version of the material; we have three manuscripts of the fourth book of the "Penitential" which make only partial use of the "Scrift boc," and only one which includes the entire text—and it is the latest.[57] There are important dif-

54. Despite the diversity of its content, this last chapter is headed "De apibus"; see Spindler, *Bussbuch*, pp. 193–194.

55. For an analysis of manuscripts containing this abridgment of Halitgar's text, which is sometimes followed by the latest of the Bedan handbooks, see Raymund Kottje, *Die Bussbücher Halitgars von Cambrai und des Hrabanus Maurus*, pp. 111–116.

56. Raith shows the parallels, in *Die altenglische Version*, pp. 60–65.

57. This is Junius 121, where the "Scrift boc" begins on fol. 87v, with the first eleven

ferences in substance which reinforce the case for the seniority of the
"Scrift boc." Unlike the "Penitential," it makes only limited use of
commutations; the practice of abbreviating periods of penance was
better established on the continent than in England in the early period, and in this regard the "Scrift boc" may well be reflecting the
earlier condition rather than the later, when—under continental influence—commutations were more widely known.[58] Nor is there reference to public penance in the "Scrift boc," while the custom is
acknowledged in the "Penitential." Again, public penance was not
well known in the eighth century in England, while it was a firmly
established tradition on the continent.[59] The tariffs themselves also
suggest that the "Scrift boc" reflects older conditions. Following
Theodore's custom, the "Scrift boc" requires a priest or bishop guilty
of homicide to submit to the king's judgment; the "Penitential" deals
with this sin twice, once to require the bishop or priest to be defrocked, and a second time to assign twelve years of penance to the
bishop and ten to the priest or monk.[60] One wonders if this deference to the king's judgment conflicted with political conditions in
the tenth century, when the church was in a stronger position in
relation to royalty than it had been in the eighth century. The "Scrift
boc" is somewhat more lenient in its penances for the clergy's sexual
offenses; while the "Penitential" requires priests and deacons (but
not bishops) to be defrocked for fornication, the "Scrift boc" assigns
penances of twelve years (for bishops) or ten (for priests) but notes

canons of the fourth book of the "Penitential" numbered as the first book of the
"Scrift boc." See *ibid.*, pp. 52–53 and 69–70. Spindler takes the *incipit* of the "Scrift
boc" (actually that of book four of the "Penitential") to indicate that a supplementary
book follows (*Bussbuch*, pp. 165–169). But in other manuscripts this describes the last
book of the "Penitential," which is also a supplementary collection. In CCCC 190 and
in Laud Misc. 482, the two books are not adjacent; the fourth book of the "Penitential" is also found in Brussels 8558-63 (see n. 39 above).

58. See Raith, *Die altenglische Version*, pp. 66–69, where cc. 4. 57–59 of the "Penitential" specify methods of reducing the period of penance; and see Spindler, *Bussbuch*,
p. 194, where cc. 39. b, c of the "Scrift boc" allow for this practice on a much smaller
scale.

59. See Raith, *Die altenglische Version*, pp. 10–11, for a description of public penance in
the "Penitential" derived from Halitgar's penitential.

60. "Scrift boc," c. 20. g (Spindler, *Bussbuch*, p. 186); "Penitential," 1. 1 and 4. 1 (Raith,
Die altenglische Version, pp. 16, 47).

that they are not to be defrocked in all cases.[61] It is obvious that the discrepancies between the "Penitential" and the "Scrift boc" would have created difficulties if both handbooks were actually being used and if their authority was considered equal. There is no manuscript evidence to indicate such a conflict, however. The discrepancies involve major rather than minor cases, and presumably when serious disciplinary questions arose the bishop did what he thought best. When we encounter contradictions in contemporary penitentials, it is important to remember that human judgment always played an important part in adjusting the regulations of the text to the circumstance of the moment. We should not, therefore, be troubled by the inconsistencies between the "Scrift boc" and the "Penitential."

Both these texts are different from the third vernacular penitential, the "Handbook for the Use of a Confessor." Only with the "Handbook" are we on new and decidedly English ground. This is apparent in almost every aspect of the work. It is not based on continental precedents alone, but on a combination of vernacular and Latin source materials. It quotes all four books of the "Penitential" but it begins with an *ordo confessionis* adapted from the *Enlarged Rule* of Chrodegang, the only portion of the "Handbook" in Latin.[62] The text also includes paragraphs instructing the priest in administering penance and special provisions for the sick and for "men of substance," those wealthy enough to shorten periods of penance with donations to the church and public mortification.[63]

The "Handbook" is a more complete guide for the confessor than either of the other vernacular texts, although like them it does not appear to have been put in final form by its compiler. The version of the "Handbook" thought to be the most complete includes a confessional prayer after the *ordo confessionis*, but there is strong evidence that this was an interpolation and not part of the compiler's original

61. "Scrift boc," cc. 1. a, b (Spindler, *Bussbuch*, p. 176); "Penitential," 4. 3 (Raith, *Die altenglische Version*, p. 48).
62. Edited by Roger Fowler, "A Late Old English Handbook for the Use of a Confessor"; see p. 16 for text and p. 13 for Fowler's suggestion that the source is a confessional formula. The resemblance to Chrodegang's text is stronger; see Max Förster, "Zur Liturgik der angelsächsischen Kirche," pp. 22–23.
63. Fowler, "Handbook," pp. 32–34.

design.[64] What distinguishes the "Handbook" is not only its format and abundant (if not efficiently executed) instruction for the confessor, but also its elimination of penances required of bishops. In several tariffs borrowed from the "Penitential," the "Handbook" reduced the clerical grades represented in this way; this may have been part of the compiler's effort to provide a new guidebook specifically for the confessor, with the jurisdiction of the text confined to the social classes in his charge.[65] The "Handbook" reduces the confessor's margin for error by reducing the number of tariffs for him to choose among. By far the shortest of the three vernacular texts, it would therefore have been the easiest to consult. In its shorter form, it includes the *ordo*, instructions for the priest's use in determining penances, a tariff manual, and additional advice for the confessor.[66] It contains only a fraction of the tariffs found in either the "Penitential" or the "Scrift boc," and unlike them it does not seem to have been intended as a compendium of penitential decisions as well as a guide for the confessor. Its tariffs are devoted chiefly to murder, sexual offenses, and superstition. This narrowed scope—signaled by the elimination of penalties due bishops—makes the "Handbook" the most practical of the vernacular penitentials; it makes few assumptions about the priest's knowledge of his duties as confessor and in fact gives nearly as much attention to advising him as to providing the tariffs themselves.[67]

The "Handbook" stands together with the "Penitential" against

64. The prayer occurs twice in Cambridge, Corpus Christi College 201, in a section of the manuscript containing the six-part text Fowler edits and in a later section containing only the *ordo* and a prayer (fols. 115–117 and 170–171). The prayer is obviously interpolated into the *ordo* on fol. 115, however: it interrupts a sentence which is then completed after the prayer concludes. Fowler's belief that the second section (the prayer) is a "genuine" part of the "Handbook" notwithstanding (see p. 4, *ibid.*), the prayer did not originally belong to the text.

65. In that part of the "Handbook" dealing with murder and fornication, bishops are omitted from the tariffs (*ibid.*, pp. 23–24); but bishops are mentioned in connection with homicide earlier (p. 21).

66. Fowler believes that the four-part form is the original version but accepts the authenticity of the six-part version as well; *ibid.*, pp. 4–5.

67. In Fowler's edition, parts one, three, and five are nearly equal in length to part four, the list of tariffs.

the "Scrift boc" in its use of commutations and its reference to public penance (taken from the "Penitential"), which states that this form of reconciliation has been only recently introduced in England but that it is known to "Christian people beyond the sea."[68]

As the homilies of Ælfric show, the Anglo-Saxons inherited the dual system of penance developed by the Carolingians. Private penance was required for private sins, and public penance for offenses public in nature. Because such sins scandalize, those guilty of them must atone before others in order to counter the bad example they have set.[69] The liturgy for the ritual was derived from continental sources. In a homily to be preached at the reconciliation rite, Wulfstan likened the sinner to Adam, expelled from Paradise for his crime and welcomed to the paradise of the holy church when he had atoned for it.[70] He derived this homily from a text by Abbo of St. Germain, one of his favorite sources, but added a note lamenting that public penance was not as well known "among this people" as it ought to have been.[71] Combined with an exhortation to public penance shared by the "Penitential" and the "Handbook," Wulfstan's observation confirms the newness of the custom in the tenth-century English church.

The Anglo-Saxons were well equipped with liturgical directions for public penance. One of the commonplace collections contains several notes about the ceremony and makes no provision for private confession or penance; this manuscript contains entries in Wulfstan's own hand and evidently was compiled as his central sourcebook for the public rite.[72] Another commonplace book contains some of the

68. Commutations are dealt with in the last part of the "Handbook," which is found only in CCCC 201 (*ibid.*, p. 4); for the quotation concerning public penance, see p. 20, and for the phrase in the "Penitential," see Raith, *Die altenglische Version*, p. 10.

69. Ælfric's homily for the Seventeenth Sunday after Pentecost, ed. and trans. Benjamin Thorpe, *The Homilies of the Anglo-Saxon Church*, 1:498.

70. "Sermo de Cena Domini," ed. Dorothy Bethurum, in *The Homilies of Wulfstan*, xv (pp. 236–238).

71. *Ibid.*, pp. 366–373, where the Wulfstan translation is printed opposite Abbo's text.

72. London, British Library, Cotton Nero A. 1; see the introduction by H. R. Loyn to the facsimile, *A Wulfstan Manuscript Containing Institutes, Laws, and Homilies*.

same information amid a collection of excerpts pertaining to both private and public penance.[73] There are, in addition, various liturgical books which include the public rite; one of them, a Cambridge manuscript from the eleventh century, copies the rite as it is found in the *Pontifical Romano-Germanique*.[74]

The public liturgies are complemented by directions provided in the non-liturgical manuscripts for the performance of the public ritual. These bits of information appear to be a synthesis—and not a systematic one—of various Frankish texts which explicate and describe public penance. The Anglo-Saxons regularly used Frankish sources in this way, excerpting needed information and making it available in new form. The penitential notes in one of the commonplace manuscripts were once, incorrectly, linked to Ælfric; the error is understandable, in a way, because these excerpts resemble Ælfric's pastoral letters, one of the most important sources for measuring the Anglo-Saxons' grasp and application of the penitential system.[75] These letters, like the commonplace excerpts, were intended to explicate all phases of penitential practice; some were addressed to the clergy, and some to Wulfstan himself. Ælfric was the most important, if not the only, synthesizer of continental sources for the Anglo-Saxon church. His letters transmitted information gleaned from penitentials, canon law, and various Frankish statutes.[76]

Ælfric's role in the reform was pivotal. His celebrated skills as an editor and compiler, witnessed in his digests and translations, were themselves the fruits of an education made possible by the reform of monastic schools. His mission was to implement that reform on a

73. CCCC 190; these excerpts are edited in part by Bernhard Fehr, *Die Hirtenbriefe Ælfrics in altenglischer und lateinischer Fassung*, pp. 234–255. Portions are also found in Cotton Nero A. I.

74. Cambridge, Corpus Christi College 163, s. xi; copied from an exemplar of the Pontifical, according to Michel Andrieu, *Les "Ordines Romani" de haut moyen âge*, 1: 96–98. Other liturgies for the public rite are listed by Bethurum, *Homilies*, p. 347.

75. Sources listed by Fehr, *Hirtenbriefe*, pp. 234–236. Fehr thought that Ælfric made these excerpts, but he did not; see Peter Clemoes, "The Old English Benedictine Office, Corpus Christi College, Cambridge, MS 190, and the Relations between Ælfric and Wulfstan."

76. On Ælfric's sources, see Fehr, *Hirtenbriefe*, pp. xcii–cxxi (they include penitentials, canons, and other non-liturgical texts).

lower level. The literacy and learning of the monastery could not be imparted to the clergy, but the clergy could be taught what the monks themselves had learned. The monks' own rules, which prescribed their habits of confession and their modes of penance, were less to the point than continental literature of the previous century aimed at clerical reform. In the tenth century, as in the eleventh and the twelfth, "it was from the monasteries that the countryside learnt its religion." But that transmission required men like Ælfric to translate monastic experiences into models for the laity.[77]

Ælfric instructed the clergy in both the theory and the practice of penance. Two of his letters repeat the requirement found in many continental statutes, as well as the preface to Egbert's penitential, that the priest must own and use the handbook.[78] Ælfric used the penitential itself as a source for information about keeping the Eucharist free from contamination (sanitation was one of the battles fought longest and hardest by the penitentials).[79] In describing the rites to be performed for the dying, Ælfric required the sick to confess and to promise to turn from their sins and pray "until their last breath."[80]

The target of at least some of Ælfric's pastoral education was Wulfstan, who seems to have relied heavily on the abbot's advice in matters both great and small. Wulfstan is often given more credit than Ælfric for an interest in the practice as opposed to the theory of penance, but his dependence on Ælfric's letters betrays this false distinction. Ælfric and Wulfstan together accomplished a task only implied by the handbooks and the orders for public penance: the instruction of the clergy whose duty it was to implement the practice of penance. For the literary history of penance, Ælfric's achievement

77. Quotation from R. W. Southern, *The Making of the Middle Ages*, p. 153. The fundamental study of clerical education and reform as one of the objectives of the tenth-century movement is Reginald R. Darlington, "Ecclesiastical Reform in the Late Old English Period."

78. See chapter four, nn. 20–22, for continental sources, and chapter three, nn. 54–55, on the text of Egbert. For Ælfric's text, see Fehr, *Hirtenbriefe*, p. 51 (Brief II, c. 137) and pp. 126–127 (Brief II, c. 157).

79. *Ibid.*, p. 29 (Brief I, c. 134).

80. *Ibid.*, pp. 150–153 (Brief III, c. 16): "oþ þa nystan orþunc3e."

assumes greater importance than Wulfstan's, since he supplied not only a digest of regulations on specific practical matters, but also some texts for the clergy's use in teaching the laity about penance and confession. The selections appended to a collection of Ælfric's homilies appear to have been intended for this purpose.[81] Their catechetical content will be examined in the following chapter, along with the homilies through which Ælfric and Wulfstan sought to popularize penitential practice.

If penitential practice had, at the end of the Anglo-Saxon period, become customary among the English, it was largely due to the legislative industry of Wulfstan, who wrote both ecclesiastical and secular laws implementing penance. His message in three important laws for the clergy is the same: the priest is to hear confessions and assign penance, and bishops are to make sure that their clergy perform these duties in accordance with canon law. It was this kind of legislation which gave traction to the penitential system and in fact made penance a systematic program in the English church.

The first of these collections is Wulfstan's *Canons of Edgar* dated (on the basis of its dependence on Ælfric's pastoral letters) between 1004 and 1008.[82] Wulfstan also drew on the vernacular "Penitential," Theodore's handbook, and various other continental sources in compiling these regulations for the clergy's conduct. Their support of the penitential system is explicit: the priest is required to "teach" confession and penance to all those who confess to him and to help them repent.[83] The link between confession and instruction is extremely common in sources from this period. Parallel exhortations can be found in the translation of the *Capitula* of Theodulf and in the translation of the *Enlarged Rule* of Chrodegang, the former of which is numbered among the *Canons'* sources.[84]

Wulfstan's *Institutes of Polity* contains his most important legal

81. The appendix to the second series of *Catholic Homilies*, in Thorpe, *Homilies*, 2:596–608.

82. Ed. Roger Fowler, *Wulfstan's Canons of Edgar*; for an overview of Wulfstan's career, see Dorothy Whitelock, "Archbishop Wulfstan, Homilist and Statesman."

83. Fowler, *Canons*, c. 68 (pp. 15–17).

84. See Hans Sauer, ed. *Theodulfi Capitula in England*, pp. 354–359, and Arthur S. Napier, ed., *The Old English Version of the Enlarged Rule of Chrodegang*, pp. 37–41. See Fowler, *Canons*, pp. xxxiv–xxxix, for Wulfstan's use of Theodulf's *Capitula*.

opinions about penance, since it was aimed at both bishops and their priests. Wulfstan instructs bishops that they are to use canonical collections when they reach decisions at synods, no doubt believing that this would enable them to develop standard, consistent practices.[85] The bishops are also told to oversee the work of their confessors, who are responsible for determining penances within their *scrift-scirs*, or confession districts. Since much was to be determined "by the confessor's direction," it was vitally important that he be subjected to the bishop's authority and punished for his sins "as the books prescribe." The confessor was reminded of his three most important obligations to his congregation: he was to preach and instruct, to heal by means of penance, and to protect them with prayer.[86]

Much emphasis was put on the clergy's penitential functions because confessors were the agents of bishops, acting in the bishops' stead. This was, historically, one of the greatest advantages of private over public penitential discipline: it was far easier to bring the individual sinner to the priest for confession than to send him to the bishop, and far easier for the layman to accept the fast imposed by the priest than to endure the public exposure of the reconciliation pronounced by the bishop. The agency of the confessor was probably most important in those areas traditionally thought of as remote from episcopal jurisdiction. In Wulfstan's case this would have meant the diocese of York, over which Wulfstan became archbishop in 1002.[87] The latest of his codes for the clergy, the *Northumbrian Priest's Law*, was issued (ca. 1020) for this area. Here the provision for the penitential system was far less extensive than in the other ecclesiastical collections, suggesting that church discipline was weaker in this region and hence more difficult to upgrade. The priest was fined for rather elementary violations of church law: he was not to refer to a layman a case which ought to have been brought before the church; he was not to refuse to hear confession or to baptize; he was not to

85. Ed. Karl Jost, *Die "Institutes of Polity, Civil and Ecclesiastical,"* pp. 67–69 (I Pol. 41–47).

86. *Ibid.*, pp. 85 (II Pol. 102) and 97–99 (II Pol. 121–124).

87. Stenton discusses the connection between the sees of Worcester and York in *Anglo-Saxon England*, pp. 436–437. For the circumstances of Wulfstan's translation to York, see Bethurum, *Homilies*, pp. 59–60.

disobey his bishop.[88] Standards in the northern province were less exacting than elsewhere; the marriage of the clergy was allowed here but not elsewhere, and the general tenor of these laws suggests that the clergy were not expected to have more than a passing acquaintance with the obligations belonging to the priest's office.[89]

Under Wulfstan, penitential discipline penetrated more deeply into secular legislation than before. As adviser to Ethelred (1008–1012) and later to Cnut (1020–1023), Wulfstan was in a position of influence not approached by earlier English ecclesiastics.[90] He had a strong hand in forming much legislation written in the early eleventh century and aimed at the establishment of Christian ethics within the secular law codes. His use of the penitential system was, in its broadest sense, traditional, continuing practices seen in Athelstan's laws and in the laws of Edmund (939–946). Just as Athelstan required the perjurer to have his penance verified before the bishop, Edmund instructed the bishop to inform one convicted of slaying in blood-feud of his legal obligations; the slayer had no recourse to the secular court until he had subjected himself to ecclesiastical penance.[91]

The laws of Ethelred do far more than merely support the church's disciplinary system. The code issued in 1008 urged every Christian to "form the habit of frequent confession" and to receive the Eucharist often. Laws issued in 1009 enforced a "general penance" before Michaelmas, requiring the laity to come barefoot to the church and confess and authorizing the reeve in each village to witness penance and almsgiving.[92] Wulfstan's hand is also evident in the laws of Cnut, especially in the secular code issued between 1020 and 1023. These laws punish violations of the Lenten fast and require the church to hear the confession of a condemned man.[93] The code twice

88. Edited by Liebermann, *Gesetze*, 1:380–385. Translated in *EHD*, pp. 471–476; see cc. 5, 8, and 45.

89. *EHD*, p. 474, c. 35 (concerning married clergy).

90. Bethurum, *Homilies*, pp. 62–64, and Dorothy Whitelock, "Wulfstan and the Laws of Cnut," *EHR* 63 (1948): 433–452.

91. See Liebermann, *Gesetze*, 1:186–192, and the translation in *EHD*, p. 428, c. 4.

92. In Liebermann, *Gesetze*, 1:238–246; in *EHD*, p. 445, c. 22 (on frequent confession), and p. 447, cc. 1–2 (on the general penance).

93. In Liebermann, *Gesetze*, 1:278–374; in *EHD*, p. 462, cc. 46–47 (on the fast) and p. 461, c. 44 (on the condemned man).

specifies that an offender must be punished according to his culpability: the man of higher rank must atone "the deeper both to God and to men for wrongdoing"; the weak and sick must not be punished as severely as the strong and powerful. These statements echo the penitentials.[94] So too does the substitution of mutilation for the death penalty: "thus one can punish and at the same time preserve the soul."[95]

Wulfstan's law codes represent the culmination of the tenth-century reforms in a cooperative legal system so Christian in character that its punishment of criminals was sometimes revised to be more corrective than retributive. Impressive though this is, it must be seen as a merely verbal accomplishment, a symbol of the interdependence which Wulfstan hoped to create between the secular and ecclesiastical worlds. How well he succeeded in bringing his society's behavior up to the standards which these codes envisage cannot, of course, be known. What can be measured, however, is the breadth of the literary achievement of Ælfric, Wulfstan, and their predecessors, and in these terms alone their success was great.

The eleventh century was not kind to the tenth-century reformers; the events of 1066 and the subsequent revolution in the English language were to age the new texts and antiquate at least some of the institutions new to England in the reform. What the tenth-century ecclesiastics did was, in a sense, simple; forced to compensate for "a century and a half's arrears"—roughly from 800 to 950—"before English knowledge of the religious life could be brought to the Continental level," they transformed a considerable portion of the Frankish reform's literature into texts suitable for use in England.[96] The institutions which the English continued to foster in the eleventh century had been built on eighth-century models as well as the earliest work of the Carolingian reformers.[97] This had the slightly odd

94. *EHD*, p. 460, c. 38. 1 (on the mighty) and p. 464, c. 68. 1 (for a statement derived from "De Confessione," in Thorpe, *Ancient Laws and Institutes*, 2:260–265). In Liebermann, *Gesetze*, p. 338 and p. 354.

95. Whitelock cites this and the above passages in "Wulfstan and the Laws," p. 447; in *EHD* see p. 459, c. 30. 5, and Liebermann, *Gesetze*, 1:332–334.

96. Bateson, "Worcester Cathedral Book," p. 690.

97. Including the *Epitome* of Benedict of Aniane (d. 821), for which see Napier, *The Old English Version*, p. xi, Alcuin's *Liber de Virtutibus et Vitiis*, and canonical collections.

effect of furnishing English bishops with new material which was, in fact, quite old, or at least old-fashioned. The "Scrift boc" is an excellent example: obviously new to the English in the tenth century, it was based on texts similar to those which the Paris Council of 829 had scorned. The second vernacular handbook, the "Penitential," had a similar history, since the English derived it from Halitgar's penitential, roughly contemporary with the Paris council.

Perhaps this explains why tenth-century English penitential practice, as seen in the handbooks, has been called a system "coming to a dishonoured end." It is true that Peter Damiani, the Italian cardinal (d. 1072), attacked Egbert's penitential as a collection of false canons, "diabolical figments instituted to deceive the souls of the simple with cunning devices," "incantations in which lost men confide with vain presumption," and "theatrical ravings." Opposition to the penitentials was nothing new, although Peter expressed it with unprecedented vigor. But it hardly justifies us in thinking that after the work of Ælfric and Wulfstan the English clergy "would have possessed garbled texts of penitentials which at their best were confused and often contradictory as well," or that "the church's long tolerance of the disorder is remarkable."[98]

One cannot reply, "What disorder?" There were contradictions between the "Penitential" and the "Scrift boc" and even between the second and fourth books of the "Penitential" itself. But there was nothing in the tenth century to equal the confusion of the seventh, before Theodore wrote his handbook (or began to collect its canons), and nothing in the English tenth-century reform to equal the controversy experienced one hundred and fifty years earlier by the Franks. Compared to its own previous history, and to the continental precedent, penitential literature in the tenth century developed quickly and consistently, if without perfect uniformity. Every significant aspect of the penitential handbook had been revised: the Anglo-Saxons supplied an introduction more informative and more detailed

98. Disagreeable conclusions in an otherwise agreeable study by Frank Barlow, *The English Church 1000–1066*, pp. 83–84. For the quotations from Peter Damian, see the *Liber Gomorrhianus*, PL 145:159–190. In c. 12 Peter complains that some penitentials claim to be Theodore's, others a "Roman penitential" (which could mean the penitential of Halitgar) or "canons of the apostles."

than any continental *ordo confessionis*, although briefer and more compact than most Latin equivalents; they overhauled the list of sins, at least in the "Penitential" and the "Handbook," producing a more efficient collection of tariffs in which sins of thought and other monastic vices were almost completely eliminated; and they revised the system of commutations which accompanied the handbook.

A single principle unified this achievement: simplification. And it was the very opposite of the final result of the Frankish reform, at least as witnessed by the *Double Penitential*—a vast and complex document, lengthy and repetitive and doubtless overwhelming to any but a highly experienced confessor. The English tradition of handbooks may be said to have culminated in the "Handbook," the bulk of whose contents related to the confessor's instructional or catechetical offices rather than to his duty to judge the sinner scrupulously. This hardly suggests a system coming to a "dishonoured" end. Rather, it suggests a healthy tradition of revision and adaptation pointing the handbooks toward a purpose which, though not itself new, nonetheless newly amplified one of the penitential's oldest functions. The short tariffs of the "Handbook" are a world away from the detailed catalogues of the early Irish penitentials, but the didactic and catechetical information included in the English penitential partakes fully of the spirit of confession in the Irish monastery. The first Irish penitentials instructed the confessor and urged him to catechize his penitents. The vernacular handbooks of tenth-century England pursue the same objectives and, it must be said, plan that pursuit with an efficiency which increased its chances of success. Their brevity and their ample advice for the confessor, seen in the "Scrift boc" introduction and in the "Handbook," as well as in many exhortatory passages to be studied in the following chapter, were concessions to the confessors' poor training. But at the same time this simplification of penitential tariffs and lists of sins and the corresponding expansion of instruction for the confessor produced penitentials newly useful and usable. In their efforts to develop handbooks suited to new purposes, the reformers succeeded in recapturing their oldest function.

The reformers acted partly in the belief that their work revived the penitential tradition of Theodore, Egbert, and even Bede. Theodore is invoked in the introduction to the "Scrift boc" as the author of a system of commutations,[99] and, as we have seen, Egbert was believed to have translated it. Other handbooks and canonical collections cite other authorities, including Augustine and St. Sylvester, and so we cannot conclude that the reformers saw the penitential system entirely as a tradition of their own church. But the "Scrift boc" at one point notes that certain customs found in its source are not attested by "old witness," implying a comparison between the source and an older text. And the *Regularis Concordia* claims to retain "the goodly customs of this land" and announces itself as a code for the "English nation."[100] This is not so much a rejection of foreign influence as an affirmation that ecclesiastical customs being revived in the tenth century were traditional, not new. Such asseverations must have made the practices, which were in fact without precedent at least in the ninth-century English church, more susceptible of success.

The contrasts between penitential texts and standards of the eighth century and the tenth are many, but one contrast points to the reformers' accomplishment better than all others: their development of a complete penitential system in vernacular literature. Only public penance remained a Latin ceremony. Everything else, beginning with the handbooks and extending to laws for the clergy as well as secular law, prayers, and homilies, was supplied in the language of the people. This made both the clergy and the laity easier to educate; hence, it increased the likelihood that confession and penance would be understood and observed. Backward-looking though the reformers were in their choice of sources, they were, in their wide use of their own language for disciplinary and devotional materials, among the most far-seeing churchmen in early medieval Europe.

99. See Raith, *Die altenglishe Version*, p. xx, for the passages attributed to Theodore.
100. See Spindler, *Bussbuch*, p. 192, c. 32; concerning the penance for one who eats a hen which has drunk a man's blood, the "Scrift boc" says: "be þysum swa þeah we nabbað ealde gewitnesse." On the *Regularis* see Thomas Symons, "Sources of the Regularis Concordia," *Downside Review* 59, n.s. 40 (1941): 34–35.

Chapter Six

Teaching Penance: Old English Homilies, Handbooks, and Prayers

THE priest who had to be taught how to administer penance by hearing confession and determining the reparation required was himself a teacher. Implicit in most handbooks of penance, and explicit in many, is a connection between the priest's judicial and educational roles. One of the most durable medieval metaphors for the priest was the mute dog: a priest without his books—his gospels, his homilies, his penitential—was like a dog without a bark. Wulfstan used a similar figure when he declared that a muzzled dog barked for naught. In supplying the priest with the administrative tools necessary to his office and teaching him how to use them, Ælfric and Wulfstan were among those who gave him voice.[1] How often or how well he barked remains unknown: we know only that the priest was expected to be heard. With this in mind, we can turn back to the administrative materials of confession and penance and to the secular laws with new questions. What was the effect of this literature on the laity? In particular, what did these texts, which insisted on educating and reforming the laity, actually teach them?

1. Ultimately derived from scripture (Isa. 65: 10), the figure was used by Gregory in the *Pastoral Care*, its probable source in Anglo-Saxon literature. See *King Alfred's West-Saxon Version of Gregory's Pastoral Care*, ed. Henry Sweet, 1: 88–89 (chapter 15, "How the teacher must be discreet in his silence and useful in his words"). Ælfric used the figure in his pastoral letter to Wulfsige; see Bernhard Fehr, ed. *Die Hirtenbriefe Ælfrics in altenglischer und lateinischer Fassung*, p. 15; see also Wulfstan's text, "Verba Ezechiel Prophete de Pigris" (xviB), in *The Homilies of Wulfstan*, ed. Dorothy Bethurum, p. 240. There is a lengthy discussion of the scriptural passage in "Langland's 'Canes Muti': The Paradox of Reform," by Alfred L. Kellogg, in *Chaucer, Langland, Arthur: Essays in Middle English Literature* (New Brunswick, N.J., 1972), pp. 51–58.

Answers to these questions begin with the penitentials and other texts written for the priest's use in teaching his congregation. Chief among these sources are the homilies. They are paralleled by the *ordo confessionis* (or analogous directions for receiving penitents) and by short, didactic passages intended for informal delivery; the homilies are complemented by prayers and, less directly, by poems. Together these texts form a coherent vernacular corpus of catechism in which confession is often seen as an opportunity for instruction. During his encounter with the penitent, the priest used confession and penance to explicate the individual's role in salvation history, linking his sinfulness to the Fall and his repentance to the Redemption. We will see that the function of penance in late Anglo-Saxon culture was not chiefly restrictive or negative, but rather catechetical. Penance was a prominent topic in Anglo-Saxon literature because it simultaneously required discipline and encouraged devotion, the twin imperatives of the Christian life.

Penitential literature becomes catechetical when its immediate subject is seen in the larger Christian framework in which penance is related to faith. In confession the priest tested the penitent's knowledge of the fundamental teachings of the church and ensured his belief in them. The penitent was then told that his faith was a mandate: if he believed in the existence of God and the devil, of heaven and hell, and if he believed that his actions would ultimately lead him to one of these two eternal homes, he would strive to shape his own life on the Christian model. Hence, catechism involved the "how" of good behavior as well as the "what" of right doctrine. The usefulness of penance in connecting behavior to belief, in directing the individual's life along the model of Christ's, is evident in much of the pastoral literature written in England in the tenth century.

The most abundant sources are the homilies intended for delivery either to the clergy or to a wider lay audience. They are traditionally divided into two classes, the anonymous homilies found in *The Vercelli Book* and *The Blickling Book*, and the homilies of Ælfric and Wulfstan. Numerous fundamental distinctions separate these categories. The theological content of the anonymous homilies is less well developed and possibly more varied; and as collections they offer imperfect evidence of systematic, liturgically specific preaching.

The homilies of Ælfric and Wulfstan, on the other hand, are theologically more sophisticated; Ælfric's, in particular, are seen as the first attempt to "arrange coherent collections of vernacular, exegetical homilies for the liturgical year."[2] If we approach the anonymous homilies separately and examine them for references to confession and penance and the integration of these practices into the layman's daily conduct, the distinction between them and the works of Ælfric and Wulfstan tends to diminish. Certainly, seen individually, many of these homilies do not deserve to be ranked as inferior to the "learned pieces" of Ælfric and Wulfstan, for they are drawn from the same Carolingian sources used by the late reformers.[3] Although the anonymous homilists have been said to be less sophisticated in their eschatological teaching than Ælfric and Wulfstan, no such invidious comparison can be made of their teaching about penance.

The *Blickling* and *Vercelli* collections both predate the mid-tenth century. On the basis of internal evidence, the *Blickling* texts are known to have been written before 971.[4] Both anthologies are based on antecedent compilations, but the nature of these earlier collections is unknown. In part they may have stemmed from the pastoral materials of the pre-Alfredian age; all that can be said with relative certainty about their chronology is that they are "at least a generation earlier" than Ælfric's earliest work, and therefore a generation earlier than 990.[5] The *Blickling* homilies may derive in part from the comparatively vigorous pastoral tradition of Mercia in the ninth century, for there are Mercian signs in their language.[6] The *Vercelli* homilies

2. For general orientation and useful specialized studies, see *The Old English Homily and Its Backgrounds*, ed. Paul E. Szarmach and Bernard F. Huppé. The standard study of both Ælfric and Wulfstan is Milton McC. Gatch, *Preaching and Theology in Anglo-Saxon England*. The quotation is taken from Gatch, "The Achievement of Ælfric," in *The Old English Homily*, p. 43.

3. They are so ranked by Joan Turville-Petre, "Translations of a Lost Penitential Homily," p. 51.

4. Richard Morris, ed., *The Blickling Homilies*, p. v, discusses the date; there is a facsimile edited by Rudolph Willard, with a full introduction.

5. Gatch, *Preaching*, p. 8.

6. The Mercian origins of the homilies are traced by Robert J. Menner, "The Anglian Vocabulary of *The Blickling Homilies*," in *Philologica*, ed. Thomas A. Kirby and Henry Bosley Woolf, pp. 56–64; he sees the texts as a "product of Mercian learning and

show traces of the language of Alfred's age, using the same word for repentance (*hreowsung*) as Alfred used in *The Pastoral Care*, rather than the term common later (*dædbot*).[7] But this is inconclusive. No evidence yet known connects these with Alfred's period, much less the ninth century.[8]

Both the *Blickling* and the *Vercelli* homilies deal with penance in two ways: they describe and recommend the acts of confession and penance, and they interpret repentance more broadly to mean a turning from evil deeds as part of the Christian's moral reorientation. Their references to penitential practice are of special interest because they attest to penance at least as an ideal put forth by the church in the pre-reform period. These homilies are usefully compared to the "Scrift boc," whose affinity with eighth- rather than ninth-century penitentials also suggests an early, pre-reform date.

Two *Blickling* homilies are devoted to the broader aspects of penance rather than the details of confession. The homily for the Fifth Sunday in Lent orders the confessor to shield the innocent and judge the guilty severely and warns that the sins of hatred and envy are among those most difficult to confess, adding that hatred is "the root of all other sins."[9] The homilist's use of the root metaphor is not casual: the homily begins by declaring that no one can bear spiritual fruit who does not hold the "root" of holy teaching in his heart.[10]

Mercian piety." Irish scholars and missionaries were active in Mercia in the ninth century; see Kathleen Hughes, "Some Aspects of Irish Influence on Early English Private Prayer," pp. 60–61.

7. *Vercelli* homilies I–VIII are edited by Max Förster, *Die Vercelli-Homilien*. The remaining homilies are edited by Paul E. Szarmach, *Vercelli Homilies IX–XXIII*. See his essay, "The *Vercelli Homilies*: Style and Structure," in Szarmach and Huppé, *The Old English Homily*, pp. 241–267. The vocabulary of penance is examined by Franz Wenish, "Kritische Bemerkungen zu angaben über die Verbreitung einiger angeblich westsächsischer Dialektwörter," *Anglia* 96 (1978): 5–44; for *dædbot* see pp. 33–39, and compare Turville-Petre, "Translations," pp. 72–74, and Robert C. Rice, "*Hreocearig*, 'Penitent, Contrite,'" *Modern Language Notes* 12 (1975): 243–250.

8. The earliest date acceptable to D. G. Scragg is "the last decade of the tenth century." See "Vernacular Homilies and Prose Saints' Lives before Ælfric," *ASE* 8 (1979): 223–277; quotation from p. 224.

9. Ed. Morris, *Homilies*, p. 65: "forþon seo synn biþ swiþe mycel þæt man oþerne hatige & tæle; sægd is þæt hit sy wyrtruma ealra oþerra synna."

10. *Ibid.*, p. 55: "se wyrtruma þære halgan gesegene."

The homilist approaches his admonition to confess and repent by first attacking immoral and corrupt clergy who excuse evildoers who offer bribes and instead condemn the poor and innocent. Good judges are necessary so that the sinner may face the heavenly judge on the Last Day; they enable Christians to "preserve ourselves from great sins, so that we may more easily amend the venial ones."[11] The homily for the feast of St. Peter and St. Paul contains a closing exhortation to confession which is not found in the homily's Latin source. The mercies of God are said to await those who cease from sin, confess fully to the priest, and abide by the confessor's judgment, promising never to return to unrighteous ways.[12] Here and in other homilies, the emphasis falls more heavily on the sinner's moral reorientation than on confession. This is true in the famous homily on the end of the world, which exhorts the sinner "to turn to the true medicine" but is really about doing good works and establishing "right belief" in one's heart.[13] The homily for Quinquagesima Sunday links penance and prayer: when sinners confess sins and pray for forgiveness, God will have mercy and pardon them.[14] The homily stresses prayer rather than confession and emphasizes the mercy of God's compassion rather than the power of the confessor to forgive sins.

Nonetheless, the *Blickling* homilies attest to private confession and penance as administered through the penitentials. The homily for the Third Sunday in Lent, like that for the Fifth, instructs priests not to be afraid of powerful men, or attracted by their bribes, but to judge them as their deeds require. It is possible that such warnings were traditional, but it may also be true that confession and penance

11. *Ibid.*, p. 63: "forþon us syndon nu to bebeorhgenne þa myccllan synna, þæt we þe eþelicor þa medmycclan gebetan magon."

12. *Ibid.*, p. 192. The source is a Latin *passio* of Peter and Paul, ed. R. Lipsius and M. Bonnet, *Acta Apostolorum Apocrypha* (1891; repr. ed., Hildesheim, 1959), I: 1. 119–177 and 223–245 (the two known versions of the *passio*, neither of which includes the exhortation to confession).

13. Morris, *Homilies*, pp. 106–115 ("Þisses middangeardes ende neah is"): "gecyrre to þam selran & to þon soþan læcedome" (p. 107).

14. *Ibid.*, p. 25: "Þæt bið seo soþe hreow þæt mon þa geworhtan synna andette & georne bete" ("that is true repentance when one confesses the sins he has committed and sincerely repents").

were sufficiently well established at the time these homilies were preached to have been the occasion for abuse. The priests, "the teachers of God's churches," are commanded to "teach" their books of penance and to "instruct, as our fathers have previously determined."[15] The same verbs—*tæcan* and *læran*—are immediately repeated by the homilist in saying that priests must tell the laity how to confess their sins rightly because sins "are so very various, and some so very impure, that a man will avoid ever telling them except the priest ask him concerning them." The confessor was not only required to assign penance properly: it was also his duty to make sure that the penitent concealed no sin through embarrassment or a failure to recognize that what he had done was, in fact, wrong. Instructions for the priest on receiving penitents, we shall see, advise the same precautions.

The *Vercelli* homilies resemble those of *The Blickling Book* in their treatment of penance and confession. The third *Vercelli* homily contains a detailed summary of sacramental confession, based on the so-called second *Capitula* of Theodulf of Orléans, as well as a list of the eight chief sins and information about fasting derived from the *Hibernensis*.[16] The third homily parallels the description of the confessor's interrogation seen in the *Blickling* text just discussed. The penitent is told that the priest will inquire about his deeds, ask if the wrong was intentional and if the sinner is sorry for it, and then assign penance.[17] The eighth *Vercelli* homily warns the sinner that pride may inhibit his candid confession and that sins concealed from the confessor will be revealed before God.[18]

More numerous are *Vercelli* homilies which urge repentance

15. *Ibid.*, p. 43: "Þa mæsse-preostas þe Godes cyricena lareowas beoþ, þa sceolan heora scrift-bec mid rihte tæcan & læran, swa swa hie ure fæderas ær demdon."

16. The sources are listed by Turville-Petre, "Translations," pp. 67–69; on the English manuscript of the second *Capitula*, see Hans Sauer, ed., *Theodulfi Capitula in England*, pp. 15–16.

17. Ed. Förster, *Vercelli-Homilien*, pp. 55–62. The *Vercelli* interrogation is related to that found in the thirty-first chapter of the Old English translation of Theodulf's *Capitula*, ed. Arthur S. Napier; see *The Old English Version of the Enlarged Rule of Chrodegang*, pp. 38–41. See Max Förster, "Zur Liturgik der angelsächsischen Kirche," pp. 47–48.

18. Ed. Förster, *Vercelli-Homilien*, pp. 150–152.

without specifically referring to sacramental confession. Here the thrust is to reform the moral life; implicit in this transformation, because it is explicit elsewhere in this same collection, is confession to the priest.[19] Some of these homilies contain information traditional in penitential literature, such as the list of major sins, and urge almsgiving and fasting, acts sometimes performed as voluntary penance, but often assigned as penance by the confessor.[20] There is nothing in the *Vercelli* homilies about penance, or in those from *The Blickling Book*, that would give even scrupulous theologians pause. In their general descriptions of confession and penance, and in their particular attention to the integrity of the confessor as the key to the integrity of the system, they conform wholly to the interests and ambitions of the later and more highly respected authorities.

What separates the anonymous homilies from the writings of Ælfric and Wulfstan is that they make no reference to public penance. Had the ritual existed when these homilies were written, it is unlikely that they would have failed to mention it in some way. This omission links them to the "Scrift boc," the only vernacular handbook not to accommodate the public ritual; since public penance was known in the sources of the anonymous homilies—in Theodulf's *Capitula*, for example—the English redactors may have omitted references to it because it was, as yet, not customary in England.[21] Such references would have been out of place in the *Vercelli* collection, which appears to have been intended for private reading; but were public penance known in the contemporary liturgy, the *Blickling* homily for Holy Thursday, the time of reconciliation, would certainly have said so.

Public penance is often discussed in Wulfstan's homilies, but

19. *Ibid.*, p. 72, the fourth homily, which urges tears and repentance for sins. The eleventh is similar; see Rudolph Willard, ed., "*Vercelli Homily XI* and Its Sources," p. 85. The fifteenth laments the immorality of the clergy; ed. Max Förster, "Der Vercelli-Codex CXVII nebst Abdruck einiger altenglischer Homilien der Handschrift," *Studien zur Englischen Philologie* 50 (1913): 20–179; see pp. 117–118.

20. See the twenty-second homily, ed. Förster, "Der Vercelli-Codex," pp. 137–148, especially p. 148; and Paul Szarmach, ed., "Vercelli Homily XX," pp. 8–9 (the homily is in part a translation of Alcuin's *Liber de Virtutibus et Vitiis*).

21. The order for public reconciliation is chapter 28 in the Old English translation; see Napier, *The Old English Version*, pp. 36–37.

not in Ælfric's, where the greatest concern is with the interior aspects of repentance. Enriched by an unequalled grasp of Latin literature about the forgiveness of sins, Ælfric's discussions of confession and penance are so extensive, allusive, and compelling that they demand full-length study on their own. His homilies are a touchstone for anyone with an interest in Anglo-Saxon penitential practice or literature; there seems to be no form of penance he did not write about, and there were few relevant patristic themes and images which he did not, at some point, weave into his prose. The traditional view, which sets him with Wulfstan in contradistinction to the anonymous homilists, is right historically but wrong in many other ways. *The Catholic Homilies* are a digest of penitential commonplaces cleverly adapted and judiciously applied, a monument which dwarfs all else written about penance in his period.[22]

Ælfric often echoes issues which figured in the Frankish controversy about penance. Like Alcuin, he insisted on oral confession, criticizing those who believed that confession to God alone, coupled with sincere contrition, was sufficient for all sins. If this were so, he asks, why do we have priests? Hence, Ælfric endorsed the three forms of reconciliation accepted by the Franks: confession to God alone was permitted for minor sins; confession to the priest was preferred for both major and minor sins; sins of public consequence required public penance.[23] Ælfric did not stress public penance, although he did emphasize the primacy of bishops in the penitential system. He held that the power to bind and to loose was theirs, handed down from the apostles; all men were to fear the bishops' words, and even the innocent were to accept the bishops' correction as an antidote to pride.[24]

22. Ed. Benjamin Thorpe, *The Homilies of the Anglo-Saxon Church*. The second series of the Catholic Homilies has been edited by Malcolm Godden, *Ælfric's Catholic Homilies*; the first series will be edited by Peter Clemoes.

23. Homily for the Third Sunday after the Epiphany, ed. Thorpe, *Homilies*, 1: 124–125.

24. *Ibid.*, pp. 234–236, homily for the First Sunday after Easter. Ælfric added a note to one manuscript of his homilies (Cambridge, Corpus Christi College 178) saying that he had no sermons for the Thursday, Friday, or Saturday of Holy Week because the church forbad preaching then. A later scribe corrected this, commenting that this was a time when the bishop was to lead the people in public penance; see N. R. Ker, "Old English Notes Signed 'Coleman,'" *MÆ* 18 (1949): 29–31.

Ælfric took special delight in the figurative richness of confession and penance. He derived most of these figures from scripture and the exegetical tradition. It is possible that the penitentials too were among his sources, since he knew handbooks and worked from them in compiling his pastoral letters. Two figures occur quite often: the pattern of binding and loosing, and the medical metaphor.

Images of binding and loosing appear in several contexts. The homily for Palm Sunday compares the ass untied for Christ to a sinner freed from his sins.[25] Later the homily supplies an image which answers this one: the devil, drawn by the "bait" of Christ's humanity, was caught on the "hook" of his own deception.[26] In his discussion of the raising of Lazarus, borrowed from Augustine, Ælfric applies these images differently. Like Lazarus, raised by Christ from the tomb, we are raised from sin and "quickened" when we confess; like the other "dead" raised by Christ, we are freed from the graveclothes and restored to life when we seek God's mercy with true repentance.[27]

Ælfric also uses the medical metaphor variously, reworking images commonplace in the penitentials. Chief among these are the figures of the confessor as the physician and of sin as the sickness which the confessor—who is also Christ—will heal.[28] Ælfric portrays sin as a destructive force more active and aggressive than disease. He compares the worms which tear the soul in hell to sins which destroy the soul; he also likens the serpents which attacked the Israelites to sins which destroy the body. These serpents he links to the serpent in the Garden, infected with the "venom" of sin; juxtaposed with them is Christ wounded on the cross, for whom the serpents raised on sticks in the desert were types. But Christ is the healer, a serpent without venom because he is without sin.[29]

25. Thorpe, *Homilies*, I: 208.

26. *Ibid.*, p. 216.

27. *Ibid.*, p. 234, homily for the First Sunday after Easter. Ælfric cites other miracles in which Christ raised the dead; see the homily for the Seventeenth Sunday after Pentecost, *ibid.*, pp. 490–494.

28. There are many examples; see the homily on the Passion of St. Bartholomew, *ibid.*, p. 472; or the homily for the Third Sunday after the Epiphany, pp. 124–128.

29. Ed. Godden, *Catholic Homilies*, homily for the Fifth Sunday in Lent, p. 135.

Not all of Ælfric's references to confession and penance are this learned or complex. Some of his catechetical homilies, collected with his works for the proper of the season as well as with texts for unspecified occasions, make straightforward exhortations to repent. One promises that the sinner who sincerely repents will be rewarded with forgiveness.[30] Another, which corresponds to one of Ælfric's pastoral letters, states that God in his might forgives all who abstain from sin with repentance.[31] These homilies are not so much hortatory as explanatory: in them Ælfric does not extol the merits of the penitential system, but merely claims that, for those who believe in God, it will work.

Ælfric's practical interest in penance is also manifest in the catechetical texts which he provided for the priest's use in teaching the laity. Some of these were specifically designed for the confessor and focus on penance; others are summaries of major points of doctrine which the priest was required to explain to his congregation. A series of these excerpts was joined to a manuscript of *The Catholic Homilies*. It includes a number of short prayers, the Lord's Prayer and two versions of the Creed among them, and a loosely organized exposition known as *De Penitentia*.[32] This text is composed of two unrelated sections. The first links penance to baptism and stresses a point made in most tenth-century homilies about repentance: it is not enough to cease evil deeds if one does not at the same time begin to perform good works. Once again Ælfric specifies that the sinner must confess not to God, but to "some man of God," if he will be forgiven; likewise, the man seeking forgiveness must first forgive those who have offended him. At this point, Ælfric takes up a new theme not clearly connected to the first. He requires the priest to know certain prayers and to explain their content, their "sense," to

---

30. See the homily for the Seventh Sunday after Pentecost, ed. John C. Pope, in *Homilies of Ælfric*, 2: 538; compare *De Doctrina Apostolica*, p. 628.

31. *Ibid.*, 1: 453–475, *De Sancta Trinitate*; see Pope's note for the relationship of this homily to Ælfric's letter to Wulfgeat, p. 463.

32. Ed. Thorpe, *Homilies*, 2: 596–609; see the discussion by Gatch, *Preaching*, pp. 52–54, and Donald G. Bzdyl, "The Source of Ælfric's Prayers in Cambridge University Library Ms. Gg 3. 28," *N & Q* 24 (1977): 98–103.

his congregation. By way of supplying his own explanation, Ælfric then sketches the core of Christian doctrine, elaborately describing the Trinity, the Incarnation, Redemption, and the Last Judgment.[33] This concludes the summary at an appropriate point, with the sinful suffering hell, "endless with ineffable tortures," and those "who in this life were pleasing to God" with him in heaven.

Less a homily than a tract, because it was not intended for delivery at a specific point in the church year, De Penitentia sums up the major concerns of penitential homilies from both the early and the late tenth century, the anonymous homilies as well as those of Ælfric and Wulfstan. Two threads unify the vernacular homiletic corpus: the priest couples the exhortation to repent with the warning that without good works repentance is futile; and he uses the opportunity to instruct the laity in fundamental points of Christian doctrine. De Penitentia illustrates this tradition and emphasizes its twofold nature: the sermon establishes no organic or overt connection between its first and second parts, and it achieves a superficial unity only with its concluding portrait of the saved and the damned.

The two-part structure of De Penitentia has many echoes in vernacular instructions for the confessor. Wulfstan's De Fide Catholica, based at least in outline on Ælfric's work, applies this teaching to specifically catechetical purpose. Wulfstan inverts Ælfric's structure; since his homily was intended to teach the essential articles of the Creed and the Lord's Prayer, Wulfstan puts doctrine first and subordinates the warning to repent and do good works.[34] This homily, like Ælfric's work, may have served as a model for the confessor's own exhortations. Wulfstan was one of the first to use Ælfric's work as if it were a manual for preachers.[35]

Public penance was a special interest of Wulfstan's, partly because it involved the exercise of episcopal jurisdiction, a power in which he believed very strongly. In addition to notes for a homily on Ash Wednesday and the Holy Thursday reconciliation homily (both

33. See Thorpe, Homilies, 2: 609, for the text.

34. On Wulfstan's use of Ælfric, see Bethurum, Homilies, p. 301.

35. See M. R. Godden, "The Development of Ælfric's Second Series of Catholic Homilies," pp. 209–216.

addressed to penitents), Wulfstan wrote homilies about private penance which fall into three different categories. Best known, and much studied, is the *Sermo Lupi ad Anglos*, but equally important in evaluating his interest in penance are two less spectacular in subject, the *Sermo ad Populum*, really a pastoral letter written for oral delivery, and *De Fide Catholica*, a catechetical homily. None of the three is solely concerned with penitential practice; each illustrates the relationship between penance and good Christian conduct.

The *Sermo Lupi* is not so much about penance as the nation's desire to avoid it. The homily catalogues sins in mounting numbers, leaving only the faintest hope that the people will turn from their evil ways. In juxtaposing the ever more terrible anger of God and the deepening shame of the guilty, Wulfstan was using a technique which the confessor shared: fear of punishment would prompt candid confession.[36] This strategy is mirrored in the other two homilies. *De Fide*, part of a series of homilies on baptism, outlines the fundamental beliefs required of the adult Christian. Sins could be forgiven through true faith, through baptism, and through repentance; unless they were confessed on earth, they would be revealed before all creation on the Last Day. Once again, the fear of punishment is used to prompt the penitent to confess.[37] The *Sermo ad Populum* makes the same point: confession to the priest, coupled with good works, will "protect ourselves against eternal torment and earn for us the kingdom of heaven."[38]

Wulfstan's habit of mentioning repentance in the context of final judgment shows only one side of penance in his homilies. He also recognized the importance of confession as an opportunity for correction and counsel. In the *Sermo ad Populum*, which outlines the church's duties to the people and their duties to the church, he encouraged confession as an occasion for spiritual direction:

36. Edited by Bethurum, *Homilies*, pp. 267–275 (XX). For recent scholarship and a close analysis, see Raachel Jurovics, "*Sermo Lupi* and the Moral Purpose of Rhetoric," in Szarmach and Huppé, *The Old English Homily*, pp. 203–220.

37. Bethurum, *Homilies*, pp. 157–165 (VII).

38. *Ibid.*, pp. 225–232 (XIII); quotation from p. 232.

Let us take heed that we hold our Christianity honorably, cast all heathenism aside and embrace right belief, attend church day and night, often and regularly, and live that life to which the confessor directs us.[39]

But Wulfstan's eye for the grand event, the "national" danger, the morality of the people, caused him to overlook the moral life as seen from a private or individual perspective, or at least not to emphasize it. This is easily explained: his homilies take the vantage point of an administrator and legislative consultant to kings—surely the long view on one's own age. As bishop, Wulfstan was chiefly responsible for the administration of the relics of the ancient system of public penance, especially in Lent. Moreover, he left comparatively few homilies, and they are of many sorts. Only in a few of them did he have an opportunity to focus on the sinner's private encounter with the confessor, which was Ælfric's chief concern when he wrote about penance.

As we examine the link between the writings of Wulfstan and Ælfric and contemporary handbooks of penance, it is important to remember the somewhat unsettled state of the evidence. Evidently Ælfric's instructional pieces for the clergy and similar, anonymous materials never received a final or fully complete form. They overlap with two of the vernacular penitentials in an instructive, if somewhat confusing, way. Both the "Handbook for the Use of a Confessor" and the introduction to the "Scrift boc" attempted to supply the confessor with instructional as well as judicial material. Sometimes this material occurs in manuscripts in which it is not connected to vernacular penitentials. The best example of this interdependence is Cambridge, Corpus Christi College 320, in which the penitential of Theodore is accompanied by vernacular instructions for the priest. These additions, made in the late tenth or early eleventh century, contain sentences close to part of *De Penitentia*; to the directions for the confessor found in Oxford, Bodleian Library, Laud Misc. 482 (a

39. *Ibid.*, p. 229: "Utan gyman þæt we urne cristendom clænlice gehealdan 7 aweorpan alcne hæðendom 7 habban rihtne geleafan, 7 lufian cyricsocne dæges 7 nihtes oft 7 gelome, 7 libban þam life þe scrift us wisige."

text for use in administering to the sick); and to a pseudo-Wulfstan homily.[40] Another set of instructions follows the "Scrift boc" in one of the earliest commonplace book manuscripts.[41]

The instructions most like *De Penitentia* occur in London, British Library, Cotton Tiberius A.iii, which does not contain a Latin or vernacular penitential, but which is rich in prayers and pieces of uncertain use. Two articles for the confessor appear amid several confessional prayers. The first exhorts its audience to repent, confess, and fast in Lent in order to atone for misdeeds committed during the year. Supplied with two sets of pronouns, first person plural and second person, this instruction could have been delivered either to the laity or to the clergy. It is composed of sections from the *Enlarged Rule* of Chrodegang, Ælfric's homily for the First Sunday in Lent, and, in small part, from the ninth *Vercelli* homily.[42]

The second exhortation in the Tiberius manuscript is both penitential and catechetical. Derived in large part from the Old English translation of the Benedictine *Rule*, this passage also depends on the introduction to the "Scrift boc" and the vernacular translation of Theodulf's *Capitula*.[43] These instructional passages appear to be a response to the requirement that the priest "teach penance" and "teach confession." They are so closely connected to the "Scrift boc" introduction and repeat so much of the initial stage of private confession that they seem to have been designed in imitation of it. Along with homilies about confession and penance, the instructions for the priest provided a rationale for penitential practice, explained the procedure of confession, and stressed the value of good works as a continuation of penitential acts. Although the priest could have deliv-

---

40. CCCC 320 is described in N. R. Ker's *Catalogue of Manuscripts Containing Anglo-Saxon*, p. 105; it contains tenth- or eleventh-century notes in Old English on a manuscript of the second half of the tenth century. Ker lists similarities between the "Scrift boc," this text, and a text in the Laud manuscript on p. 106 (for the Laud codex, see pp. 419–422).

41. Cambridge, Corpus Christi College 190; *ibid.*, p. 72. The instructions are edited by Benjamin Thorpe, *Ancient Laws and Institutes of England*, 2: 224–228.

42. Edited with commentary by Hans Sauer, "Zwei spätaltenglische Beichtermahnungen aus Hs. Cotton Tiberius A. III," pp. 21–23 ("Confession II"). See pp. 8–9 for sources.

43. *Ibid.*, pp. 9–12.

ered these instructions to his people at any time, it is most likely, to judge from internal references, that they were made at the beginning of Lent. Some, in fact, are specifically designated for delivery at that time.[44]

Certainly the most effective linking of penitential and catechetical teaching occurred during private confession itself, when the priest would have spoken with the penitent alone rather than addressed a congregation. In preparing the penitent to confess, the priest first questioned him concerning the fundamental ideas of the faith; his faith thus confirmed, the penitent was asked about his sins and his desire to atone for them. Because this procedure was derived from Frankish models, it is well to examine it first in a continental *ordo*, somewhat fuller than the Old English evidence. The following text is the procedure for receiving penitents which accompanies an anonymous eighth-century Frankish handbook, possibly from Fleury; its primary stress is catechetical.

> (The priest) is required to hold forth the word of salvation and to give the penitent an explanation: how the devil through his pride fell from the angelic dignity and afterward drove the man out of paradise, and (how) Christ accordingly for human salvation came into the world through the virgin's womb and after his resurrection both conquered the devil and redeemed the world from sin, and afterward gave the Apostles the grace of baptism by which he (the priest) should deliver man from his sin; and that he who has sinned, if he does not do penance, shall be sent to hell to be tormented forever; and he who gives his confession to the priests after the commission of an offense shall obtain eternal rewards; or how in the end of the age, "He shall come to judge the living and the dead" and to "render to every man according to his work." Let him be questioned as to his belief in the resurrection, or all those things that he is told, or whether he has faith of confession, by which to obtain pardon before God through the judgment of the priest. But if he confesses everything and does not doubt that there is a

44. N. R. Ker, "Three Old English Texts in a Salisbury Pontifical, Cotton Tiberius c. i." These are directions for the Lenten fast.

blessed life for the righteous in Paradise after death, and that
the gehenna of fire is prepared for sinners, let him be questioned as to what he has done that causes him fear.[45]

The penitent first professed to accept the faith and its obligations and
then admitted to having failed in them. Through this process he
came to understand himself as sinful, and with this belief firmly established, he confessed.

The introduction to the "Scrift boc" shortens this procedure but
imitates it closely. The substance of the interrogation corresponds
closely to both parts of De Penitentia, embracing both doctrine and a
declaration of willingness to repent:

When anyone goes to his confessor, he shall prostrate himself
before him with the utmost fear of God and humility, and in a
doleful voice beg him to prescribe for him penance for all
those faults which he has committed against God's will; and he
shall confess to him his misdeeds, so that the priest may know
what kind of penance he should prescribe for him. Then the
confessor must ask him what beliefs he has in God, and must
charge and warn him concerning his soul's need, and speak
thus: "Do you believe in God the Almighty, and in the Son,
and in the Holy Spirit? Do you believe that all men must arise
from death on the Last Day? Do you remember all the evil you
have committed in work, word, and thought? Will you forgive

45. Edited by F. W. H. Wasserschleben, *Die Bussordnungen der abendländischen Kirche*,
pp. 422–423: "Oportet eum exhortari verbum salutis et dare illi rationem, qualiter
diabulus per superbiam suam de angelicam cecidit dignitatem et postea hominem
expulit de paradiso, et proinde Christus ad salutem humanam per uterum virginis in
mundum venit atque post resurrectionem et diabulum vicit et mundum de peccato
redemit, et postea per apostolos baptismi gratiam tradidit, per quod hominem levaret
de peccato, et qui peccasset, si poenitentiam non agebat, in infernum mitteretur per-
petuo cruciandum; et qui sacerdotibus dabit confessionem post crimina perpetrata,
aeterna consequeretur praemia, vel qualiter in finem seculi venturus est judicare vivos
et mortuos et reddere unicuique secundum opera sua. Interrogatur ei, si credit resurrectionem vel ista omnia, quod dictum est ei, vel si habeat fidem confessionis, per
judicium sacerdotis veniam consequi apud Dominum. Quodsi omnia confitetur et
non dubitat, vitam esse justis in paradiso beatam post mortem, et quod peccatoribus
gehenna ignis praeparatur, interrogatur ei, quod egit, unde timet." Translated by
John T. McNeill and Helena M. Gamer, *Medieval Handbooks of Penance*, pp. 280–281;
the manuscript of this text is lost and the date, therefore, is conjectural.

each of those who have offended you?" If he (the penitent) says, "I am willing," say to him: "May God forgive you, and grant me (grace) so that I might."[46]

The priest then commanded the penitent to fast each day in Lent until the ninth hour and avoid the eight chief sins. The penitent was instructed in the Golden Rule and told that if he did good works, he would enjoy eternal happiness with the Father. Only then did he confess his sins. This ceremony closely resembles the liturgy of baptism, in which initiates were instructed in the mysteries of the faith (the *traditio*, or "handing over" of sacred teaching) and later questioned concerning their belief in them (the *redditio symboli*).[47] Nowhere is the connection between baptism and penance clearer: baptism first washed away man's sins, and penance, the second baptism, renewed the cleansing each time the sinner confessed and accepted penance.[48]

The "Handbook" offered the priest additional advice on securing a sincere confession. The order for receiving penitents in this manual resembles a ceremony, well attested in contemporary manuscripts, for public confession followed by general absolution. But

46. Ed. R. Spindler, *Das altenglische Bussbuch*, p. 170: "Þonne man to his scrifte gange, þonne sceall he mid swyðe mycelum Godes ege *and* eadmodnesse beforan him hine aþenian *and* hine biddan wependre stefne þæt he him dædbote tæce ealra þæra gylta þe he ongean Godes willan gedon hæbbe; *and* he sceal hi*m* andettan his misdæda, þæt se sacerd wite hwylce dædbote he him tæcan scyle. Þonne sceal se sacerd hine axian hwylcne geleafan he to Gode hæbbe, *and* hine mænigfealdlice to his sawle þearfe tihtan *and* mynegian *and* ðus cweþan: 'Gelyfst ðu on God Ælmihtigne *and* on þæne Sunu *and* on ðone Halgan Gast?' *Respondeat.* 'Gelyfst ðu þæt ealle men sculon arisan on domes dæg of deaþe?' *Respondeat.* 'Oðþinceð þe ealles þæs þe ðu to yfele hæfst geþoht *and* gecweden *and* geworht?' *Respondeat.* 'Wilt ðu forgyfon ælcon þæra þe wið þe æfre agyltan?' Gyf he cweð: 'Ic wille,' cweð him þonn*e* to: 'God Ælmihtig gemildsige þin *and* me geunne þ*æt* ic mote.'"

47. See Milton McC. Gatch, "The Medieval Church: Basic Christian Education from the Decline of Catechesis to the Rise of the Catechisms," forthcoming, and Josef A. Jungmann, *Handing on the Faith: A Manual of Catechetics*, trans. A. N. Fuerst from the 2d ed. (New York, 1962).

48. See J. D. C. Fisher, *Christian Initiation: Baptism in the Medieval West, A Study in the Disintegration of the Primitive Rite of Initiation*, Alcuin Club Collections, vol. 47 (London, 1965). Ælfric wrote that confession and penance were used "to wash us a second time from the sins which we commit after Baptism." See *De Paenitentia*, ed. Thorpe, *Homilies* 2:602.

because the textual tradition of the "Handbook" establishes this *ordo* as part of the penitential, it will be considered in the private context first, and the second, or communal, ceremony examined later. The *ordo* was not an interrogation concerning faith, but instead a recitation of the Creed, apparently following a litany, after which the penitent began the confession of his sins "before God and before the priest."[49]

There is a good deal about this ceremony which suggests a ritual other than the simple reception of the penitent by the confessor. It is in Latin, whereas the "Scrift boc" introduction is in the vernacular; its parallels and probable sources are found in liturgies for public penance, whereas those of the introduction are chiefly in the penitentials; it does not quiz the penitent on his beliefs, but rather assumes that he holds them and, in fact, that he can recite the Creed.[50] But the best reason for doubting the applicability of the *ordo* to private confession is that the "Handbook" later supplies simpler, and clearer, instruction of its own. Both the third and the fifth sections advise the priest on making judgments about penitents. The instructions in the third are especially important, since they require the priest to be certain that the penitent understands his sins and is sorry for them. But the priest is warned: "If he (the penitent) does not know how to confess his deeds and examine his sins, question him concerning his habits and extract his sins (from them), and explain what he has done."[51] The "Handbook" does not supply an interrogation concerning the penitent's faith, here or elsewhere. Evidently its compiler trusted to the *ordo* which began the penitential to accomplish this, although in fact the Latin ritual makes no such inquiry. It is unlike the "Scrift boc" introduction and related instructional pieces in an important aspect: it does not teach doctrine or an acceptance of the

49. Ed. Roger Fowler, "A Late Old English Handbook for the Use of a Confessor"; see pp. 16–17.

50. Fowler, "Handbook," p. 13, suggests that the source is a Latin letter from Othmar of St. Gall (ca. 720), a text closer to the second than the first part of the "Handbook."

51. *Ibid.*, pp. 19–20 (part three), pp. 26–32 (part four); Fowler suggests that these two sections may be related to Wulfstan (pp. 9–11); translation from p. 19: "Gif he ne cunne his dæda andettan *and* his giltas asmeagan, acsa hine his wisena *and* atred him þa giltas ut *and* asec his dæda."

faith, but rather articulates beliefs already held. It is a devotional, rather than a pedagogical or catechetical, document.

In a taxonomy of late Anglo-Saxon penitential texts, this *ordo* belongs among the liturgies and the prayers, rather than among the juridical or catechetical literature. Anglo-Saxon penitents were supplied with words as well as good deeds at the end of their confessions. This we know from the abundant and various confessional prayers found in both Latin and the vernacular. Penitential in content, they are not catechetical in purpose, at least not in every case. Unlike the prayers which were used to teach the faith—the Lord's Prayer, the Creed, and the short prayers found in the appendix containing *De Penitentia*—certain of these prayers are expiatory; as pleas for intercession and forgiveness, they express devotion based on faith but rooted in a conviction of one's sinfulness, and hence one's unworthiness to call for much-needed divine assistance.

The English acquired these prayers and patterns for using them from continental sources. Some of these prayers entered England as parts of canonical and psalter collections. A continental manuscript in Oxford, Bodleian Library, Bodley 311, contains a confession "before God, the angels, and men" in the margin, before beginning the text of the Nicene Councils.[52] A late ninth-century manuscript, possibly from Rheims (containing a list of saints from Rheims), includes a confessional prayer among psalter texts.[53] In Bodley 311 there is no connection between the prayer and the penitential of Cummean, or other content related to penance, found in the manuscript. But Bodley 718 contains a lengthy confessional prayer as part of an order for confession, one of two which follow the penitential of Egbert in this manuscript. In the first the penitent was asked about his faith; he agreed to turn from sin and then confessed as many sins as he could recollect. The priest blessed the "trustworthy" penitent and recon-

---

52. Later at Exeter, according to Ker, *Catalogue*, p. 360; a tenth- or eleventh-century gloss in Old English on a tenth-century manuscript.

53. Cambridge, Corpus Christi College 272; see M. R. James, *A Descriptive Catalogue of Manuscripts in the Library of Corpus Christi College*, 2 vols. (Cambridge, 1911–1912), 2:31. The manuscript was later at Christ Church, Canterbury. On the origin and provenance of the manuscript, see K. Gamber, *Codices Liturgici Latini Antiquiores*, Spicilegii Friburgensis Subsidia, vol. 1 (2 vols.) (Freiburg, 1968), p. 609, 1686b.

ciled him after his penance was complete; the dimwitted penitent
was reconciled at once.[54]

The second Bodley *ordo* gives the full version of the one which
accompanies the "Handbook." After reciting the litany, the penitent
rises and is interrogated concerning his faith. Then he confesses his
sins, "humbly, before the priest." He does not confess his own sins,
however, but the long list provided in the confessional prayer which
begins at this point and continues for three full pages in the manuscript.[55] This was not private confession, but a devotional exercise,
and it was probably performed by a community rather than by an
individual, alone, with the priest. It concluded with a form of absolution recited by the priest before the altar. This *ordo* has all the signs
of a liturgical rite and none of the juridical material essential to assigning penance for the sins confessed.

This kind of extensive confessional prayer has been accepted as
the second of the "Handbook's" parts, but on the basis of the Bodley
ordo and that found in London, British Library, Cotton Vespasian
D. xx, the combined *ordo* and prayer should be taken as devotional
instead. The London manuscript prefaces its confessional prayer
with a note directing the priest to read the prayer if the penitent is
literate (that is, educated). The prayer asks forgiveness for all the
sinner's wrongdoing since he was baptized. The priest absolves him
and begins to read a long series of prayers, interspersed with psalms.
This manuscript repeats a pattern seen in Bodley 718: first it gives an
order for private confession, including tariffs for specific sins; next
comes a devotional *ordo* in which a general confession is followed by
an absolution and the recitation of prayers.[56]

54. For Bodley 718, see F. Madan and H. Craster, *A Summary Catalogue of Western
Manuscripts in the Bodleian Library at Oxford*, 7 vols. (Oxford, 1895–1953), 2:459–461.
The first *ordo*, specifying immediate reconciliation for the "simplex vel brutus," and
later reconciliation for the trustworthy, is on fols. 14v–15v.

55. The second *ordo* is on fols. 15v–21r; the longest prayer is on fols. 19r–20r.

56. See Ker, *Catalogue*, p. 278, mid-tenth century. An *ordo* apparently based on
Halitgar's penitential, but also similar to that which accompanies the *Double Penitential*, is on fols. 2r–15r; the second *ordo* is on 23r–51r, this last folio containing a ritual
for the imposition of hands. Additional confessional prayers follow, including fols.
87r–92v, a prayer in Old English. This is a very small manuscript (written space 152 ×
95 mm.), and although it contains fragmentary passages of penitential tariffs, it appears to be a devotional manual rather than a guide for private confession.

Elsewhere in tenth- and eleventh-century manuscripts, confessional prayers made before the priest (or, in one case, the bishop) are separated from the directions for receiving penitents or the Latin *ordo*. An example is found in one of the early commonplace books.[57] In addition, there are many prayers evidently intended for private recitation. Another British Library manuscript, Cotton Vespasian D. xv, contains an Old English title for a Latin confessional prayer. Although the title claims that the prayer is made "to gode seolfum," the text confesses sins to God, the angels and saints, and "to you, a man of God."[58]

Prayers which actually contain a confession to God alone are legion, in both Latin and vernacular manuscripts. They echo many of the themes and devices of the earliest English prayer collections, such as *The Book of Cerne*, but clearly derive from the *libelli precum* of the ninth century. Included among these prayers are translations of devotions by Alcuin, including a partial translation of the prayer he is believed to have written for Charlemagne.[59] Some of them fortify the long list of sins with a catalogue of the parts of the body, proving the durability and appeal of this early Irish motif.[60] Some of the prayers in Latin are glossed in Old English, and this evidence, coupled with the many translations taken from known continental originals, shows the effort of the late Anglo-Saxon church to supply devotional materials to accompany and complement its disciplinary and catechetical texts.[61]

These collections of private prayers were not intended for gen-

57. cccc 190 (*ibid.*, p. 365) contains a confessional prayer to be recited before the bishop; see Förster, "Zur Liturgik," p. 14.

58. See Ker, *Catalogue*, pp. 277–278, mid-tenth century; the manuscript contains a version of the penitential of Theodore, fols. 84r–101v. The reference to the "homini dei" is on fol. 68r.

59. Alcuin's prayer is partly translated in London, British Library, Cotton Tiberius A. iii, fols. 44r–45v, and Royal 2 B. 5, fols. 197r–198v; see Förster, "Zu den AE. Texten aus MS. Arundel 155," pp. 52–55.

60. An example is the prayer which forms the second section of Fowler's "Handbook," versions of which are also found in Cotton Vespasian D. xx and Cotton Tiberius C. i; see Fowler, "Handbook," pp. 17–19.

61. For examples, see Ferdinand Holthausen, "Altenglischen Interlinearversionen lateinischer Gebete und Beichten," edited from London, British Library, Arundel 155, s. xi^{med}.

eral consumption. They would have belonged to monks or to the educated nobility, some of whom sought to live a religious life similar to the monks'. How successfully these elaborate and sophisticated prayers could have been taught to less pious laymen, or understood by them, is a matter of doubt.[62] Merely that the prayers were written in the vernacular neither proves nor even increases the likelihood of their use among laymen; in an age when priests were reminded of their obligations to learn Latin, little should be taken for granted in assessing the literacy of those whom the priests were supposed to teach. It was probably expected that the laity would learn the Creed and the Lord's Prayer and hoped that they would absorb the sense of these prayers as well as their words.

There is slight evidence that confessional prayers were recited by lay people. In Cotton Tiberius A. iii, a Latin note before such prayers tells the priest how to dismiss the penitent: the sinner is to turn from evil, retire to his home, pray, and keep the commands of the priest. This may mean that the vernacular prayers were to be used "when the penitent returned *in domum suam, orans.*"[63] But the same direction concludes the second, elaborate *ordo* in Bodley 718, at which point the manuscript ends.[64] Any layman devout enough to participate in this *ordo*, with its litany and long prayers, may have practiced a similar form of devotion in his own home. This might have been expected of the trustworthy penitent, but not of the low-born sinner, whose speedy absolution indicated that little piety was expected of him.

62. See Gatch, *Preaching*, p. 49, for evidence that devout laymen modeled their spiritual lives on those of monks. An example of a prayer collection for such a layman, or a monk, is London, British Library, Cotton Galba A. xiv, s. xi[1]; see Ker, *Catalogue*, pp. 198–202, and the description by Edmund Bishop, *Liturgica Historica*, pp. 384–391. This manuscript contains, among the prayers, a version of the introduction which accompanies the "Scrift boc," an odd choice for a prayer collection, but interesting evidence of reading habits (it is unlikely that this manuscript ever served as a handbook for confession, of course, since it contains no penitential tariffs).

63. Fol. 44v, printed by Lars-G. Hallander, "Two Old English Confessional Prayers," p. 92.

64. Fol. 21r: "Postea dicat sacerdos illi qui confessus est peccata sua ante altare dicens, Deuerte ab omni malo usque in finem. Et post haec recedat humiliter in domum suam orans et custodiens mandata sacerdotis. Finit liber paenitentiale Ecgberhti archepiscopi."

Among especially devout laymen, confessional prayers would have formed only a small part of devotional practice. A layman who assumed the full responsibility for his spirituality allowed by the sources would take up a great burden indeed. It was not enough that he submit to teaching from his confessor and worship regularly. He was required to be sure of his confessor's honesty; instructions for the Lenten fast of the laity at one point instruct penitents who do not trust their confessor to seek out another.[65] Laymen probably knew if the local confessor was corrupt—warnings about this danger are frequent enough in the homilies—and were evidently obliged to select a different confessor if circumstances required. This duty, of course, had another side: those who felt that their confessor was unjustly demanding might seek out one who imposed less weighty burdens.

Taken together, the homilies, handbooks, sets of instructions for the clergy, and, to a lesser extent, the prayers are remarkably consistent in language, if not in form. Many of the same words and phrases can be found in these sources, often slightly modified, frequently shaped to a new context. By a process of selection, synthesis, and adaptation, the tenth-century reformers produced a corpus of vernacular literature which has no immediate counterpart in its sources, either in size or in scope. The eleventh-century reformers attacked the problems of penitential discipline from many directions. It appears that they were headed toward the creation of some new forms. One might have been that represented by the "Scrift boc" introduction, the English version of the *ordo confessionis*. The introduction differs from continental orders for private confession in its inclusiveness: it provides not only a form for the interrogation of the penitent, but also supplementary material for the priest's use in determining penances. Although continental penitentials are rich in this information, they do not combine with the *ordo* guidelines for shortening penance or the twelve remissions of sin. The introduction combines all this material. It may have been a short, separate manual meant to be used with various sets of penitential tariffs. The "Handbook" can be seen as a parallel, since it too is a group of texts not new in themselves, but new in their combination. The important points

65. Ker, "Three Old English Texts," p. 279.

are two: the Anglo-Saxons attempted a new synthesis of the penitential texts they inherited, and they did not finish the adaptations or record their final intentions. The juridical literature—like the instructional pieces and the collections of prayer—has come down to us in a state of flux. The manuscripts preserve stages of development, attempts at synthesis and recombination; sometimes the evidence appears highly unsatisfactory, and often it is incomplete. We cannot judge the reformers' abilities on the basis of this evidence alone.[66]

One additional source remains to be examined: vernacular poetry relevant to Anglo-Saxon penitential practice. The acts and ideas substantiated by the handbooks, homilies, and instructional passages are mirrored in the poems. Some of the poems are merely versified prayers; others use the materials of the penitential tradition more imaginatively. In an important way the poems are one with the prose: they never invoke confession and penance without exhorting their audience to practice them. In this respect, the poems are more than reflections of the Anglo-Saxon penitential tradition; they are part of the reformers' spiritual and social design.

66. Evidence for the ignorance of the Anglo-Saxon clergy presented by C. E. Hohler is damning but perhaps exaggerated. See "Some Service Books of the Later Anglo-Saxon Clergy," in *Tenth-Century Studies*, ed. David Parsons, pp. 60–83. For convincing criticism of Hohler's views, see Eric John's comments in *EHR* 92 (1977): 411–412.

Chapter Seven

Penance as Theme and Image in Old English Poetry

I N the *Canons of Edgar*, Wulfstan twice ordered his priests to teach laymen how to pray and how to instruct their children. Every adult, the archbishop wrote, was to train his children in the ways of the church and teach them the Lord's Prayer and the Creed; he who would not do this was not to be considered a Christian.[1] No specific texts would have been required to fulfill these and similar commands: certainly Wulfstan nowhere recommended using poetry to educate the laity. Nonetheless, his command to teach provides a background for the versified prayers found in several eleventh-century manuscripts. Both the Creed and the Lord's Prayer were elaborately enlarged and explicated, each line translated and then provided with commentary itself in the form of prayer. A Cambridge manuscript mixes legislative prose with prayers of this type, the Lord's Prayer among them:

> *Et dimitte nobis debita nostra.*
> Forgif us ure synna,   þaet us ne scamige eft,
> drihten ure,   þonne þu on dome sitst
> and ealle men   up arisað
>
> .   .   .   .
>
> Ne magon we hit na dyrnan,   for ðam þe hit drihten wat,

---

1. *Wulfstan's Canons of Edgar*, ed. Roger Fowler, pp. 6–7, cc. 17 and 22. This text is a set of ecclesiastical regulations, written chiefly for priests but including much about lay piety.

and þar gewitnesse beoð   wuldormicele,
heofonwaru and eorðwaru,   helwaru þridde.[2]
(ll. 83–86, 93–95)

This passage is more than an explanation of the prayer: it is an interpretation. The translator expands his source—which says simply, "Forgive us our trespasses"—to include a new idea: forgiveness granted now will spare sinners the shame of a second confession or revelation of sins before the assembled hosts of heaven, earth, and hell. Of all the arguments for confession and penance advanced in early medieval England, none was more popular: one should repent in this life in order to avoid eternal penance in the next. The argument is made more explicitly in other sources which contrast confession to one man with disclosure before all creation; homilies and instructional pieces for confessors, including the introduction to the "Scrift boc," state the argument so systematically that it has been called a "penitential motif."[3] Common though the idea was in prose, it occurs in poetry only in the long eschatological poem known as *Christ III* and in the Cambridge *Lord's Prayer*, where it takes a slightly less specific form.

The popularity of the motif can be attributed to the irrefutable logic of its underlying assumption: it *is* better to suffer short-term, immediate humiliation than to be damned before all and forever. Confession is here juxtaposed with judgment before God, the angels, the devils, and all mankind; penance is juxtaposed with life everlasting in hell. The motif does not stress the positive aspects of confession and penance, but instead offers them as the lesser of two evils: voluntary disclosure is to be preferred to forcible exposure. The objective of these juxtapositions was to prompt the sinner to be contrite and to confess; they appeal to his piety less than they play on his fears

2. Ed. Elliott van Kirk Dobbie, *The Anglo-Saxon Minor Poems*, pp. 70–74; for a description of the manuscript (Cambridge, Corpus Christi College 201), see pp. lxix–lxx. Translations are my own.

"Forgive us our sins, that we may not be ashamed again, when you, our Lord, sit in judgment and all men rise [from the dead]. . . . Nor may we conceal it [all that we have done] by any means, for the Lord knows it, and there will be many witnesses there—the tribes of heaven, earth and hell."

3. Analyzed by M. R. Godden, "An Old English Penitential Motif," pp. 235–236. Its earliest form is a homily by Boniface (*PL* 89:851).

of God's wrath. Such fear occupies a prominent place in the scriptural tradition, and that is why it had a place in the motif. It is paralleled by another fear, the fear of shame, which is commonplace in Old English elegiac and heroic poetry. The fear of shame belongs to a public code of honor. If shame is defined as the scorn visited on one who fails to meet the reciprocal obligations of his social role, Anglo-Saxon values, as reflected in both the law and poetry, can be said to be "shame-dominated."[4] The laws define an intricate network of duties linking members of Anglo-Saxon society, inside the kinship unit (a father and son) or outside it (a retainer and his lord). Infidelity to one's loyalties—oathbreaking, desertion of one's husband, failure to pay church dues—was severely punished.[5] Unfaithful retainers are condemned in two heroic poems, *Beowulf* and *The Battle of Maldon*, because they deserted their lords in battle.[6] Society honored the loyal and dishonored, punished, and scorned the disloyal; their families shared in their triumph or their shame.

Honor and shame are corresponding public values, originating outside the individual among his kinsmen and members of his community and resting on the individual's need for the respect of those with whom he lived. Shame figures prominently in Wulfstan's *Sermo Lupi ad Anglos* for that reason. Wulfstan repeatedly invoked the "public shame" of Englishmen in their defeat at foreign and heathen hands. The cause of their collapse was pride; they were "more

4. There is an interesting analysis of guilt and shame and their interrelationship in John F. Benton, "Consciousness of Self and of 'Personality' in the Renaissance of the Twelfth Century," in *The Renaissance of the Twelfth Century*, ed. Robert L. Benson and Giles Constable.

5. Laws of Cnut issued between 1020 and 1023 punish one who deserts his lord or his companions with forfeiture of "all that he owns and his own life" (II Cnut 77); a woman who committed adultery forfeited all her goods to her husband and lost her nose and ears so that she might "become herself a public disgrace" (II Cnut 53); ed. Felix Liebermann, *Die Gesetze der Angelsachsen*, 1:278–371. The laws are translated by Dorothy Whitelock, *EHD*, pp. 454–567. There is an excellent introduction to the concept of loyalty by Milton McC. Gatch, *Loyalties and Traditions*, pp. 115–137; the examples from Cnut's laws are discussed on p. 127.

6. Beowulf's unfaithful retainers bear their shields in shame to the fallen hero (ll. 2850–2852; see F. Klaeber, *Beowulf*, 3d ed. [Lexington, Mass., 1950], p. 107). The similarity of their disgrace to that of the unfaithful retainers in *The Battle of Maldon* is noted by Eric V. Gordon in his edition of the poem, pp. 23–24, and by Stanley B. Greenfield, *A Critical History of Old English Literature* (New York, 1965), pp. 100–101.

ashamed of good deeds than of misdeeds" and perversely were "not ashamed, though they sin greatly and commit crimes against even God himself." Great though their wrongs were, the people were "ashamed to repent their misdeeds as the books teach" because of "idle calumny."[7] Here public shame is described as working in two ways, both wrong: shame kept sinners from repenting because a stigma was attached to doing penance, and shame also kept sinners from performing good acts, presumably because departing from widespread evil ways was scorned as well. As Wulfstan knew, shame was a "retarding factor" in the penitential system, an obstacle which had to be overcome forcibly.[8] There was, admittedly, a benefit to be derived from fear. The penitential of Egbert advised the priest to mete out stiff penances to hardened sinners so that others, seeing them suffer, would have fear and cease their own sinning.[9] But in the early medieval period, the shame of confession was not seen as beneficial, and the "chief virtue" of confession was certainly not "derived from the shame it engendered" when the penitent faced the priest.[10] Confession had to be followed by acts of penance before serious sins could be forgiven. The more serious the sin, the greater the penance—and hence the greater the shame it brought.

Only the fear of God was powerful enough to overcome this fear of shame. Old English homilies and poems invested great energy in portraying the Last Judgment, the horrors of hell, and the decay of the corpse in the grave. Their objective was to persuade sinners to

7. Ed. Dorothy Bethurum, *The Homilies of Wulfstan*, p. 273 (xx). My translation follows that in *EHD*, pp. 932–933. "Hy ne scamað na þeah hy syngian swyðe 7 wið God sylfne forwyrcan hy mid ealle, ac for idelan onscytan hy scamað þæt hy betan heora misdæda, swa swa bec tæcan."

8. I borrow the concept from Erik Berggren, *The Psychology of Confession*, p. 11.

9. Ed. F. W. H. Wasserschleben, *Die Bussordnungen der abendländischen Kirche*, p. 233: "Ergo qui perseverat in malo, non ignosce, sed judica districtum judicium secundum canones, ut alii timorem habeant."

10. Thomas N. Tentler argues that the shame of confessing was seen as satisfaction for sin in the ninth and tenth centuries; see *Sin and Confession on the Eve of the Reformation*, p. 20: "The historical origins of the idea are evident: to explain the substantial lightening of works of satisfaction they saw in contemporary discipline, [some theologians] simply concluded that shame made confession itself a work of satisfaction." Penances assigned in tenth-century Anglo-Saxon England were in no danger of becoming too soft.

overcome their reluctance to confess and to be candid in naming their sins. This technique appears somewhat oppressive, but it based fear on faith and used fear only as a means to an end. Unless the penitent believed in death and resurrection, and redemption, he would have no reason to fear the consequences of his wrongdoing. Alcuin's *Liber de Virtutibus et Vitiis* contains an extensive discussion of fear of the Lord which was very likely known to Ælfric and Wulfstan. Alcuin distinguished filial from servile fear: one feared his father because he loved him, and feared his master only because he dreaded the master's punishment.[11] The first fear was a consequence of love; it was the basis for perfect, as opposed to imperfect, contrition. Ultimately fear and love were inconsistent, however, as Alcuin knew from the first letter of John: "There is no room for fear in love; perfect love banishes fear. For fear brings with it the pains of judgment, and anyone who is afraid has not attained to love in its perfection." It is probable that the tenth-century reformers settled for less than perfect contrition and filial love, but also probable that they saw the wisdom of Alcuin's maxim: "Fear of God drives out the fear of hell."[12] In other words, he who lived in fear could die without it. The objective of the motif, then, was to lead the sinner to the love of God.

Literature which makes use of the motif or images and themes specifically associated with confession and penance would appear to constitute a special category of Old English texts. In invoking confession and penance and the analogous acts of prayer and mortification, these texts either describe or directly parallel the essential elements of the church's penitential system. The prose texts, especially

11. The link between fear and faith is analyzed by F.-D. Joret, *The Eucharist and the Confessional* (a translation of *Aux sources de l'eau vive*), pp. 94–95. The scriptural tradition of the fear of God is traced by R. H. Pfeiffer, "The Fear of God," *Israel Exploration Journal* 5 (1955): 41–48. For Alcuin's text, see *PL* 101: 613–638. Wulfstan was particularly fond of Alcuin's work; see Dorothy Bethurum, "A Letter of Protest from the English Bishops to the Pope," pp. 98–99.

12. John's letter reads: "Timor non est in charitate: sed perfecta charitas foras mittit timorem, quoniam timor poenam habet: qui autem timet, non est perfectus in charitate" (1 John 4:18). *Liber de Virtutibus et Vitiis*, c. 15, "De timore Domini": "Timor Dei timorem gehennae expellit. Sic (ergo) timeamus Deum, ut diligamus eum; quia *perfecta charitas foras mittit timorem* servilem" (*PL* 101:624).

the homilies and instructions for confessors, are most clearly "penitential" literature because they were used to implement the system. Can we define a corresponding "penitential" poetry? A list of poems which make either direct or analogous reference to the penitential system includes works so dissimilar in form and theme that they can scarcely be considered a cohesive class. On the one hand are catechetical texts so plainly didactic in intent that only a liberal definition of imaginative literature would include them; on the other are elaborate hagiographical verses and lyrics ranked among the finest Old English poems. At this point it is useful to note that catechetical poems such as the Cambridge version of the Lord's Prayer, *Christ III*, and *The Seasons for Fasting, Almsgiving, An Exhortation to Christian Living, Instructions for Christians, A Summons to Prayer*, and others have rarely if ever been called "penitential," although they do contain exhortations to confess and repent or to perform voluntary ascetic acts of repentence.

There is, of course, no law which insists that "penitential" must refer to sacramental penance. Nor should there be, for there is no evidence that the Anglo-Saxons thought of penitential poetry as a particular kind of poetry, or that they consciously sought to create poetry rooted in either confession or penitential practice. On the other hand, there are a number of Old English poems which derive some elements from the penitential system, and the better we understand the system, the more likely we are to understand its use in poetry. For that reason, it is worthwhile to investigate poetic themes and images which recall penance or confession and to distinguish poems which contain explicit exhortations to repent from those which do not.

Because penitential poetry has been written about more extensively than any other literature related to penitential practice, it is necessary to review previous terms of inquiry. There appear to have been two approaches to penitential poetry, one based on content, the other on form. The first approach leads to a far greater number of poems definable as penitential—far too many for any more than a brief survey. The second, more firmly based on principles of penitential practice and hence in every way more useful, is also less well known. Poems were probably called "penitential" long before *The*

Seafarer was linked to the pilgrimage *pro amore dei* seen in the lives of saints.[13] From pilgrimage it was but a short step to exile, and the journey into exile, as a "figural motif" for the journey of the soul to God, soon became one of the criteria of penitential poetry.[14] Three poems fit the category: *The Wanderer, The Seafarer,* and *Resignation* (also known as *The Penitent's Prayer*).[15] Not everyone accepted this classification: it was pointed out that the voyage could have been performed as an act of voluntary asceticism, independent of penance assigned by the confessor.[16] More telling was the observation that because neither poem expressed sorrow for sin, neither *The Wanderer* nor *The Seafarer* should have been called "penitential."[17] Then *Resignation* was proven to be not one poem but the parts of two, accidentally joined, so that the "figurative" journey of the soul in the first part and the sea journey in the second were totally unrelated.[18] Penitential poetry had fallen on hard times: it was a category of Old English poetry without poems.

The formal approach to penance in poetry worked with different texts and fared much better. Five poems in the Cambridge manuscript mentioned earlier were interpreted as a sequence modeled on confession and penance. Beginning with *Judgment Day II* and the "heart-searching" of the sinner, the series progressed to *The Exhortation to Christian Living, A Summons to Prayer, The Lord's Prayer,* and the *Gloria*; this was seen as a movement from contrition and confession to absolution and prayer.[19] Another reading of peni-

13. See Dorothy Whitelock, "The Interpretation of 'The Seafarer.'"

14. E. G. Stanley, "Old English Poetic Diction and the Interpretation of *The Wanderer, The Seafarer,* and *The Penitent's Prayer.*" These poems, in Stanley's view, share "symbolic poetic diction" (using the journey figuratively).

15. This is the canon as set by P. L. Henry, *The Early English and Celtic Lyric,* pp. 176–180, in an analysis based largely on Stanley's.

16. See reviews of Henry's study by T. P. Dunning in *English Language Notes* 6 (1968): 45–48, and M. N. Nagler, *ES* 52 (1971): 255–259.

17. Morton Bloomfield, "Understanding Old English Poetry," p. 25; see also John C. Pope, "Second Thoughts on the Interpretation of *The Seafarer,*" *ASE* 3 (1974): 78.

18. Alan Bliss and Allen J. Frantzen, "The Integrity of *Resignation.*"

19. See L. Whitbread, "Notes on Two Minor Old English Poems," *SN* 29 (1957): 123–129; and Graham D. Caie, *The Judgment Day Theme in Old English Poetry,* pp. 115–116.

tential poems focused on their relationship to the formal divisions of the sacrament (contrition, confession, satisfaction, and absolution) or to non-sacramental ascetic practice. Having thus established a technical basis for classifying the poetry, this study examined elements of penitential practice in *Elene*, *Juliana*, other poems by Cynewulf, and *The Dream of the Rood*. The approach to *Christ I, II*, and *III* was slightly different. These poems were seen as representative of distinct stages of the process of penance, the first two parts emphasizing the need for release from sin, and the third showing how that release is effected by confession to the priest.[20] Although to be preferred to arguments about exile and pilgrimage, the formal analysis has limitations of its own, for it seeks to impose on a series of poems a single, cohesive framework which subordinates the integrity of each individual poem.[21] Without a certain battering of the text, few poems seem to fit any definition of penitential poetry so far proposed.

It is time not to redefine the term but to recognize the disadvantages of pigeonholing Old English poems, many of which fall into several categories and hence defy the labels fixed to them. Poems which refer to confession and penance intersect with these generic classifications; they do not form a self-contained or cohesive group. They make specific use of the materials of penitential practice and should be separated from those poems which merely express sorrow for sin and stop short of naming confession or penance. Rather than redefine "penitential poetry," I prefer to examine several poems which can be better understood in the light of penitential practice. Aware of the practical aspects of penance, we have a better idea of what these poems are about and how they relate to the Anglo-Saxon spiritual tradition.

Poems in the first group are peripherally related to penance and confession. Catechetical, and hence without narrative context, they share few of the sentiments of the heroic or elegiac traditions. In-

20. Robert C. Rice, "Soul's Need," pp. 1–17, and Rice's article, "The Penitential Motif in Cynewulf's *Fates of the Apostles* and in his Epilogues."

21. For example, it is difficult to see how the *Gloria* could belong to prayers recited by the penitent or the confessor when confession was completed. It is not a prayer of reconciliation.

stead they teach. *Almsgiving* derives its image from a scriptural figure also used by Wulfstan: just as water quells flames, alms remove the "wounds of sin" and cure the soul.[22] *The Seasons for Fasting* explains when and why Christians fast, recommends almsgiving, and stresses the importance of the priest's duties to teach, urge repentance, and lead his people.[23] There is little specifically about confession or penance in these poems because they were written for a larger purpose: they direct the moral life along the broader lines of good conduct and rarely explicate the sacramental observances which belong to Christian living.

The Lord's Prayer in the Cambridge manuscript is catechetical, but it differs from related poems in its focus on the hereafter. Although all poems which exhort Christians to devout and honest conduct point ahead to the eternal rewards of good behavior and belief, very few imagine the judgment scene. Those which do constitute a second and much larger group of poems about penance. Unlike the catechetical poems, which appear to have been written first in the tenth century, some of these poems may have descended from the earlier period. Among them, only *Christ III* follows the "penitential motif" closely. The final section of the poem recounts the Last Judgment first from the perspective of the saved and then from that of the damned.[24] Three horrors will "shame" sinners before they are condemned: they will see the torments of hell, the corruption of their own souls, and the bliss of the saved (ll. 1263–1288). "Overwhelmed with shame," the damned will be exposed to the gaze of all assembled; God, the angels, and "the sons of men" watch:

Ealle eorðbuend   ond atol deofol,
mircne mægencræft,   manwomma gehwone

22. Joseph B. Trahern, Jr., "The Old English 'Almsgiving,'" *N & Q* 16 (1969): 46–47, and Bethurum, *Homilies*, p. 356; the figure is used by Wulfstan in the *Sermo Lupi* (xx). For the poem, see *The Exeter Book*, ed. George Philip Krapp and Elliott van Kirk Dobbie, p. 223.

23. Text in Dobbie, *The Anglo-Saxon Minor Poems*, pp. 98–104; see the discussion by Kenneth Sisam, *Studies in the History of Old English Literature*, pp. 45–60.

24. Text in Krapp and Dobbie, *The Exeter Book*, pp. 3–49. On the relationship of the three major sections of the poem, see Colin Chase, "God's Presence through Grace as the Theme of Cynewulf's *Christ II* and the Relationship of this Theme to *Christ I* and *Christ III*," *ASE* 3 (1974): 87–101.

> magum þurh þa lichoman,   leahtra firene,
> geseon on þam sawlum.   Beoð þa syngan flæsc
> scandum þurhwaden   swa þæt scire glæs,
> þæt mon yþæst mæg   eall þurhwlitan.   (ll. 1278–1283)[25]

The poet explains how this awful fate could have been averted:

> Wære him þonne betre   þæt hy bealodæde,
> ælces unryhtes,   ær gescomeden
> fore anum men,   eargra weorca,
> godes bodan sægdon   þæt hi to gyrne wiston
> firendæda on him.   Ne mæg þurh þæt flæsc se scrift
> geseon on þære sawle,   hwæþer him mon soð þe lyge
> sagað on hine sylfne,   þonne he þa synne bigæð.
> Mæg mon swa þeah gelacnigan   leahtra gehwylcne,
> yfel unclæne,   gif he hit anum gesegð,
> ond nænig bihelan mæg   on þam heardan dæge
> wom unbeted,   ðær hit þa weorud geseoð.   (ll. 1301–1311)[26]

Were men able to see the sins on their souls, the poet concludes, no one could describe the zeal with which they would try to prolong their lives so that adequate penance could be performed (ll. 1312–1321). Those who do repent will live "blameless and unashamed" among men and will enjoy eternal happiness in the hereafter. Shaming oneself before the confessor was a way to earn immediate as well as eternal honor; the public disgrace attached to penitential practice elsewhere here becomes the price of an honorable life among men.

---

25. "And all the earth's inhabitants and the vile devil, too, shall behold their evil might and their stains of guilt. They may see the transgressions of sin through the body on the soul. The sinful flesh shall be pierced with disgrace as though it were clear glass that man may most easily see through." The image of the bodies as glass is analyzed by Thomas D. Hill, "Vision and Judgment in the Old English *Christ III*," *SP* 70 (1973): 233–243.

26. "It would have been better had they previously been ashamed for crime, for each injustice, for evil works, and had said to the messenger of God that they knew to their sorrow the evil deeds within them. The confessor cannot see the soul through the flesh and does not know whether man tells him truth or falsehood about himself when he avows his sins. But one can cure every disease, every unclean evil, if he will tell it to one. And none may conceal an uncompensated iniquity on that severe day when multitudes shall see it."

Christ III is not the only Old English poem which offers confession and penance as sacramental counterparts to judgment and punishment. *Judgment Day II* is another poem which employs this analogy in order to establish a reference in the reader's life for the great events imagined in the poem. *Christ III* juxtaposes the eschatological and the penitential and so derives from the Last Judgment a mandate for mankind in "the little span of life that is here" (l. 1322). This poem works from the king's pronouncement to the priest's; *Judgment Day II* reverses this strategy, beginning with confession and ending with an eschatological vision. This confession is made not to the priest but to God alone and is coupled at the outset with a statement of the poet's contrition. His vision of himself as a condemned sinner is prompted by his fear of God's judgment and of "eternal wrath for myself and for each of the sinful ones." [27] If we are to call this a penitential poem, however, it is because the poem is a devotional confession—a form of confession which was, throughout the early medieval period, an accepted method of obtaining remission for the punishment due to sin. [28] All references to confession in *Judgment Day II* are of this type: the confessor is not mentioned, for the "physician" referred to is always God, never man. The speaker dreads eternal punishment "before God himself" ("æt sylfum gode," l. 18). He claims that the miserable soul can find salvation only by revealing its wounds to the "supreme physician" ("uplicum læce," l. 46), and his model for the repentant sinner is the Good Thief, who as he neared death "offered his prayer with the thoughts of his breast" ("his bena bebead breostgehigdum," l. 60). Before the eschatological vision is launched, the poet warns that weeping and lamentation for sin are not to be scorned "in the fitting time for repentance" ("forgifnesse gearugne timan," l. 91); anyone who hesitates to judge himself for his sins on earth should remember how great will be the terror produced by the judgment of all men before God (ll. 92–98).

27. Text in Dobbie, *The Anglo-Saxon Minor Poems*, pp. 58–67 (ll. 17–18); see Richard L. Hoffman, "Structure and Symbolism in the *Judgment Day II*," *Neophilologus* 52 (1968): 170–178; and comments by Caie, *The Judgment Day Theme*, pp. 115–159.

28. This development is discussed above, chapter three, nn. 96–100. The tradition of confessional prayers in England in the tenth century would have had Carolingian and Frankish roots; for the continental background to this kind of confession, see Cyrille Vogel, *Les "Libri Paenitentiales*," pp. 55–57.

In both this poem and *Christ III*, the torments of hell are imagined with splendid vigor. Worms tear the damned souls, flames surge, and hell-dwellers suffer all manner of misery. The fear of God translates into fear of such punishments as these, and the rewards of heaven pale when compared to them. This may be a modern judgment, but it seems not to be too far removed from the poets', both of whom invest much less energy in depicting the fates of the just.[29] *Judgment Day II* does, however, conclude with a vision of heavenly happiness which prompts the poet to ask what earthly hardship can be compared to the gladness to be had in Paradise.

Judgment Day II takes the form of a confessional prayer. It uses a convention which we might call the "anatomical motif," or catalogue of parts of the body, common in Latin confessions; and it echoes an axiom of Theodulf to explain how such prayers and oral confession worked: what man once remembered, God would forget.[30] When penitential acts are mentioned in this poem, there is no certain indication that they are penances assigned by a priest; they appear instead to be voluntary acts of mortification undertaken as a response to the sinner's confession to God.

Another penitential poem about voluntary asceticism is known as *Soul and Body*; here again there is no mention of the confessor and no indication that the ascetic acts mentioned have been assigned by him.[31] Yet this too can be called a poem about a penance—in this case, fasting—which the Anglo-Saxons would have undertaken in

29. In *Christ III* the disproportion is glaring: the address to the good souls is barely twenty lines long; that to the damned is nearly one hundred and fifty, and the subsequent description of their torment in hell continues for one hundred more (see ll. 1344–1361 and 1379–1523).

30. Theodulf's first *Capitula* states, "Quanto nos memores sumus peccatorum nostrorum, tanto horum Dominus obliviscitur" (*PL* 105:200). At this point Theodulf is discussing confession to God alone. The poem says that God will avenge man's sins only once (l. 89).

31. There are two versions of *Soul and Body*. That in *The Vercelli Book*, longer and more complete, is the one discussed here (ed. George Philip Krapp, *The Vercelli Book*, pp. 54–59); in Krapp and Dobbie, *The Exeter Book*, see pp. 174–178. On the relationship of the two versions, see P. R. Orton, "The Old English 'Soul and Body': A Further Examination," *MÆ* 48 (1979): 173–179; see also Orton, "Disunity in the Vercelli Book *Soul and Body*," *Neophilologus* 63 (1980): 592–603.

Lent, the "fitting time" for repentance. In *Christ III* and *Judgment Day II*, our attention is drawn to the poems' penitential content by exhortations to confess. These poems are about the Last Judgment and the apprehension which precedes it; *Soul and Body* shows instead life and death in an interim period, when the soul and body are separated by physical death and are waiting to be reunited for final judgment. The judgment has yet to be pronounced, but the two souls—one saved, one damned—anticipate it in their speeches to the bodies when they visit their graves. Each soul measures the body's conduct in terms of fasting. The evil soul accuses its body of feeding itself and starving the soul, while the good soul praises its body for doing the opposite. Neither soul mentions confession or penance, and so we can say no more than that this poem describes the acts which were regularly assigned by confessors. But when we analyze the souls' speeches more closely, we begin to see a strong resemblance between this poem and others more explicitly penitential.

Soul and Body recalls *Judgment Day II* and *Christ III* in its use of the body as an image for the soul. The evil soul reviles its body's corruption and invites comparison between the distress the body suffers in the grave and that it will suffer in hell: in both pits worms tear the body, and foulness encloses it (l. 64, ll. 89–91). The poet reinforces this comparison. Following the evil soul's account of the Last Judgment is the poem's most celebrated passage, a description of the worms as they destroy the flesh (ll. 103–126). As a sequel, the good soul's speech is an anticlimax. Not surprisingly, the good soul quickly passes over the body's decay (a single reference, ll. 135–136) and recounts the body's good deeds and the waiting glories of heaven. The good body's decay must be de-emphasized because the poet has portrayed physical corruption as a sign of moral rot. That is why the evil soul dwells so long on the subject, and why the good soul, although confronted with the same unpleasant sight, focuses its speech on a happier topic. Strictly speaking, physical decay is the consequence of the Fall, not retribution for the individual's unrepented sins, but the poet is less concerned with theological precision than with the graphic possibilities of his theme. His poem could be said to rest on a maxim found in the penitentials: he who sins through the body must repent through the body.[32] What the flesh fails to do on earth, it must do in the hereafter. In *Soul and Body*, the hereafter begins in the grave, in circumstances suitable only for sinners (saints' bodies were often spared decay). This is a good poem but a lopsided one—the emphasis on the negative may be exaggerated because the leaf containing the good soul's speech and the poem's conclusion is missing in one of the manuscripts.[33]

Cynewulf's poems manipulate the premises of *Christ III* and *Judgment Day II* and go beyond them. The Last Judgment is described in the epilogues to *Elene*, *Juliana*, and *The Fates of the Apostles*, but only the first two poems contain confessions of the poet's sinfulness. In them Cynewulf uses penitential materials for concluding exhortations, but he also adapts these commonplaces to realize fully, in a non-fictional mode, the theme of conversion central to both poems. *Juliana* concludes with the poet's lament that he has turned to penance too late, and that he will be one of the sheep "stained with sin" before the Judge.[34] Unsure of his fate, the poet calls on those who recite his song and on Juliana herself to pray for him (ll. 715–721). He uses several commonplace expressions of sinfulness and inadequate repentance to describe the uncertainty of his own conversion. More than an autobiographical gesture of self-effacing piety, the poet's portrait serves as a model for his audience. Like him, we do not know where our souls will go; like him, we "trembling shall await what He shall judge" (ll. 700–707). Sharing his anxiety, we are meant to seek the resolution he proposes and which Juliana herself demonstrates.

One of the poem's most important episodes recalls the confessional encounter; as if she were a priest interrogating a penitent, Juliana quizzes the devil to learn how he wins souls. He causes "the

---

32. "Per corpus peccat, per corpus emendet"; the idea is quoted here from Egbert's penitential (ed. Wasserschleben, *Bussordnungen*, p. 245, c. 14); it is found in several sources from the later Old English period. I develop the link between this theme and the poem in "The Body in *Soul and Body I*," forthcoming in *Chaucer Review* 17 (1982).

33. See Krapp's introduction to *The Vercelli Book*, pp. xxxviii–xxxix.

34. For the text, see Krapp and Dobbie, *The Exeter Book*, pp. 113–133. For a good critical introduction, see Joseph Wittig, "Figural Narrative in Cynewulf's *Juliana*," *ASE* 4 (1975): 37–55.

beginning and end of all evils" by clever temptation: when the sinner has determined to do God's will, the devil exposes him to the "vices of the mind" and leads him into sin (ll. 352–365). Before the devil will struggle for his soul, the Christian must have accepted God's will; only when man's will actively turns to the good can it be perverted, and for this reason the devil tempts when man least expects it—when he is at prayer. When he is successful, the devil persuades the devout to cease praying and leave the place of prayer (ll. 373–376).

The devil's confession (really a boast) glosses the action he has just taken at this point in the poem in his temptation of Juliana.[35] Pitched into prison after hanging by her hair for six hours, she prays. Disguised as an angel, the devil appears and urges her to stop and offer sacrifices to the false gods she has rejected (ll. 247–256). Juliana's entire character in the poem can be summed up in a single word: steadfastness. With Christ fast in her breast, she dwells in prison steadfastly and, deep in prayer when the "angel" arrives, will not swerve from her resolution. She strengthens her prayer and her call to God for help, successfully overcomes the temptation, and learns from a mysterious heavenly voice who her visitor is. She forces him to confess his evil deeds to her, and as he does he complains that those who resist his lures shame him; falsely contrite, he pleads for her mercy: "Pity me, the miserable one, that all unblessed I perish not" (ll. 449–450). Herself unbound, she binds the devil, who once again pleads, "Put not upon me fresh indignity, reproach before men" (ll. 541–542). But when he admits that she punishes him justly, he vanishes, at least for a time, in disgrace.

Juliana may well be the only ironic confessional poem in Old English. It certainly contains a rare, insincere statement of contrition, as well as a hypocritical plea for forgiveness. This is part of the poem's inverted design, seen again when the evil judge condemns the saint to be burned. The fires rage, but the inferno cannot harm the innocent; instead, it is the judge who is destroyed (ll. 580–600). Before her own death, Juliana delivers an exhortation to her people, urging them to pray, warning them that they do not know the hour

---

35. Rice has an excellent discussion of this confession in "Soul's Need," pp. 127–135.

of their own death, and asking for mercy (ll. 660–669). Cynewulf's epilogue continues her departing speech but installs the poet as the departing figure. The tone shifts from the high spirits of Juliana's triumphs and her humorous mortification of the devil to the uncertainty and fear of the poet's self-reflection. As a final tribute to the saint's example, Cynewulf transforms his epilogue into a prayer for her intercession.

Elene too offers an important link between the epilogue and the central event of the poem. Judas is to this poem what the devil is to *Juliana*: a resister of the saint's powers, the object of her catechetical preaching, and finally her convert (although the devil's conversion, seen in his plea for mercy, is obviously a sham). *Elene* is about the saint's efforts to discover the True Cross, whose location is a secret of the Jews. She accuses five hundred of their wisest of having wrought a foolish deed and rejected the cure for their blindness in rejecting holy scripture ("blindnesse bote forsegon," l. 389).[36] But the wise men do not know the sin she accuses them of, and after her speech they hold counsel in an attempt to discover it. It is not that they refuse to confess their wrongdoing but rather that they cannot imagine what it might be. They call on Judas to explain, and he tells them that their forefathers were guilty of Christ's death and that in order to preserve the integrity of their religion—the ancient texts and wise teaching ("frod fyrngewritu ond þa fæderlican lare," ll. 431–432)— they must keep this crime a secret. Judas, therefore, knows the people's sin and argues against its disclosure.

But he himself shares in their blame and knows that it would be better to acknowledge it. The wise man Sachias had told Judas's father that if anyone were to ask about this crime he was to confess it— the Old English is *cyðan*, "to testify" or "to confess" (l. 446). The father declared himself innocent of Christ's death because he kept himself apart from the guilt of the Jews "and wrought no shame to my soul." But he too counseled Judas to acknowledge the deed if asked about it because God is merciful:

36. For the text, see Krapp, *The Vercelli Book*, pp. 66–102; there is a good critical reading by Robert Stepsis and Richard Rand, "Contrast and Conversion in Cynewulf's *Elene*," *NM* 70 (1969): 273–282.

"þeah we æbylgð wið hine   oft gewyrcen,
synna wunde,   gif we sona eft
þara bealudæda   bote gefremmaþ
ond þæs unrihtes   eft geswicaþ." (ll. 513–516)[37]

The wise men are summoned once more by Elene. She does not ask them about the cross but asks instead if they acknowledge the truth of Christ's life and death. This they refuse to do, and for their defiance Elene promises them hell on earth—a funeral pyre ablaze with the hottest of fires (ll. 579–584). At this point they elect to have Judas speak for them, and of him she asks a different question: the location of the cross. He replies that he does not know, and this appears to be the truth, but combined with questions about the cross are questions about his knowledge of Christ's death and other matters which he can answer. But he refuses to speak and so incurs Elene's wrath:

"Ic þæt geswerige   þurh sunu meotodes,
þone ahangnan god,   þæt ðu hungre scealt
for cneomagum   cwylmed weorðan,
butan þu forlæte   þa leasunga
ond me sweotollice   soð gecyðe." (ll. 686–690)[38]

The verb for "torment" here is *cwylman*; in the Latin source of the poem it glosses *cruciare*, "to crucify." Cynewulf reinforces this meaning by having Elene swear on the body of the crucified Christ.[39] Judas will be "crucified with hunger," therefore, when he is forced to fast seven days, a penance both symbolic and real. So imprisoned,

37. God is merciful "even though we offend him and often work the wounds of sin, if we immediately afterwards undertake repentance for the evil deeds and afterwards forsake wrongdoing."

38. "I swear by the son of God, the crucified one, that you will be tormented with hunger before your kinsmen unless you forsake falsehoods and plainly tell me the truth."

39. In a Latin version of Helen's life, Judas is cast into the pit "sine cibo . . . ut ibidem famis molestia cruciari"; see Ferdinand Holthausen, "Zur Quelle von Cynewulf's 'Elene,'" *Zeitschrift für deutsches Philologie* 37 (1905): 13. This point was brought to my attention by David W. Burchmore, who is preparing a study of the poem.

Judas soon admits his error. Because it will shortly become evident that he does not yet know where the cross lies, we see that his mistake was to deny the meaning of the cross, not the cross itself. God sends him a sign, and he finds the cross; but immediately after the ensuing celebration the devil challenges him, and when Judas renounces Satan, Elene sees the cross in his bosom, a catechetical prelude to his baptism (ll. 935–1045). Only when he believes in Christ can Judas be forgiven: only when the penitent acknowledged the truth of the redemption could he confess.

The conversion of Judas, which leads him from sinful secrecy to revelation and repentance, is paralleled by the conversion of the bishop Eusebius, renamed Cyriacus. He too receives a sign, and it leads him to find the nails with which Christ was crucified. In this way the bishop turns to repentance ("to bote gehwearf," l. 1125), his new name signaling his renewed faith. The second conversion modeled on that of Judas is Cynewulf's, which is recounted in the epilogue. Like Judas and Cyriacus, he finds the meaning of the cross by fixing his thoughts on it. This revelation frees him from the oppression of his sin—it "unbinds" him, and it will unbind those who hear his poem and imitate him by affixing their thoughts to the cross. The means of the audience's conversion is, of course, the poem and the poet's skill; Cynewulf emphasizes the dual agency of art and artist by embedding his runic signature in the epilogue. The epilogue, like that of *Juliana*, is not an appeal to penance and confession but instead an appeal to prayer and the devout life—an appeal already made several times within the narrative. The confession of Judas, extorted by Elene, is actually a profession of faith; neither *Elene* nor *Juliana* is a poem about confession and penance, but both use the vocabulary of penitential literature and employ motifs of revelation analogous to confession. Both poems focus on the intercessory power of prayer as an aid to those who believe and repent and fear the moment of their final judgment. If we look for the language and motifs of penitential literature in these poems, we immediately confront their central themes and techniques. But no one could rigidly classify either narrative as a penitential poem without slighting its manifold riches.

Poems indebted specifically to the penitential system differ from other Old English verse in more than theme and image. The subject matter is evident in their vocabulary, which consists of stock expressions (the medical metaphor, words meaning "confess," "repent," and so forth), the arrangement of these traditional materials into a motif, and sometimes direct exhortation. Penitential poems also share a quality more difficult to identify but no less distinctive; it might be called a state of mind, and it can be seen in one of the most peculiar Old English poems, the fragmentary *Resignation B*. Here the speaker claims that God is angry with him but repeatedly insists that he does not know why. Having expressed discomfort with his world and anxiety about his spiritual state, the speaker reaches a conclusion poised oddly between the penitential and stoic modes:

> Giet biþ þæt selast,   þonne mon him sylf ne mæg
> wyrd onwendan,   þæt he þonne wel þolige.   (ll. 117–118)[40]

The speaker has complained too much about his uncaring acquaintances and the unjust and unexplained accusations against him to allow belief in his patient endurance. Each year brings him greater sorrow, and his attempts to love have been rewarded with contempt (ll. 115–118). He can neither tolerate this world nor leave it. His resolution is suspect: a stoic would not complain, and no penitent would go into exile with this indecorous hesitation. *Resignation B* looks like an attempt to fabricate a poem out of fundamentally inconsistent clichés. The poem sits no better with *The Wanderer* and *The Seafarer*, or others in the "wisdom" tradition, than with poems about penance.[41] The speaker in *Resignation B* announces that he will tell a "true tale" about himself, and this suggests a similarity between this "tale" and the "true song" of *The Seafarer*. We also think of *The Wanderer* and *The Wife's Lament*, since the speaker in each makes a song (as the Wife says) "of my deep sadness." Each knows some

40. Text in Krapp and Dobbie, *The Exeter Book*, pp. 215–218: "Still it is best, when a man cannot change his own destiny, that he should endure it patiently."

41. On the "wisdom" tradition, see T. A. Shippey, *Poems of Wisdom and Learning in Old English* (Totowa, N.J., 1976). Referring to *The Wanderer*, *The Seafarer* and *Deor*, Bloomfield writes: "Although they may refer to God and end with a prayer to him, they are didactic and addressed to men, not a plea for forgiveness addressed to God"; their "true generic siblings" are "meditative, reflective wisdom poems" ("Old English Poetry," p. 25).

misery and is moved by that misery to sing—to tell, as the *Resignation B* speaker says, "a painful story primarily about myself" (ll. 96–97).[42] In each case the speaker's misery clearly connects with his or her need to share it; their unhappiness drives their stories forward.

The autobiographical poems in the wisdom tradition are only in a limited sense like poems incorporating penance; what links Cynewulf's epilogues and *Judgment Day II*, and possibly *The Dream of the Rood*, to wisdom poems is the anxiety of the reflective mind. But the poems offer different solutions to that anxiety. Wisdom poems are stoic; the alienation of the speaker remains intact at the end of the poem. Seeing that he cannot change his destiny, the Wanderer, like the speaker in *Resignation B*, concludes that he must suffer it for the time being and trust to happiness in the next world.

This decision to contain one's dissatisfaction and accept hardship as one's lot has important consequences which set the wisdom poems apart from penitential themes. Wisdom poems maintain a strong sense of the speaker's individuality by withholding the resolution of his or her unhappiness. In poems informed by penance, this separation must be overcome: the objective of penitential practice, seen in the *ordo confessionis* and in the motif of shame used in *Christ III*, *The Lord's Prayer*, and much penitential prose, is to intensify the sinner's awareness of his isolation from the community of the saved and to make him see his sin as the cause of his separation. The sinner's contrition, confession, and acts of penance restore him to the community. His fear of God is aroused by images of judgment and prompts him to overcome his fear of shame: he confesses and performs penance, and so prepares himself to accept and return God's love.

Wisdom poems follow a different pattern and subscribe to a different ethic, seen in many poems in *The Exeter Book*. An example is *Precepts*, a poem of advice given from father to son. Like *The Wanderer*, this poem cautions against disclosing one's thoughts. Instead, one should be wary of his speech, ponder his fortunes "in his breast" and not aloud:

42. "Ic bi me tylgust / secge þis sarspel"; for the text of *The Wife's Lament*, see Krapp and Dobbie, *The Exeter Book*, pp. 210–211. It begins, "I compose this lay about my own wretched self, about my own experience" ("Ic þis giedd wrece bi me ful geomorre, / minre sylfre sið").

"Wærwyrde sceal   wisfæst hæle
breostum hycgan,   nales breahtme hlud." (ll. 57–58)[43]

The wise man journeys through life with his thoughts bound firmly in his breast because the world is treacherous. Self-revelation must be avoided: it endangers the speaker or invites him to trust the world's fleeting consolations. The conclusion to *The Wanderer* makes a similar point:

Til biþse þe his treowe gehealdeþ,   ne sceal næfre his torn
to rycene
beorn of his breostum acyþan,   nemþe he ær þa bote
cunne. (ll. 112–113)[44]

In the penitential system, self-revelation buys security, and that is why exposure must be endured. Penance reduces tensions between the self and society by promoting peace and reconciliation in this world as the price of comfort in the next. Much of the finest in Old English poetry promotes tension instead, by leaving the speaker to support his sense of alienation and his anxiety. This code is the converse of penance, which formulated, articulated, and, through prescribed acts of mortification, relieved anxiety. Within the penitential tradition, one cannot stand stoically when faced with misery and loss: one must pray and seek the remedy for sin. Prayer and confession would be unthinkable in *The Wanderer* because they would undercut the tension between self and society which distinguishes the poem. Here, anxieties are articulated—that creates the Wanderer's poem—but repressed rather than released. This distinguishes *The Wanderer* from *The Seafarer*, in which the speaker's individuality finally vanishes in a generalized statement about all human experience.[45] Because the Wanderer does not speak, because he does not

43. *Precepts* is a lame title for a most interesting poem. The text is on pp. 140–143, *ibid.*: "The prudent man, cautious in speech, must ponder (silently) in his breast, not aloud with noise."

44. Text on p. 137, *ibid.*: "Good is he who keeps his trust; nor must the warrior ever divulge the anger in his heart, unless he first knows how to remedy it." This poem begins with the speaker's declaration that there is no one living to whom he dare reveal his thoughts ("modsefan minne durre / sweotule asecgan," ll. 10–11).

45. Pope notes a "fading away of the speaker's vigorous individuality," in "Second Thoughts," p. 82.

ask for assistance, he retains a powerful individual identity. His theology is not suspect, as his final invocation of the Father shows, but his spiritual outlook does not compromise his anxiety; he remains a man both in and of the world. *The Wanderer's* famous *ubi sunt* passage laments the passing of earthly beauties without denouncing the beauties themselves. His stoicism dignifies circumstances which poems about penance seek to transcend.[46]

The Wanderer, Homiletic Fragment II, and, to an extent, *Resignation B* show that the wise man does not share the secrets of his heart. Penitential practice demanded confession from the recesses of the heart, leaving no evil undisclosed. In wisdom poems, the unknown is sacred; in poems about penance, the unknown is potentially fatal. The wisdom poems would be destroyed by the revelation of their mysteries, while without systematic and full disclosure, penitential poems would have no resemblance to either confession or penance. Poems which refer to penance and confession teem with images of revelation—wounds are opened, thoughts unveiled, bodies seen through—and abound with references to speech. They are poems about disclosure. In wisdom poems it is enough that the speaker contemplate his unhappiness and formulate a resolution in his mind. But penance requires that thoughts lead to acts: contrition must lead to confession, as it does in *Judgment Day II*.

It becomes easy to see why poems concerned with penance are not the favorites of Old English literary criticism. Their speakers channel their sorrows and anxieties into a single, sacramental process which focuses attention on propitiation and reconciliation. The wisdom poems contain their mysteries and so invite continued speculation on the speakers' circumstances: we attempt to understand how this person reaches a compromise between resignation and a desire to flee the world which has brought so much sorrow. There is nothing in the cultural milieu of early medieval England to suggest that authors of either kind of poem needed to explore the stereotypes they invoked. Poetry about penance is highly systematic, relying on

46. For a similar reading, see T. P. Dunning and A. J. Bliss, eds., *The Wanderer*, pp. 96–104. They argue that the *ubi sunt* passage expresses a "specifically Christian" idea in "heroic terms" (pp. 96–97) and conclude that the Wanderer does not reject the world of his past but instead rises above it (see p. 101).

well-established images and familiar themes used by the homilists and authors of the handbooks. There was no need to go beyond these materials, because the poetry shared, at least in part, the objective of the prose: to explicate, to illustrate, to educate, and sometimes to exhort. The poetry could, and did, accomplish more because it was capable of greater formal beauty and wider imaginative range. It was not created as a distinct kind of penitential literature; it worked together with the prose to encourage penitential practice, but that was not its only, or even its chief, function. Poems informed by penance had many uses, some of them shared with the poems of the wisdom tradition. One of these was to reduce complex situations to clearly formulated generalizations about human behavior and the life to come and to offer examples of individuals whose experience conformed to the general truths maintained by the poetry. This didactic purpose unifies all Anglo-Saxon poetry and prose; literature about confession and penance was but one specific, systematic, and consistent approach to realizing that objective.

Epilogue

A Look Ahead to New Questions

Astudy as broadly focused as this may best be concluded by a review of its immediate and long-range objectives, a retrospective which inevitably raises important and unanswered questions about both penitentials and penance. In the following pages I discuss directions for further research in the literature of penance and speculate about the link between early medieval penitential traditions and the customs and literature of the later Middle Ages, a subject to which I hope to return.

The most important problems in the history of penance are concealed by the penitentials. My immediate objectives in this study of the handbooks have been, first, to analyze Irish, English, and Frankish penitentials in the context of the ecclesiastical literature contemporary with them and, second, to distinguish some of the changes which these cultures produced in the handbooks and in penitential practice. One pursues such objectives out of curiosity about the changes which penitentials and penance produced in these societies. But there is little point in further study of the penitential tradition without better editions of the penitentials themselves. It is remarkable that we know so little about their manuscript traditions, their authors, and their relationship to daily life. Most of the available editions are sadly out of date, either because they reflect archaic editorial principles or because new manuscript evidence has undermined established theories about the texts. Analysis built on foundations so unsteady can tell us nothing that we need to know. Fortunately the Frankish penitentials are now being re-edited as part of a vast project in which uniform methods will be used to reassess the manuscripts and construct reliable and authoritative editions.[1] It is well that the Frankish texts are the first to be re-examined, for, even apart from their value to continental history, they are pivotal. Frankish penitentials are important evidence of Irish and English missions to the continent. More numerous in the manuscripts than either Irish or English handbooks, those written on the continent unquestionably reflect contemporary insular customs and hence amplify our knowledge of them. The continental penitentials are also the source for the vernacular handbooks written in England in the tenth century. The more we know about the Frankish texts, therefore, the more we will know about the continental origins of some of Anglo-Saxon England's most important pastoral literature.

New editions will also enable us to fit the handbooks into the picture of early medieval pastoral education and reform. In this regard both Frankish and English sources seem to have been more thoroughly explored than the Irish—a paradox, considering that it was the Irish who bequeathed the penitentials to the western church. Indeed, if we date the earliest of the Irish handbooks to the mid-sixth century, we can place them near the beginnings of Hiberno-Latin literature. Their pre-eminence over Frankish and English sources is almost too obvious to stress. Historians of the early Irish church and its prose should be urged to take a closer look at these texts. Bieler's edition of the Irish penitentials is already some twenty years old; masterful in many respects, it is not without flaw, and it is unfortunate that so little new research has followed in its path. Without new work, we will never move beyond the approximations now forced upon us when we inquire into Welsh analogues to the penitentials or attempt to link the handbooks to Irish canonical collections and the native law codes.

New editions of the penitentials will, in their turn, make possible a whole range of studies in the history of penitential literature and practice. Armed with evidence which ties certain handbooks to certain monastic centers, historians will be able to pair the penitentials and civic evidence with a certitude now wholly beyond us.

1. Under the direction of Professor Raymund Kottje of the University of Bonn. Publication of the new editions is forthcoming in the *Corpus Christianorum, Continuatio Mediaevalis*.

Social historians, for example, might be able to study population growth in the light of the church's attempts to regulate the laity's sexuality: were the sexual prohibitions of the penitentials part of an economic rather than a spiritual maneuver, or an attempt to hold down the size of the population as well as to redeem it?

Such studies will allow us to understand for the first time the full meaning of penitentials and penance in medieval life and literature. But we can improve our view of the penitential tradition as we await new work, and that has been my third and indeed my overriding objective: to help release the penitentials from the stigma identifying them as harsh, inhibiting, primitive, and exotic. That stigma springs from two sources, the more obvious one being our reluctance to accept lists either as literature or as historical evidence. Lists appear to be arbitrary, even meaningless, catalogues hovering awkwardly between fiction and fact. I have shown that the penitentials are not mere lists of sins but that they are instead texts centered on a process both disciplinary and devotional. So long as we dismiss the handbook as a mere inventory of sins, penance will be characterized as mechanical, an automatic gesture emptied of meaning by ritualistic repetition. Yet we have become too aware of the importance of ritual and its implications to condescend to penance in this way. Rather than regard the penitential as a crude means of dispensing retribution, we should try to see it, in a light more subtle and sophisticated, as a text essential to one of the church's most important and life-giving sacraments—that is, to see it in a medieval perspective.

The lesser source of discontent with the penitentials is that they seem to present the medieval church as manipulative and invasive of private lives. Many adults have as one of their earliest memories of religion the terror of confessing to the parish priest. One counted his sins, perhaps supplying a few extra minor offenses (so many marshmallows with which to bombard the confessor) in order to balance out a more serious one. Among the young—unfortunately they for many years felt the pressure of confession most acutely—this calculus of the conscience encouraged rigidity and even contempt for oneself. Such is the confession about which Foucault has written—an exchange which put the sinner at the mercy of an inquisitive confessor's interrogation about his most private habits.[2] It was perhaps in an attempt to escape this stigma that the church recently renamed penance the sacrament of "reconciliation." Readers of this book will see this gesture as something other than a post—Vatican II relaxation of strict standards, another departure from venerable tradition. If the church has chosen to de-emphasize the severity of penance and confession, it has in doing so merely returned to its ancient concept of penance as an opportunity for counsel as well as for correction. Throughout this study I have sought to present the early penitential system in that twofold aspect which is unquestionably its earliest character in medieval Europe.

Much written about penitential practice disregards its devotional character and stresses instead its disciplinary function and hence its harshness. We perpetuate this stereotypical half-truth if we reduce penance among medieval Christians to a compulsory social observance. The early evidence argues against the possibility that penitential practice was universally observed and suggests that it was instead part of the religious life of the few. The first among the laity to undertake penance did so voluntarily in an effort to pattern their spiritual lives on the lives of monks. These men and women were not barbarians forcibly subjected to penance, but Christians with a refined sense of wrong and right. For them the austerity of penance as the early handbooks describe it—harsh though it seems to us—was not too great; indeed, it was precisely what they sought.

The history of penance was a movement away from the strictest mortification toward a discipline less exacting and more likely to be widely observed. It is usually assumed that the austerity of penance was gradually eroded by the introduction of commutations and vicarious penances. But such practices were known in early Ireland

2. Michel Foucault, *The History of Sexuality, I: An Introduction*, trans. Robert Hurley. Foucault gives interesting ammunition to those who maintain the theory of social control. It is worth noting that sexuality has always been the main focus of confession—no sins outnumber sexual offenses in the early penitentials—even in non-Christian cultures. See R. Pettazzoni, "La confession des péches dans l'histoire des religions," in *Mélanges Franz Cumont*, Annuaire de l'institute de philologie et d'histoire orientales et slaves, vol. 4: 2 (Bruxelles, 1936; repr. ed., 1969): 893–901.

and England as well as in the later Middle Ages, and we cannot explain a change in the history of penance merely by pointing to them. Neither system was an escape or an evasion of the burden of penance; commuted penances, although brief, were extremely difficult to perform, and vicarious penances were penances still; that is, they atoned for sin, and atonement, not the punishment of wrongdoing, was the purpose of penance.

Nonetheless, the contrast between early and later penitential practice cannot be denied, even though it has yet to be satisfactorily explained. Penances did not soften because the Lateran Council of 1215 made annual confession an obligation, thereby mandating penances of moderate character.[3] Annual confession had been urged on the faithful long before. The period immediately preceding this declaration was a most important one for both penance and penitential literature, and it is there, among the theological conflicts of the twelfth century, that we shall have to search for turning points. By the time Gratian published his concordance to the canons (1140), a serious disagreement about confession had arisen: the followers of Peter Abelard argued that any sin could be forgiven so long as the sinner was genuinely sorry for it, but the followers of Bernard of Clairvaux insisted on oral confession to be followed by penance and absolution.[4] Gratian left this dispute unresolved; Peter Lombard took the decisive step when, in his *Sentences*, he required the sinner at least to have the intention to confess orally if oral confession could not be made.[5] Contemporary with this debate about the necessity of confession to the priest is a controversy about the severity of penances. The two disputes were, of course, closely linked. Abelard, Robert of Flamborough, Alan of Lille, and others all complained

3. There is a concise survey of this development in Oscar D. Watkins, *A History of Penance*, 2:735–749.

4. See Joseph de Ghellinck, *Le mouvement théologique de XIIe siècle*, for an analysis of this complex development. There is also a survey in Thomas N. Tentler, *Sin and Confession on the Eve of the Reformation*, pp. 3–27.

5. Gratian's *Decretum* is edited by Emil Albert Friedberg, *Corpus Iuris Canonici*, vol. 1 (Leipzig, 1879). See also Peter Lombard, *Quatuor Libri Sententiarum*, 2 vols. (Quaracchi, 1916).

that some priests gave penances so mild that forgiveness could not flow from them.[6] Obviously a matter as vital as atonement for sin could not be left to the care of easily corrupted priests. It was because confessors had become lax that the necessity of oral confession itself came into question.

Abelard's role in this dispute is especially important to the difference between early and late medieval penitential customs. More clearly than any other theologian, he formulated a concept of sin dependent on interior rather than exterior conditions. He separated a sin from an evil action on the basis of the sinner's intention in sinning; he thus made it possible for one to do an evil deed without sinning. Logically, then, he could define "fruitful repentance" as "sorrow and contrition of mind" which proceeded "from love of God, whom we consider to be so kind, rather than from fear of punishments."[7] Abelard was seeking to prove that forgiveness depended not on the power of the keys, which Christ had given to the apostles, but on the sinner's interior disposition. He maintained that priests could merely "declare" whether a sin had or had not been forgiven, and that God alone could know if the sinner was genuinely contrite—if his contrition stemmed from love rather than from fear.[8]

Given these arguments, it is not surprising that Abelard should be identified as an "abolitionist" of the old penitential system and the enemy of much seen in the early handbooks, especially their reliance on the priest's judgment. But as Luscombe has shown, much in Abelard's penitential teaching is in fact deeply traditional. It is especially important that he recommended the use of handbooks of the

6. For a general overview and references, see Tentler, *Sin*, pp. 17–18.

7. *Peter Abelard's "Ethics,"* ed. and trans. D. E. Luscombe, Oxford Medieval Texts (Oxford, 1971; repr. ed., 1979): "Et haec quidem reuera fructuosa est penitentia peccati, cum hic dolor atque contritio animi ex amore Dei, quem tam benignum adtendimus, potius quam ex timore penarum procedit" (p. 88). Abelard's influence is studied by Luscombe, *The School of Peter Abelard*, Cambridge Studies in Medieval Life and Thought, vol. 14 (Cambridge, 1969).

8. See the section of the *Ethics* entitled, "That sometimes confession may be dispensed with," in Luscombe, *Ethics*, pp. 100–111. Abelard maintained that the power of the keys was given to the apostles only, and that it was not passed on to bishops and priests.

older, more severe kind, to combat the proneness of confessors to error and corruption.[9] When we understand the balance of Abelard's approach to penance, we may begin to distrust interpretations which show him to be a reformer, an "abolitionist," or a reviser of the older system. But Abelard's importance rests only partly on his penitential teaching. His chief significance for the history of ideas is not that he defined sin in terms of the sinner's intention, but that his concern for intention seems linked to the renewed interest in interiority which marks the twelfth century. This "concern about inner attitudes"[10] is, we are told, new in the age of Abelard. Recent studies have claimed that before this time "mentally and physically human life had narrow limits,"[11] that men of the early Middle Ages were unaware of the importance of interiority in assessing the individual's morality,[12] that "there was no interest in probing the mind of the sinner and obtaining interior repentance."[13]

These are rather severe charges. Rereading them after one has become acquainted with the early Irish and English penitentials, one must conclude that the charges are unfounded, or at least exaggerated. We have seen that many early penitentials, including the earliest written in Ireland, specifically require the priest to probe the penitent's sincerity and to make sure that his sorrow for his sins is genuine. The evidence of the early handbooks has been overlooked because it does not conform to the harshness which we traditionally associate with early medieval piety. A closer examination of the evidence will show that just as the later Middle Ages continued to make use of early handbooks—a Norman manual for priests from the twelfth century requires the use of a penitential by Bede or The-

9. See Luscombe's comments on the *Ethics* in *Peter Abelard*, ed. E. M. Buytaert, Proceedings of the International Conference at Louvain, Mediaevalia Lovaniensia, vol. 1: 2 (Leuven, 1974), pp. 73–84.

10. Colin Morris, *The Discovery of the Individual 1050–1200*, p. 73 (confession is here treated in the chapter "The Search for the Self"). See also John F. Benton, "Consciousness of Self and of 'Personality' in the Renaissance of the Twelfth Century," and M.-D. Chenu, *L'éveil de la conscience dans la civilisation médiévale*, pp. 22–24, where Abelard is seen as the "first modern man."

11. R. W. Southern, *Medieval Humanism*, p. 32.

12. Morris, *Discovery*, p. 73; see also Morris, "A Critique of Popular Religion," p. 60.

13. Charles M. Radding, "Evolution of Medieval Mentalities," p. 588.

odore[14]—the early Middle Ages manifested a concern with interiority which became more pronounced in the twelfth century.

If we compare devotional materials known in the later period with those of the period studied here, we will see a clear but limited continuity. Unquestionably the later period was richer in imaginative and contemplative texts concerned with penance. Confession required the penitent to examine his conscience, to study his behavior, and to search out and resist his own weaknesses. In the thirteenth century we find manuals for contemplatives which traced these objectives and so, by their inward-looking intensity, enriched the literature of penance. As the author of the *Ancrene Riwle* stated, all that an anchorite suffered was to be thought of as penance, and the most perfect contemplative life was to be achieved by willingly hanging on Christ's cross and turning those sufferings into joy.[15] In the voices of the Middle English mystics, we may hear a faint echo of the Old English confessional prayers, a few of which center on the Passion, and perhaps of *The Dream of the Rood*. But the Middle English texts speak out of a new sensibility and a new spirituality, hinted at in Anselm's prayers, themselves based on the Old English prayers and some of those in *The Book of Cerne*.[16]

These devotional and didactic texts helped to make the images and acts associated with penitential practice more familiar. At the same time, the church's efforts to educate the laity made the faithful better acquainted with confession and the preparation for it. These and other developments made it possible for confession and penance to assume new prominence in the narrative literature of the Middle English period. A well-known example is found in *Sir Gawain and the Green Knight*, where we see a confession undertaken as a perfunctory social gesture of no consequence to the penitent's subsequent behavior and a confession which flows from Gawain's deep sense of

---

14. Pierre Michaud-Quantin, "Un manuel de confession archaïque dans le manuscrit Avranches 136," *Sacris Erudiri* 17 (1966): 5–54. Later confessional manuals are studied by Michaud-Quantin, *Sommes de casuistique et manuels de confession au moyen âge (XII–XVI siècles)*, Analecta Mediaevalia Namurcensia, vol. 13 (Louvain, 1962).

15. Ed. Mabel Day, *The English Text of the "Ancrene Riwle,"* pp. 157–160.

16. See Thomas Bestul, "St. Anselm and the Continuity of Anglo-Saxon Devotional Traditions."

his own wrongdoing and his resolve to amend his ways.[17] We glimpse a confessor of dubious integrity in *Confessio Amantis* when Amans seeks counsel from Genius, a priest more inclined to serve Venus than the church.[18] No one tapped the richness of confession and penance more skillfully than Chaucer, and no one looked more critically at the system than Langland. The freedom of artistic scrutiny which informs so many references to confession and penance in fourteenth-century literature was unknown three centuries earlier.[19]

More directly than narrative poetry, handbooks for spiritual guidance in the Middle English period taught in detail both the logic and the procedure of penance and confession. These manuals were part of the catechetical literature spawned by the Lateran Council's decree. In addition to new manuals for the priest, the thirteenth and fourteenth centuries produced handbooks explicitly for lay people. These small treatises helped them to examine their conscience before confession, taught them the text of important prayers, and sometimes educated them by means of *exempla*. Like the narrative poems, but more serious in purpose, these manuals required the reader's imaginative participation. Some were very traditional. *The Book of Vices and Virtues*, which was written for priests to use in teaching the laity, advised that a Christian would learn to hate sin if he would "forget his body once a day," seek hell with his mind, and spur his own repentance by envisaging the sorrow of unforgiven sinners.[20] The objective of this text hardly differs from that of *Christ III, Soul and Body*, or various other Old English poems.

Other didactic texts broke new ground. *Handlyng Synne* (1303), for example, a manual written for lay people, illustrates each of the Ten Commandments with *exempla* and so supplements its teaching with samples of the vices and virtues in action. The manual explains

17. See Michael J. Foley, "Gawain's Two Confessions Reconsidered," *Chaucer Review* 9 (1974): 73–79.

18. See comments on the identity of Genius by Russell A. Peck, ed., *Confessio Amantis*, pp. xiv–xv, and Denis N. Baker, "The Priesthood of Genius: A Study of the Medieval Tradition," *Speculum* 51 (1976): 277–291.

19. See H. G. Pfander, "Some Medieval Manuals of Religious Instruction in England and Observations on Chaucer's *Parson's Tale*."

20. *The Book of Vices and Virtues*, ed. W. Nelson Francis, p. 71.

that it is for "handlying with honde": since we handle the foulness of sin every day, we should permit another "handlying" with "shryfte of mouþe to clense."[21] The last of its stories describes the shriving of the devil, who, wishing to be transformed through confession into a creature of brightness and beauty, thinks he can confess his sins without repenting. After his "fals shryving," he is sent away still "blak and foule." His confessor explains that spiritual beauty comes not from mouthing the words of confession, but from "gode repentaunce."[22] It was only one of hundreds of ways in which fourteenth-century Christians were told that the forgiveness of their sins hinged on their inner disposition, not on formal observance of religious rituals.[23]

The teaching was traditional; its form, at least in the Anglo-Saxon perspective, was not. Most Middle English penitential literature was written for and about the sinner himself, and that is its chief distinction from Old English prose and poetry about confession and penance. Old English handbooks were written for bishops and their priests, the keepers of the keys which Christ gave to the apostles. Old English literature which united with the penitentials in the service of disciplinary and catechetical ideals seems to express a single guiding principle, formulated here by Gregory: "The word of admonition is a key, for it unlocks and opens the sins which he who committed it was not aware of."[24] It was the lasting innovation of the Middle English period to shape the keys of admonition, the keys to the Kingdom, into poems, prayers, catechisms, and even pageants about penance and to place them, in those forms, within every man's reach.

In the later period confession and penance were easily assimilated into a literature which explored—as Old English poetry and prose almost never did—the experience of sin and the resolution of guilt through confession. In Anglo-Saxon England confession and penance were rarely referred to without exhortation. Poets, like the homilists, chose to write and speak as if Christianity were still a reli-

21. *Handlyng Synne*, ed. Frederick J. Furnivall, p. 4.

22. *Ibid.*, p. 395.

23. Middle English instructional literature has been catalogued by P. S. Jolliffe, *A Check-List of Middle English Prose Writings of Spiritual Guidance*.

24. *King Alfred's West-Saxon Version of Gregory's Pastoral Care*, ed. Henry Sweet, 1:90.

gion in its first flowering and as if no opportunity to reinforce faith in unstable hearts could be neglected. The interior problems of the spiritual life were explored in a literature that was chiefly monastic—oblique, subtle, thoughtful. That was the milieu of the elaborate confessional prayers. Literature of a less personal and sophisticated kind addressed a wider audience for whom the problems of the moral life were posed in simple and clearly contrasting patterns. By envisioning the end of life in either the glories of heaven or the horrors of hell, eschatological poems sought to shape the attitudes and ultimately the behavior of their audiences. Penitential literature in Middle English, more elegantly imagined, more varied, more engaging to modern readers, is without this compelling moral preoccupation. The earlier literature loses little in the comparison, for it speaks with an urgency which commands attention and a moral certitude which commands respect.

Bibliography

Ælfric. For editions, see Godden, Pope, Skeat, and Thorpe.

Albers, Bruno. "Wann sind die Beda-Egbert'schen Bussbücher verfasst worden, und wer ist ihr Verfasser?" *Archiv für katholisches Kirchenrecht* 81 (1901): 393–420.

Anciaux, Paul. *La théologie du sacrement de pénitence au XIIe siècle.* Louvain and Gembloux, 1949.

Ancient Laws of Ireland. 6 vols. Rolls Series. Dublin, London, 1865–1901.

Anderson, A. O., and M. O. Anderson, eds. and trans. *Adomnan's Life of St. Columba.* London, 1961.

Andrieu, Michel, ed. *Les "Ordines Romani" de haut moyen âge.* 5 vols. Spicilegium Sacrum Lovaniense, Etudes et Documents. Louvain, 1931–1961.

Arnould, E. J. *Le manuel des péchés: étude de littérature anglo-normande.* Paris, 1940.

Aronstam, Robin Ann. "Penitential Pilgrimages to Rome in the Early Middle Ages." *Archivum Historiae Pontificae* 13 (1975): 65–83.

———, ed. "The Latin Canonical Tradition in Late Anglo-Saxon England: The *Excerptiones Egberti.*" Ph. D. dissertation, Columbia University, 1974.

Asbach, Franz Bernd, ed. *Das Poenitentiale Remense und der sogen. Excarpsus Cummeani.* Regensburg, 1975.

Assmann, Bruno, ed. *Angelsächsische Homilien und Heiligenleben.* BAP, vol. 3. Repr. ed., with an introduction by Peter Clemoes, Darmstadt, 1964.

Attenborough, F. L., ed. and trans. *The Laws of the Earliest English Kings.* Cambridge, 1922.

Banks, R. A. "Some Anglo-Saxon Prayers from British Museum MS. Cotton Galba A. xiv." *N&Q* 210 (1965): 207–213.

Barlow, Frank. *The English Church 1000–1060: A Constitutional History*. Hamden, Conn., 1963.

———, et al. *Leofric of Exeter: Essays in Commemoration of the Foundation of Exeter Cathedral Library in A.D. 1072*. Exeter, 1972.

Bateson, Mary. "Rules for Monks and Secular Canons after the Revival under King Edgar." *EHR* 9 (1894): 690–708.

———. "A Worcester Cathedral Book of Ecclesiastical Collections, Made ca. 1000 A.D." *EHR* 10 (1895): 712–731.

Beck, Henry G. J. *The Pastoral Care of Souls in South-East France during the Sixth Century*. Analecta Gregoriana, vol. 51. Rome, 1950.

Belfour, A. O., ed. *Twelfth-Century Homilies in MS Bodley 343*. Part 1: Text and Translation. EETS, o.s. 137. London, 1909.

Benson, Robert L., and Giles Constable, eds. *The Renaissance of the Twelfth Century*. Cambridge, Mass., in press.

Benton, John F. "Consciousness of Self and of 'Personality' in the Renaissance of the Twelfth Century." In *The Renaissance of the Twelfth Century*, edited by Benson and Constable. Cambridge, Mass., in press.

Berggren, Erik. *The Psychology of Confession*. Studies in the History of Religions, vol. 29. Leiden, 1975.

Best, R. I., and Rudolf Thurneysen. *Ancient Laws of Ireland*. Irish Manuscripts Commission Facsimile in Collotype of Irish Manuscripts. Dublin, 1931.

Bestul, Thomas H. "St. Anselm and the Continuity of Anglo-Saxon Devotional Traditions." *Annuale Mediaevale* 18 (1977): 20–41.

Bethurum, Dorothy. "Archbishop Wulfstan's Commonplace Book." *PMLA* 57 (1942): 916–929.

———. "A Letter of Protest from the English Bishops to the Pope." In *Philologica: The Malone Anniversary Studies*, edited by Thomas A. Kirby and Henry Bosley Woolf, pp. 97–104. Baltimore, 1949.

———. "Wulfstan." In *Continuations and Beginnings: Studies in Old English Literature*, edited by Eric Gerald Stanley, pp. 210–246. London, 1966.

———, ed. *The Homilies of Wulfstan*. Oxford, 1957.

Bieler, Ludwig. "The Irish Penitentials: Their Religious and Social Background." *Studia Patristica* 8 (1966): 329–339.

———, ed. and trans. *The Irish Penitentials*. Scriptores Latini Hiberniae, vol. 5. Dublin, 1963.

————, and James Carney, eds. "The Lambeth Commentary." *Ériu* 23 (1972): 1–55.

Binchy, D. A. "The Linguistic and Historical Value of the Irish Law Tracts." *Proceedings of the British Academy* 29 (1943): 195–227.

————. "The Pseudo-Historical Prologue to the *Senchas Már.*" *Studia Celtica* 10/11 (1975–1976): 15–28.

————. "St. Patrick's 'First Synod.'" *Studia Hibernica* 8 (1968): 49–59.

————. "A Text on the Forms of Distraint." *Celtica* 10 (1973): 72–86.

————, ed. *Corpus Iuris Hibernici.* 6 vols. Dublin, 1978.

————, ed. *Críth Gablach.* Mediaeval and Modern Irish Series, vol. 11. Dublin, 1970.

————, ed. "The Old-Irish Table of Penitential Commutations." *Ériu* 19 (1962): 47–72.

————, trans. "Penitential Texts in Old Irish: Translation." In *The Irish Penitentials,* edited by Ludwig Bieler, pp. 258–283. Dublin, 1963.

Birch, Walter de Gray, ed. *An Ancient Manuscript of the Eighth or Ninth Century; Formerly Belonging to St. Mary's Abbey, or Nunnaminster, Winchester.* London, 1889.

Bischoff, Bernhard. *Lorsch im Spiegel seiner Handschriften.* Münchener Beiträge zur Mediävistik und Renaissance-Forschung. Munich, 1974.

————. *Mittelalterliche Studien.* 2 vols. Stuttgart, 1966–1967.

————. "Turning-Points in the History of Latin Exegesis in the Early Middle Ages." In *Biblical Studies: The Medieval Irish Contribution,* edited by Martin McNamara, pp. 74–160. Proceedings of the Irish Bible Association, vol. 1. Dublin, 1976. (Translation by Colm O'Grady of "Wendepunkte in der Geschichte der lateinischen Exegese im Frühmittelalter." *Sacris Erudiri* 6 [1954]: 189–279.)

Bishop, Edmund. *Liturgica Historica.* Oxford, 1918; repr. ed., 1962.

Bishop, T. A. M. *English Caroline Minuscule.* Oxford, 1971.

Bliss, Alan, and Allen J. Frantzen. "The Integrity of *Resignation.*" *RES* 27 (1976): 385–402.

Bloomfield, Morton. *The Seven Deadly Sins.* East Lansing, Mich., 1952.

————. "Understanding Old English Poetry." *Annuale Mediaevale* 9 (1968): 5–25.

Bonser, Wilfred. *Anglo-Saxon and Celtic Bibliography*. 2 vols. Oxford, 1957.

Bossy, John. "The Social History of Confession in the Age of the Reformation." *Transactions of the Royal Historical Society*, 5th ser. 25 (1975): 21–38.

Boswell, John. *Christianity, Social Tolerance, and Homosexuality*. Chicago, 1980.

Bradshaw, Henry. *The Early Collection of Canons Known as the Hibernensis: Two Unfinished Papers*. Cambridge, 1893.

Brommer, Peter. "Die bischöfliche Gesetzgebung Theodulfs von Orléans." *Zeitschrift für Savigny-Stiftung für Rechtsgeschichte*, kan. Abt. 60 (1974): 1–120.

———. "Capitula episcoporum: Bemerkungen zu den bischöflichen Kapitularien." *Zeitschrift für Kirchengeschichte* 2/3 (1980): 207–236.

———. "Die Rezeption der bischöflichen Kapitularien Theodulfs von Orléans." *Zeitschrift der Savigny-Stiftung für Rechtsgeschichte*, kan. Abt. 61 (1975): 113–160.

Bromwich, Rachel. *Medieval Celtic Literature: A Select Bibliography*. Toronto Medieval Bibliographies, vol. 5. Toronto, 1974.

Brow, Louis. *The Psalter Collects*. Henry Bradshaw Society, vol. 83. London, 1949.

Bullough, Donald A. "The Educational Tradition in England from Alfred to Ælfric: Teaching *Utriusque lingua*." *Settimane* 19 (1972): 453–494.

———. "Roman Books and Carolingian Renovatio." *Studies in Church History* 14 (1977): 23–50.

Cabrol, Ferdinand, and H. Leclercq, eds. *Dictionnaire d'archéologie chrétienne et de liturgie*. 15 vols. Paris, 1907–1953.

Caie, Graham D. *The Judgment Day Theme in Old English Poetry*. Publications of the Department of English, University of Copenhagen, vol. 2. Copenhagen, 1976.

Campbell, Jackson J. "Prayers from MS. Arundel 155." *Anglia* 81 (1963): 82–118.

Campbell, James. "Observations on English Government from the Tenth to the Twelfth Century." *Transactions of the Royal Historical Society*, 5th ser. 25 (1975): 39–54.

Caraman, P. G. "The Character of the Late Saxon Clergy." *Downside Review* 63, n.s. 44 (1945): 171–189.

Carney, James. *Studies in Irish Literature and History*. Dublin, 1955.

Chadwick, Owen. *John Cassian*. Cambridge, 1969.

Chaney, William A. *The Cult of Kingship in Anglo-Saxon England*. Manchester, 1970.

Chenu, M.-D. *L'éveil de la conscience dans la civilisation médiévale*. Paris, 1969.

————. *Nature, Man, and Society in the Twelfth Century*. Edited and translated by Jerome Taylor and Lester K. Little. Chicago, 1968.

Chickering, Howell D., Jr. "Some Contexts for Bede's *Death-Song*." *PMLA* 91 (1976): 91–100.

Clemoes, Peter A. M. "The Chronology of Ælfric's Works." In *The Anglo-Saxons: Studies in Some Aspects of Their History and Culture Presented to Bruce Dickins*, edited by Peter Clemoes, pp. 212–247. London, 1959.

————. "The Old English Benedictine Office, Corpus Christi College, Cambridge, MS 190, and the Relations between Ælfric and Wulfstan: A Reconsideration." *Anglia* 78 (1960): 265–283.

————, and Kathleen Hughes, eds. *England before the Conquest: Studies in Primary Sources Presented to Dorothy Whitelock*. Cambridge, 1971.

Clercq, Carlo de. *La législation religieuse franque de Clovis à Charlemagne: etudes sur les actes des conciles et les capitulaires, les statuts diocésains et les régles monastiques*. 2 vols. Paris, 1936; Antwerp, 1958.

Coens, Maurice. "Les litanies Bavaroises du 'Libellus precum' dit de Fleury." *Analecta Bollandiana* 77 (1959): 373–391.

Colgrave, Bertram, ed. *Two Lives of St. Cuthbert*. Cambridge, 1940.

————, and R. A. B. Mynors, eds. and trans. *Bede's Ecclesiastical History of the English People*. Oxford, 1969.

Colledge, Eric. *The Mediaeval Mystics of England*. New York, 1961.

Contreni, John J. *The Cathedral School of Laon from 850 to 930: Its Manuscripts and Masters*. Münchener Beiträge zur Mediävistik und Renaissance-Forschung. Munich, 1978.

Crawford, Jane. "Evidences for Witchcraft in Anglo-Saxon England." *MÆ* 32 (1963): 99–116.

Cross, J. E. "The Literate Anglo-Saxon: On Sources and Disseminations." *Proceedings of the British Academy* 58 (1972): 67–100.

Darlington, Reginald R. "Ecclesiastical Reform in the Late Old English Period." *EHR* 51 (1936): 385–428.

Dauphin, H. "Le renouveau monastique en Angleterre au xe siècle et ses rapports avec le réforme de S. Gérard de Brogne" (with a response by Eric John). *RB* 70 (1960): 177–196.

Day, Mabel, ed. *The English Text of the "Ancrene Riwle."* EETS, o.s. 225. London, 1952.

Deanesly, Margaret. *The Pre-Conquest Church in England.* New York, 1961.

Devisse, Jean. *Hincmar, archevêque de Reims.* 3 vols. Geneva, 1976.

Dickins, Bruce, and Alan S. C. Ross, eds. *The Dream of the Rood.* London, 1934; repr. ed., 1963.

Dobbie, Elliott van Kirk, ed. *The Anglo-Saxon Minor Poems.* ASPR, vol. 6. New York, 1942; repr. ed., 1969.

Dornier, Ann, ed. *Mercian Studies.* Leicester, 1977.

Duckett, Eleanor Shipley. *Alfred the Great: The King and His England.* Chicago, 1956; repr. ed., 1975.

Dudley, Louise. "An Early Homily on the 'Body and Soul' Theme." *JEGP* 8 (1909): 225–253.

Dunning, G. C. "Trade Relations between England and the Continent in the Late Anglo-Saxon Period." In *Dark Age Britain,* edited by D. B. Harden, pp. 218–233. London, 1956.

Dunning, T. P., and A. J. Bliss, eds. *The Wanderer.* London, 1969.

Eisenhofer, Ludwig, and Joseph Lechner. *The Liturgy of the Roman Rite.* Translated by A. J. and E. F. Peeler. Freiburg, 1961.

Ellard, Gerald. *Master Alcuin, Liturgist: A Partner of Our Piety.* Chicago, 1956.

Ewig, Eugen. "Saint Chrodegang et la réforme de l'église franque." In *Saint Chrodegang,* pp. 25–54. Metz, 1967.

Farrell, Robert, ed. *Bede and Anglo-Saxon England.* British Archeological Reports, British Series, vol. 46. Oxford, 1978.

Fehr, Bernhard. "Altenglische Ritualtexte für Krankenbesuch, heilige Ölung, und Begräbnis." In *Texte und Forschungen zur englischen Kulturgeschichte: Festgabe für Felix Liebermann,* edited by Max Förster and K. Wildhagen, pp. 20–67. Halle, 1921.

———, ed. *Die Hirtenbriefe Ælfrics in altenglischer und lateinischer Fassung.* BAP, vol. 9. Repr. ed., with an introduction by Peter Clemoes, Darmstadt, 1966.

Finsterwalder, Paul Willem, ed. *Die Canones Theodori Cantuariensis und ihre Überlieferungsformen.* Weimar, 1929.

Firth, J. J. Francis, ed. *Robert of Flamborough: Liber Poenitentialis.* Toronto, 1971.

Fisher, D. J. V. "The Church in England between the Death of Bede and the Danish Invasions." *Transactions of the Royal Historical Society,* 5th ser. 2 (1952): 1–19.

Fleming, John V. "'The Dream of the Rood' and Anglo-Saxon Monasticism." *Traditio* 22 (1966): 43–72.

Fleuriot, Léon. "Le 'saint' Breton *Winniau* et le pénitentiel dit 'de Finnian'?" *Etudes Celtiques* 15 (1978): 607–614.

Flower, Robin. *The Irish Tradition.* Oxford, 1947; repr. ed., 1970.

Förster, Max. "Der Inhalt der altenglischen Handschrift Vespasianus D. xiv." *Englische Studien* 54 (1920): 46–68.

———. "Zu den AE. Texten aus MS. Arundel 155." *Anglia* 66 (1942): 52–55.

———. "Zur Liturgik der angelsächsischen Kirche." *Anglia* 66 (1942): 1–51.

———, ed. *Die Vercelli-Homilien zum ersten Male herausgegeben.* BAP, vol. 12. Repr. ed., Darmstadt, 1964.

Foucault, Michel. *The History of Sexuality, 1: An Introduction.* Translated by Robert Hurley. New York, 1978.

Fournier, Paul. "Le décret de Burchard de Worms." *Revue d'Histoire Ecclésiastique* 12 (1911): 451–473, 670–701.

———. "Etudes sur les pénitentiels." *Revue d'Histoire et de Littérature Religieuses* 6 (1901): 289–317; 7 (1902): 59–70, 121–127; 8 (1903): 528–553; 9 (1904): 97–103.

———, and G. Le Bras. *Histoire des collections canoniques en occident depuis les Fausses Décrétales jusqu'au Décret de Gratien.* 2 vols. Paris, 1931–1933.

Fowler, Roger. *Wulfstan's Canons of Edgar.* EETS, o.s. 266. London, 1972.

———, ed. "A Late Old English Handbook for the Use of a Confessor." *Anglia* 83 (1965): 1–34.

Fox, Cyril, and Bruce Dickins, eds. *The Early Cultures of North-West Europe: H. M. Chadwick Memorial Studies.* Cambridge, 1950.

Francis, W. Nelson, ed. *The Book of Vices and Virtues.* EETS, o.s. 217. London, 1942; repr. ed., 1968.

Frantzen, Allen J. "The Significance of the Frankish Penitentials." *JEH* 30 (1979): 409–421.

———. "The Tradition of Penitentials in Anglo-Saxon England." *ASE* 11 (1982): 23–56.

Furnivall, Frederick J., ed. *Handlyng Synne.* EETS, o.s. 119, 123. London, 1901, 1903; repr. ed., 1975.

Ganshof, F. L. *The Carolingians and the Frankish Monarchy.* Translated by Janet Sondheimer. London, 1971.

———. *Frankish Institutions under Charlemagne.* Translated by Bryce and Mary Lyon. New York, 1970.

Gasquet, F. A., and Edmund Bishop, eds. *The Bosworth Psalter.*
London, 1908.
Gatch, Milton McC. "Eschatology in the Anonymous Old English
Homilies." *Traditio* 21 (1965): 117–165.
———. *Loyalties and Traditions.* New York, 1971.
———. *Preaching and Theology in Anglo-Saxon England: Ælfric and
Wulfstan.* Toronto, 1977.
Gaudemet, Jean. "Les statuts épiscopaux de la première décade du
ixe siècle." In *Proceedings of the Fourth International Congress on
Medieval Canon Law,* edited by Stephan Kuttner, pp. 303–349.
Monumenta Iuris Canonica, vol. 5. Vatican City, 1976.
Ghellinck, Joseph de. *Le mouvement théologique du xiie siècle.* 2d ed.
Museum Lessianum, Section historique, vol. 10. Bruges, 1948.
Gibson, Margaret. "The Continuity of Learning, c. 850–1050." *Via-
tor* 6 (1975): 1–13.
Gneuss, Helmut. *Hymnar und Hymnen in englischen Mittelalter.*
Tübingen, 1968.
Godden, M. R. "The Development of Ælfric's Second Series of
Catholic Homilies." *ES* 54 (1973): 209–216.
———. "An Old English Penitential Motif." *ASE* 2 (1973): 221–239.
———, ed. *Ælfric's Catholic Homilies: The Second Series (Text).*
EETS, s.s. 5. London, 1979.
Godel, Willibrord. "Irisches Beten im frühen Mittelalter." *Zeitschrift
für katholische Theologie* 85 (1963): 261–321, 390–439.
Gordon, Eric V., ed. *The Battle of Maldon.* London, 1937; repr. ed.,
with supplement by D. G. Scragg, 1976.
Gordon, Ida L., ed. *The Seafarer.* London, 1960.
Gougaud, Louis. *Christianity in Celtic Lands.* Translated by Maud
Joynt. London, 1932.
———. "Les conceptions du martyre chez les Irlandais." *RB* 24
(1907): 360–373.
Green, D. H. *The Carolingian Lord.* Cambridge, 1955.
Gretsch, Mechthild, ed. *Die Regula Sancti Benedicti in England.*
Texte und Untersuchungen zur englischen Philologie, vol. 2.
Munich, 1973.
Grierson, Philip. "Grimbald of St. Bertins," *EHR* 55 (1940):
529–561.
———. "The Relations between England and Flanders before the
Norman Conquest." *Transactions of the Royal Historical Society,*
4th ser. 23 (1941): 71–112.
Gwynn, E. J., ed. "An Irish Penitential." *Ériu* 7 (1914): 121–195.

————, and W. J. Purton, eds. "The Monastery of Tallaght." *Proceedings of the Royal Irish Academy* 29 (1912): 115–179.

Haddan, Arthur West, and William Stubbs, eds. *Councils and Ecclesiastical Documents Relating to Great Britain and Ireland.* 3 vols. Oxford, 1869–1873.

Haimerl, Franz Xaver. "Mittelalterliche Frömmigkeit im Spiegel der Gebetbuchliterature Süddeutschlands." *Münchener theologische Studien*, hist. Abt., vol. 4. Munich, 1952.

Hallander, Lars-G., ed. "Two Old English Confessional Prayers." *Stockholm Studies in Modern Philology*, n.s. 3 (1968): 87–110.

Hammer, Carl I., Jr. "Country Churches, Clerical Inventories, and the Carolingian Renaissance in Bavaria." *Church History* 49 (1980): 5–17.

Hanssens, Ioanne Michaele, ed. *Amalarii Episcopi Opera Liturgica Omnia.* 3 vols. Studi e Testi, vols. 138–140. Vatican City, 1948–1950.

Harden, D. B., ed. *Dark-Age Britain: Studies Presented to E. T. Leeds.* London, 1956.

Hardinge, Leslie. *The Celtic Church in Britain.* London, 1972.

Hartmann, Wilfried. *Das Konzil von Worms 868: Überlieferung und Bedeutung.* Abhandlungen der Akademie der Wissenschaften in Göttingen, philologische-historische Klasse, dritte Folge, vol. 105. Göttingen, 1977.

Hautkappe, F. *Über die altdeutschen Beichten und ihre Beziehungen zu Cäsarius von Arles.* Münster, 1917.

Henry, P. L. *The Early English and Celtic Lyric.* London, 1966.

Hillgarth, J. N. "The East, Visigothic Spain and the Irish." *Studia Patristica* 4 (1961): 442–456.

————. "Visigothic Spain and Early Christian Ireland." *Proceedings of the Royal Irish Academy* 62 (1962): 167–194.

Holthausen, Ferdinand. "Altenglische Interlinearversionen lateinischer Gebete und Beichten." *Anglia* 65 (1941): 230–254.

Hörmann, W. von. "Bussbücherstudien: Das sog. 'Poenitentiale Martenianum.'" *Zeitschrift der Savigny-Stiftung für Rechtsgeschichte*, kan. Abt. 1 (1911): 194–250; 2 (1912): 111–181; 3 (1913): 413–492; 4 (1914): 358–483, 610.

Hughes, Kathleen. "The Changing Theory and Practice of Irish Pilgrimage." *JEH* 11 (1960): 143–151.

————. *The Church in Early Irish Society.* London, 1966.

————. *Early Christian Ireland: Introduction to the Sources.* London, 1972.

———. "Some Aspects of Irish Influence on Early English Private Prayer." *Studia Celtica* 5 (1970): 48–61.

Hull, Vernon, ed. "*Abgitar Chrábaid*: The Alphabet of Piety." *Celtica* 8 (1968): 44–89.

John, Eric. *Orbis Britanniae and Other Studies*. Studies in Early English History, vol. 4. Leicester, 1966.

———. "The Sources of the English Monastic Reformation: A Comment." *RB* 70 (1960): 197–203.

Jolliffe, P. S. *A Check-List of Middle English Prose Writings of Spiritual Guidance*. Subsidia Mediaevalia, vol. 2. Toronto, 1974.

Joret, F.-D. *Aux sources de l'eau vive*. Paris, 1928. (Translated as *The Eucharist and the Confessional*. London, 1955.)

Jost, Karl, ed. *Die "Institutes of Polity, Civil and Ecclesiastical": Ein Werk Erzbischof Wulfstans von York*. Swiss Studies in English, vol. 47. Bern, 1959.

Jungmann, Josef A. *The Early Liturgy to the Time of Gregory the Great*. Translated by F. A. Brunner. London, 1960.

———. *Die lateinischen Bussriten in ihrer geschichtlichen Entwicklung*. Innsbruck, 1932.

Kanner, Barbara, ed. *The Women of England from Anglo-Saxon Times to the Present*. Hamden, Conn., 1979.

Kenney, James F. *The Sources for the Early History of Ireland, 1: Ecclesiastical*. New York, 1929; repr. ed., with revisions by Ludwig Bieler, 1966.

Ker, N. R. *Catalogue of Manuscripts Containing Anglo-Saxon*. Oxford, 1957.

———. *Medieval Libraries of Great Britain: A List of Surviving Books*. 2d ed. Royal Historical Society Guides and Handbooks, vol. 3. London, 1964.

———. "Three Old English Texts in a Salisbury Pontifical, Cotton Tiberius C.i." In *The Anglo-Saxons: Studies in Some Aspects of Their History and Culture Presented to Bruce Dickins*, edited by Peter Clemoes, pp. 262–278. London, 1959.

Kerff, Franz, ed. "Der *Quadripartitus*: Überlieferung, Quellen, und Bedeutung." Ph.D. dissertation, Rheinisch-Westfälische Technische Hochschule, 1979.

Kirby, D. P. *The Making of Early England*. London, 1967.

Kirby, Thomas A., and Henry Bosley Woolf, eds. *Philologica: The Malone Anniversary Studies*. Baltimore, 1949.

Kleinclausz, Authur. *Alcuin*. Annales de l'Université de Lyon, 3d ser., vol. 15. Paris, 1948.

Knowles, David M. *The Monastic Order in England: A History of Its Development from the Times of St. Dunstan to the Fourth Lateran Council: 940–1216.* 2d ed. Cambridge, 1966.

Kottje, Raymund. *Die Bussbücher Halitgars von Cambrai und des Hrabanus Maurus: Ihre Überlieferung und ihre Quellen.* Beiträge zur Geschichte und Quellenkunde des Mittelalters, vol. 8. Berlin, 1980.

————. "Einheit und Vielfalt des kirchlichen Lebens in der Karolingerzeit." *Zeitschrift für Kirchengeschichte* 76 (1965): 323–342.

————. "Kirchenrechtliche Interessen im Bodenseeraum vom 9. bis 12. Jahrhundert." In *Kirchenrechtliche Texte im Bodenseegebiet,* edited by J. Autenrieth and R. Kottje, pp. 23–41. Vorträge und Forschungen, vol. 18. Sigmaringen, 1975.

Krapp, George Philip, ed. *The Vercelli Book.* ASPR, vol. 2. New York, 1932; repr. ed., 1969.

————, and Elliott van Kirk Dobbie, eds. *The Exeter Book.* ASPR, vol. 3. New York, 1936; repr. ed., 1966.

Kuypers, A. B., ed. *The Prayer Book of Aedelauld the Bishop Commonly Called the Book of Cerne.* Cambridge, 1902.

Laeuchli, Samuel. *Power and Sexuality.* Philadelphia, 1972.

Laistner, M. L. W. *Thought and Letters in Western Europe, A.D. 500–900.* Rev. ed. Ithaca, 1957.

————. "Was Bede the Author of a Penitential?" In *The Intellectual Heritage of the Early Middle Ages,* edited by Chester G. Starr, pp. 165–177. Ithaca, 1957.

Laporte, Jean, ed. *Le pénitentiel de Saint Columban: introduction et édition critique.* Tournai, 1958.

Lauer, P., ed. and trans. *Nithard: histoire des fils de Louis le Pieux.* Paris, 1926.

Le Bras, G. "Iudicia Theodori." *Revue Historique de Droit Français et Étranger,* 4th ser. 10 (1931): 95–115.

Lea, Henry Charles. *A History of Auricular Confession and Indulgences in the Latin Church.* 3 vols. Philadelphia, 1896.

Levison, Wilhelm. *England and the Continent in the Eighth Century.* Oxford, 1946.

Liebermann, Felix, ed. *Die Gesetze der Angelsachsen.* 3 vols. Halle, 1903–1916.

Little, Lester K. "Les techniques de la confession et la confession comme technique." In *Faire Croire: Modalités de la diffusion et de la réception des messages religieux du XIIe au XVe siècle,* pp. 87–99. Collection de l'école Française de Rome, vol. 51. Rome, 1981.

Logeman, Henri, ed. "Anglo-Saxon Minora." *Anglia* II (1889): 97–120; *Anglia* 12 (1889): 497–518.

Lowe, E. A., ed. *The Bobbio Missal: A Gallican Mass-Book.* Henry Bradshaw Society, vol. 58. London, 1920.

———, ed. *Codices Latini Antiquiores.* II vols., with Supplement. Oxford, 1934–1971.

Loyn, H. R. *Anglo-Saxon England and the Norman Conquest.* London, 1962.

———, ed. *A Wulfstan Manuscript Containing Institutes, Laws, and Homilies: British Museum Cotton Nero A. I.* Early English Manuscripts in Facsimile, vol. 17. Copenhagen, 1971.

Lyonnet, Stanislas, and Leopold Sabourin. *Sin, Redemption, and Sacrifice: A Biblical and Patristic Study.* Analecta Biblica, vol. 48. Rome, 1970.

McKitterick, Rosamond. *The Frankish Church and the Carolingian Reforms, 789–895.* London, 1977.

McNally, Robert E. "The Evangelists in the Hiberno-Latin Tradition." In *Festschrift Bernhard Bischoff,* pp. 111–122. Stuttgart, 1971.

Mac Neill, Eoin. *Early Irish Laws and Institutions.* Dublin, 1934.

McNeill, John T. *The Celtic Penitentials and Their Influence on Continental Christianity.* Paris, 1923. (Also published in *Revue Celtique* 39 [1922]: 257–300; 40 [1923]: 51–103, 320–341.)

———. "Folk-Paganism in the Penitentials." *Journal of Religion* 13 (1933): 450–466.

———. *A History of the Cure of Souls.* New York, 1951.

———. "Medicine for Sin as Prescribed in the Penitentials." *Church History* 1 (1932): 14–26.

———, and Helena M. Gamer. *Medieval Handbooks of Penance.* New York, 1938; repr. ed., 1965.

Mac Niocaill, Gearóid. *Ireland before the Vikings.* The Gill History of Ireland, vol. 1. Dublin, 1972.

Malnory, A. *Saint Césaire, évêque d'Arles.* Paris, 1894.

Mansi, Giovanni Domenico, ed. *Sacrorum Conciliorum, Nova et Amplissima Collectio.* 31 vols. Florence, 1759–1798.

Mayr-Harting, Henry. *The Coming of Christianity to England.* New York, 1972.

Menner, Robert J. "The Anglian Vocabulary of *The Blickling Homilies.*" In *Philologica: The Malone Anniversary Studies,* edited by Thomas A. Kirby and Henry Bosley Woolf, pp. 56–64. Baltimore, 1949.

Meyer, H. B. "Alkuin zwischen Antike und Mittelalter: Ein Kapitel frühmittelalterliche Frömmigkeitgeschichte." *Zeitschrift für katholische Theologie* 81 (1959): 306–350, 405–454.

Mirgeler, Arthur. *Mutations of Western Christianity.* Translated by Edward Quinn. London, 1964.

Mitchell, Gerard. "The Origins of Irish Penance." *Irish Theological Quarterly* 22 (1955): 1–14.

———. "St. Columbanus on Penance." *Irish Theological Quarterly* 18 (1951): 43–54.

Mordek, Hubert. "Kanonistische Aktivität in Gallen in der ersten Hälfte des 8. Jahrhunderts." *Francia* 2 (1974): 19–25.

———, ed. *Kirchenrecht und Reform im Frankenreich: Die Collectio Vetus Gallica.* Beiträge zur Geschichte und Quellenkunde des Mittelalters, vol. 1. Berlin, 1975.

Morris, Colin. "A Critique of Popular Religion: Guibert of Nogent on *The Relics of the Saints.*" In *Studies in Church History* 8 (1972): 55–60.

———. *The Discovery of the Individual 1050–1200.* New York, 1972.

Morris, Richard, ed. *The Blickling Homilies.* EETS, o.s. 58, 63, 73. London, 1874–1880; repr. ed., 1967.

Mortimer, Robert Cecil. *The Origins of Private Penance in the Western Church.* Oxford, 1939.

Murphy, Gerard, ed. and trans. *Early Irish Lyrics.* Oxford, 1956; repr. ed., 1970.

Napier, Arthur S. *The Old English Version of the Enlarged Rule of Chrodegang; An Old English Version of the Capitula of Theodulf; An Interlinear Old English Rendering of the Epitome of Benedict of Aniane.* EETS, o.s. 150. London, 1916; repr. ed., 1971.

Nelson, Janet. "On the Limits of the Carolingian Renaissance." *Studies in Church History* 14 (1977): 51–69.

Noonan, John T. *Contraception: A History of Its Treatment by the Catholic Theologians and Canonists.* Cambridge, Mass., 1965.

Oakley, Thomas P. "Celtic Penance: Its Sources, Affiliations, and Influence." *Irish Ecclesiastical Review* 52 (1938): 198–264, 589–601.

———. "The Cooperation of Medieval Penance and Secular Law." *Speculum* 7 (1932): 515–524.

———. "Cultural Affiliations of Early Ireland in the Penitentials." *Speculum* 8 (1933): 489–500.

———. *English Penitential Discipline and Anglo-Saxon Law in Their Joint Influence.* New York, 1923; repr. ed., 1969.

———. "The Origins of Irish Penitential Discipline." *Catholic Historical Review* 19 (1933–1934): 320–332.

———. "The Penitentials as Sources for Medieval History." *Speculum* 15 (1940): 210–223.

———. "Some Neglected Aspects of the History of Penance." *Catholic Historical Review* 24 (1938): 293–309.

O'Neill, Patrick. "The Background to the *Cambrai Homily*." *Ériu* 32 (1981): 137–147.

———. "A Middle Irish Poem on the Maledictory Psalms." *Journal of Celtic Studies* 3 (1981): 40–58.

Paetow, Louis J., ed. *Sacraments and Forgiveness: History and Doctrinal Development of Penance, Extreme Unction, and Indulgences.* Sources of Christian Theology, vol. 2. London, 1959.

Parsons, David, ed. *Tenth-Century Studies: Essays in Commemoration of the Millennium of the Council of Winchester and "Regularis Concordia."* London, 1975.

Payen, J.-C. *Le motif du repentir dans la littérature française médiévale (des origines à 1230).* Publications romanes et françaises, vol. 98. Gênes, 1967.

Peck, Russell, ed. *Confessio Amantis.* New York, 1968.

Pettazzoni, R. *La confession des péchés.* Translated by R. Mannot. 2 vols. Paris, 1931–1932.

———. "Confession of Sins in the Classics." *Harvard Theological Review* 30 (1937): 1–14.

Pfander, H. G. "Some Medieval Manuals of Religious Instruction in England and Observations on Chaucer's *Parson's Tale*." *JEGP* 35 (1936): 243–258.

Pierce, Rosamond. "The 'Frankish' Penitentials." *Studies in Church History* 11 (1975): 31–39.

Plummer, Charles, ed. *Venerabilis Baedae Opera Historica.* 2 vols. Oxford, 1896; repr. ed., 1966.

———, ed. *Vitae Sanctorum Hiberniae.* 2 vols. Oxford, 1910; repr. ed., 1968.

———, ed. and trans. *Bethada Náem nÉrenn.* 2 vols. Oxford, 1922; repr. ed., 1969.

Pollock, F., and F. W. Maitland. *The History of English Law before the Time of Edward I.* 2d ed. 2 vols. Cambridge, 1968.

Pope, John C., ed. *Homilies of Ælfric: A Supplementary Collection.* 2 vols. EETS, o.s. 259, 260. London, 1967–1968.

Porter, H. B. "The Rites for the Dying in the Early Middle Ages, 1: Theodulf of Orléans." *JTS* 10 (1959): 43–62.

Poschmann, Bernhard. *Die abendländische Kirchenbusse im Ausgang des christlichen Altertums*. Munich, 1928.

———. *Die abendländische Kirchenbusse im frühen Mittelalter*. Breslauer Studien zur historischen Theologie, vol. 16. Breslau, 1930.

———. *Der Ablass im Licht der Bussgeschichte*. Theophaneia, vol. 4. Bonn, 1948.

———. *Penance and the Anointing of the Sick*. Translated and revised by Francis Courtney. Freiburg, 1964.

Prinz, Friedrich. *Frühes Mönchtum im Frankenreich*. Munich, 1965.

———. "Monastische Zentren im Frankenreich." *Studi Medievali* 19 (1978): 571–590.

Radding, Charles M. "Evolution of Medieval Mentalities: A Cognitive-Structural Approach." *American Historical Review* 83 (1978): 577–597.

Raith, Josef. *Die altenglische Version des Halitgar'schen Bussbuches (sog. Poenitentiale Pseudo-Ecgberti)*. BAP, vol. 13. Repr. ed., with a new introduction, Darmstadt, 1964.

Rand, E. K., and L. W. Jones. *The Earliest Books of Tours*. Studies in the Script of Tours, vol. 2. Cambridge, Mass., 1934.

Rice, Robert C. "The Penitential Motif in Cynewulf's *Fates of the Apostles* and in his Epilogues." *ASE* 6 (1977): 105–119.

———. "Soul's Need: A Critical Study of the Penitential Motif in Old English Poetry." Ph.D. dissertation, University of Oregon, 1974.

Riché, Pierre. *Education and Culture in the Barbarian West*. Translated by John J. Contreni. Columbia, S.C., 1978.

———. *La vie quotidienne dans l'empire carolingien*. Paris, 1973. (Translated as *Daily Life in the World of Charlemagne*, by Jo Ann McNamara. Philadelphia, 1978.)

Robertson, D. W., Jr. "The Cultural Tradition of *Handlyng Synne*." *Speculum* 22 (1947): 162–185.

———. "A Note on the Classical Origin of 'Circumstances' in the Medieval Confessional." *SP* 43 (1946): 6–14.

Robinson, J. Armitage. *The Times of Saint Dunstan*. Oxford, 1923; repr. ed., 1969.

Rochais, H. M. "*Liber de Virtutibus et Vitiis* d'Alcuin." *Revue Mabillon* 4 (1951): 77–86.

Ryan, John. *Irish Monasticism: Origins and Early Development.* Dublin, 1931; repr. ed., with new bibliography, Ithaca, N.Y., 1972.

Salmon, Pierre. "Livrets de prières de l'époque carolingienne." *RB* 86 (1976): 218–234.

Sauer, Hans, ed. *Theodulfi Capitula in England.* Texte und Untersuchungen zur englischen Philologie, vol. 8. Munich, 1978.

———. "Zur Überlieferung und Anlage von Erzbischof Wulfstans 'Handbuch.'" *Deutsches Archiv für Erforschung des Mittelalters* 36 (1980): 341–384.

———. "Zwei spätaltenglische Beichtermahnungen aus Hs. Cotton Tiberius A. III." *Anglia* 98 (1980): 1–33.

Schmitz, H. J., ed. *Die Bussbücher und das kanonische Bussverfahren.* Düsseldorf, 1898; repr. ed., Graz, 1958.

———. *Die Bussbücher und die Bussdisziplin der Kirche.* Mainz, 1883; repr. ed., Graz, 1958.

Schmitz, Wilhelm, ed. *Regula Canonicorum: S. Chrodegangi Metensis Episcopi.* Hanover, 1889.

Seckel, Emil. "Zu den Akten der Triburen Synod 895." *Neues Archiv* 20 (1895): 291–353.

Sheehan, Michael M. *The Will in Medieval England.* Pontifical Institute of Mediaeval Studies, Studies and Texts, vol. 6. Toronto, 1963.

Short, D. D. "The Old English *Gifts of Men* and the Pedagogic Theory of the *Pastoral Care.*" *ES* 57 (1976): 497–501.

Sims-Williams, Patrick. "Thought, Words, and Deed: An Irish Triad." *Ériu* 29 (1978): 78–111.

Sisam, Kenneth. *Studies in the History of Old English Literature.* Oxford, 1953.

Skeat, Walter, ed. *Ælfric's Lives of Saints.* 2 vols. EETS, o.s. 76, 82, 94, 114. London, 1881–1900; repr. ed., 1966.

Smetana, Cyril. "Second Thoughts on 'Soul and Body I.'" *MS* 29 (1967): 193–205.

Southern, R. W. *The Making of the Middle Ages.* London, 1953; repr. ed., 1970.

———. *Medieval Humanism.* New York, 1970.

Spindler, Robert, ed. *Das altenglische Bussbuch (sog. Confessionale Pseudo-Egberti).* Leipzig, 1934.

Stanley, Eric Gerald. "Old English Poetic Diction and the Interpretation of *The Wanderer, The Seafarer,* and *The Penitent's Prayer.*" *Anglia* 73 (1956): 413–466.

————. *The Search for Anglo-Saxon Paganism*. Cambridge, 1975.

————, ed. *Continuations and Beginnings: Studies in Old English Literature*. London, 1966.

Steinmeyer, Elias von, ed. *Die kleineren althochdeutschen Sprachdenkmäler*. Berlin, 1916; repr. ed., 1963.

Stenton, Frank M. *Anglo-Saxon England*. 3d ed. Oxford, 1971.

Stokes, Whitley. *Lives of the Saints from the Book of Lismore*. Oxford, 1890.

————, and John Strachan, eds. and trans. *Thesaurus Palaeohibernicus*. 2 vols. Cambridge, 1903; repr. ed., Oxford, 1975.

Storms, G. *Anglo-Saxon Magic*. The Hague, 1948.

Stubbs, William, ed. *Memorials of Saint Dunstan*. Rolls Series, vol. 63. London, 1874.

Sweet, Henry, ed. and trans. *King Alfred's West-Saxon Version of Gregory's Pastoral Care*. 2 vols. EETS, o.s. 45, 50. London, 1871; repr. ed., 1973.

Symons, Thomas. "The English Monastic Reform of the Tenth Century." *Downside Review* 60, n.s. 41 (1942): 1–22, 196–222, 268–279.

————, ed. *Regularis Concordia Anglicae Nationis Monachorum Sanctimonialumque*. London, 1953.

Szarmach, Paul E., ed. *Vercelli Homilies IX–XXIII*. Toronto, 1981.

————. "Vercelli Homily XX." *MS* 35 (1973): 1–26.

————, and Bernard F. Huppé, eds. *The Old English Homily and Its Backgrounds*. Albany, 1978.

Teetaert, Amédée. *La confession aux laïques dans l'église latine depuis le VIIIe jusqu'au XIVe siècle*. Dissertationes ad gradum magistri in Facultate Theologica vel in Facultate Iuris Canonici (Louvain), ser. 2: 17. Paris, 1926.

Tentler, Thomas N. *Sin and Confession on the Eve of the Reformation*. Princeton, 1977.

————. "The Summa for Confessors as an Instrument of Social Control" (with "Response and *Retractatio*"). In *The Pursuit of Holiness in Late Medieval and Renaissance Religion*, edited by Charles Trinkaus with Heiko Oberman, pp. 101–126, 131–137. Leiden, 1974.

Thorpe, Benjamin, ed. and trans. *Ancient Laws and Institutes of England*. 2 vols. London, 1840.

————, ed. and trans. *The Homilies of the Anglo-Saxon Church: The First Part, Containing the "Sermones Catholici" or Homilies of Ælfric*. 2 vols. London, 1844–1846.

Thurneysen, Rudolf, Nancy Power, *et al. Studies in Early Irish Law.* Dublin, 1936.

Trahern, Joseph B., Jr. "Caesarius of Arles and Old English Literature: Some Contributions and a Recapitulation." *ASE* 5 (1976): 105–120.

Turville-Petre, Joan. "Translations of a Lost Penitential Homily." *Traditio* 19 (1963): 51–78.

Ullmann, Walter. "Canonistics in England." *Studia Gratiana* 2 (1954): 519–528.

————. *The Carolingian Renaissance and the Idea of Kingship.* London, 1971.

Ure, James M., ed. *The Benedictine Office: An Old English Text.* Edinburgh University Publications on Language and Literature, vol. 11. Edinburgh, 1957.

Vacant, A., E. Mangenot, and E. Amann, eds. *Dictionnaire de théologie catholique.* 15 vols. Paris, 1930–1950.

Vogel, Cyrille. "Composition légale et commutations dans le système de la pénitence tarifée." *Revue de Droit Canonique* 8 (1958): 289–318; 9 (1959): 1–38, 341–359.

————. *La discipline pénitentielle en Gaule des origines à la fin du VIIe siècle.* Paris, 1952.

————. "La discipline pénitentielle en Gaule des origines à la fin du IXe siècle: Le dossier hagiographique." *Revue des Sciences Religieuses* 30 (1956): 1–26, 157–186.

————. *Les "Libri Paenitentiales."* Typologie des Sources du Moyen Age Occidental, vol. 27. Turnhout, 1978.

————. "Le pèlerinage pénitentiel." *Revue des Sciences Religieuses* 38 (1964): 113–153.

————. "Les rites de la pénitence publique aux Xe et XIe siècles." In *Mélanges René Crozet,* edited by Pierre Gallais and Yves-Jean Riou, 1:137–144. Poitiers, 1966.

————, and Reinhard Elze, eds. *Le Pontifical Romano-Germanique du dixième siècle.* Studi e Testi, vols. 226, 227, 269. Vatican City, 1963–1972.

Walker, G. S. M., ed. and trans. *Sancti Columbani Opera.* Scriptores Latini Hiberniae, vol. 2. Dublin, 1957; repr. ed., 1970.

Wallace-Hadrill, J. M. *Early Germanic Kingship in England and on the Continent.* Oxford, 1971.

————. *Early Medieval History.* Oxford, 1975.

————. *The Long-Haired Kings and Other Studies in Frankish History.* London, 1962.

Wallach, Luitpold. *Alcuin and Charlemagne: Studies in Carolingian History and Literature*. Ithaca, 1959.

Warner, George F., ed. *The Stowe Missal*. 2 vols. Henry Bradshaw Society, vols. 31, 32. London, 1906, 1915.

Warren, F. E., ed. *The Antiphony of Bangor*. 2 vols. Henry Bradshaw Society, vols. 4, 10. London, 1893, 1895.

Wasserschleben, F. W. H., ed. *Die Bussordnungen der abendländischen Kirche*. Halle, 1851; repr. ed., Graz, 1958.

―――. *Die irische Kanonensammlung*. 2d ed. Leipzig, 1885.

―――. *Reginonis Abbatis Prumiensis, Libri Duo de Synodalibus Causis et Disciplinis Ecclesiasticis*. Leipzig, 1840.

Watkins, Oscar D. *A History of Penance*. 2 vols. New York, 1920; repr. ed., 1961.

Wenzel, Siegfried. *The Sin of Sloth: Acedia in Medieval Thought and Literature*. Chapel Hill, N.C., 1960.

Werner, Karl Ferdinand, "Le rôle de l'aristocratie dans la christianisation du nord-est de la Gaulle." *Revue d'Histoire de l'Église de France* 62 (1976): 45–73.

Whitbread, L. "The Old English Poem *Judgment Day II* and Its Latin Source." *PQ* 45 (1966): 635–656.

Whitelock, Dorothy. "Archbishop Wulfstan, Homilist and Statesman." *Transactions of the Royal Historical Society*, 4th ser. 24 (1942): 25–45.

―――. "The Interpretation of 'The Seafarer.'" In *The Early Cultures of North-West Europe*, edited by Cyril Fox and Bruce Dickins, pp. 261–272. Cambridge, 1950.

―――, ed. *Sermo Lupi ad Anglos*. 3d ed. London, 1963.

―――, and David C. Douglas, eds. and trans. *English Historical Documents, I: c. 500–1042*. 2d ed. London, 1979.

Willard, Rudolph. "The Address of the Soul to the Body." *PMLA* 50 (1935): 957–983.

―――, ed. *The Blickling Homilies*. Early English Manuscripts in Facsimile, vol. 10. Copenhagen, 1960.

―――, ed. "*Vercelli Homily XI* and Its Sources." *Speculum* 24 (1949): 76–87.

Wilmart, André. *Auteurs spirituels et textes dévots du moyen âge latin: etudes d'histoire littéraire*. Paris, 1932; repr. ed., 1971.

―――. "Lettres de l'époque carolingienne." *RB* 34 (1922): 234–245.

―――. "Le manuel de prières de saint Jean Gualbert." *RB* 48 (1936): 259–299.

————, ed. *Precum Libelli Quattor Aevi Karolini*. Rome, 1940.

————, E. A. Lowe, and H. A. Wilson. *The Bobbio Missal: Notes and Studies*. Henry Bradshaw Society, vol. 61. London, 1924.

Wilson, H. A., ed. *The Pontifical of Magdalene College*. Henry Bradshaw Society, vol. 29. London, 1910.

Wormald, Patrick. "Bede, Beowulf, and the Conversion of the Anglo-Saxon Aristocracy." In *Bede and Anglo-Saxon England*, edited by Robert T. Farrell, pp. 32–95. Oxford, 1978.

————. "*Lex Scripta* and *Verbum Regis*: Legislation and Germanic Kingship, from Euric to Cnut." In *Early Medieval Kingship*, edited by P. H. Sawyer and I. N. Wood, pp. 105–138. Leeds, 1977.

Wulfstan. For editions see Bethurum, Fowler, Jost, and Whitelock.

Zettinger, J. "Das 'Poenitentiale Cummeani.'" *Archiv für katholisches Kirchenrecht* 82 (1902): 501–540.

Index

A

Abelard, Peter, 116, 202–204
Absolution, 5–6, 114–115, 118, 169–170, 181–182
Adomnan, *Life of Columba*, 35–36
Ælfheah (bishop), 123 n. 4
Ælfric (abbot):
achievement of, 123, 142–143
and *De Penitentia*, 160–161, 163–164, 167 n. 48
homilies of, 141, 144, 157–160
pastoral letters of, 142, 143, 151 n. 1, 159, 160
and public penance, 141, 157–158
and Wulfstan, 143, 163
Æthelbald (king), *Privilege* of, 84
Æthelwold (abbot), 122–123, 129
Aidan, 63
Alan of Lille, 202–203
Alcuin:
and acts of penance, 111, 115–116
penitential theology of, 114–116, 147 n. 97, 157 n. 20, 158, 179
prayers of, 89–90, 114–115, 171
Alfred (king), 124–129, 154
laws of, 125–127
Almsgiving, 180, 183
Almsgiving, as penance, 9, 16, 82, 146, 157
Alphabet of Piety, 50
Anatomical motif, 85–90, 171, 186.
See also Prayers, confessional
Ancrene Riwle, 205
Ansegius, canons of, 101

Anselm, prayers of, 205
Asceticism, voluntary, 25–26, 54, 55, 82, 95, 157, 180, 181, 183, 186, 201
Athelstan (king), 125
laws of, 146

B

Baptism, 12, 79, 85, 111, 112, 160, 162, 167
Battle of Maldon, 177
Beati. *See* Psalms, *Beati* (Psalm 118)
Bede:
and the Irish, 61, 63
letter to Egbert, 83, 114
Life of Cuthbert, 63, 83
penitentials attributed to:
authorship of, 1–2, 69–71, 73
date of, 71–72
and *Double Penitential*, 109, 117–119, 120, 149
and Egbert's penitential, 69–72, 108–109
manuscripts of, 69–72, 77, 107–109, 113, 130, 131, 133
sources of, 71–72, 76–77
and Theodore's penitential, 70, 75–76, 204. *See also* Pseudo-Bede, tradition of
Benedictine Reform, 122–129, 147–150, 173–174
Benedict of Aniane, *Epitome* of, 147 n. 97
Benedict of Nursia, *Rule* of, 27, 49, 164

Beowulf, 177
Bernard of Clairvaux, 202
Bigotian Penitential:
  date and sources of, 36–37
  structure of, 49, 51
Binding and loosing, 22, 158, 159, 192
Bishops:
  penances for, 75, 138, 140
  powers of, 33–34, 41, 81–82, 125,
    144–146
  and public penance, 5–6, 98, 158,
    161–162
Blickling homilies, 152–155, 156, 157
Blood-feud, 67, 76, 146
Bobbio Missal, 52, 105
Bobbio Penitential, 101
Boniface (archbishop), 95–96
Book of Aicill, 44 n. 75
Book of Cerne, prayers of, 84–90,
  113, 171, 205
Book of Nunnaminster, 84–85
Book of Vices and Virtues (Middle
    English), 206
Brigit, *Life* of, 53
Brittany, 128–130

C

Caesarius (bishop), 24, 25, 97, 113,
  115
Cáin Lánamna, 44–45
Cambrai Homily, 29 n. 24, 77 n. 66
Canones Gregorii, 130
Canterbury, 62–63, 78, 122
Capitula a Sacerdotibus Proposita, 100
Cassian, John, 21, 24–26
Céli-Dé reform, 43, 58, 113
Charlemagne, 6, 89, 97–98, 100, 171
Charles Martel, 96
Charles (son of Louis), 111–112
Charters, Anglo-Saxon, 84
Chaucer, Geoffrey, 13, 206
Christ I and II, 182–183
Christ III, 176, 180, 182, 183–185,
  194, 206
Chrodegang, *Rule* of, 96, 118, 139
  in Old English, 121, 144, 164

Circumstances (used in confession),
  7–8, 31, 117–118, 139
Clergy:
  instruction of, 81, 83, 143, 144,
    151–152, 156, 160–161, 163–165
  penances for, 37–38, 82, 96–97,
    137–138
Cnut, laws of, 146, 177 n. 5
Collectio Dacheriana, 99 n. 15, 109,
  132
"Collection books," 110
Collectio Vaticana, 99 n. 15
Columba (Columcille), 35–36, 61
Columbanus:
  letters of, 95
  Life of, 35, 37
  mission to continent of, 26–27,
    30, 33, 35, 95–96
  penitential of, 21
    date of, 94–95
    and native law, 42
    and public penance, 52
    sources of, 36
    structure of, 37, 57
  rules of, 26–29, 37, 47
Commonplace books, 123–124, 129,
  141–142, 164
  penitentials in, 132–133
Commutations of penance, 16, 18
  on the continent, 73, 138
  in England, 73–74, 81–82
  in Ireland, 24, 52, 54–55
  later history of, 201–202
  in Old English texts, 135, 138–139,
    141, 149, 150
Compensation, 42–43, 44, 76, 79,
  125
Confession:
  devotional (to God alone), 29–
    30, 87–88, 104, 114–115, 119,
    158, 170, 185, 186
  mutual, 45, 87
  open (informal), 35, 53, 63
  private (to priest):
    exaggerated, 35
    frequency of, 15, 36, 112, 146,
      202

monastic origins of, 19–25
monastic practice of, 28–30,
    35–36
necessity of, debated, 202–203
used to teach, 9–10, 144, 152,
    164–167
used to test faith, 117–119, 152,
    168, 169, 170
in public penance, 5, 113, 171
Confessor:
instructions for, 7–8, 30–32, 38–
    39, 106, 145, 149, 156, 163–
    168. *See also Ordo confessionis*
    (private penance)
roles of, 9–10, 30–32, 145
Contraries, theory of, 50, 84, 87
Contrition, in confession, 8, 194
necessary for forgiveness, 115–119,
    202–204
Councils, ecclesiastical:
Arles (813), 100 n. 18
Chalon (813), 98, 99, 100, 102
Chalon-sur-Saone (644–656), 97
Clovesho (747), 74, 81, 84
Constantinople, 33
Fourth Lateran (1215), 15, 117, 202,
    206
Grately (828), 125
Mainz (852), 100
Paris (829), 99, 148
Rheims (813), 100 n. 18
Tours (813), 98, 101
Worms (868), 117
Counsel, in confession, 27–30, 77,
    162
Críth Gablach, 45–46
Cross vigil, 55
cumal, 44
Cummean (abbot), penitential of, 3
    n. 5, 9–10, 31, 117
date of, 36
manuscripts of, 68, 92, 107, 130,
    132, 169
and native law, 42
and public penance, 51–52
structure of, 38–39, 47–48, 49,
    50, 57, 65–66, 88, 103

and Theodore's penitential, 68.
    See also Pseudo-Cummean,
    penitential of
Cursing, 33, 48, 86
Cuthbert, *Life* of, 63, 83
Cynewulf, poetry of. *See Elene;*
    Juliana

D

"Discipulus Umbrensium." *See*
    Theodore (archbishop), pen-
    itential of
Discretion, in confession, 7–8, 14,
    117–118, 168
Double Penitential. See Bede, peni-
    tentials attributed to
Dream of the Rood, 182, 194, 205
Druids, 32, 33
Dunstan (archbishop), 122–123

E

Eadwig (king), 122
Easter, date of, 61, 66, 95
Ebbo (archbishop), 103
Edgar (king), 122
Edmund (king), 122
    laws of, 146
Edward, treaty with Guthrum, 125
Egbert (archbishop), 70, 73, 74
    Dialogue of, 82–83
    penitential of, 25 n. 15, 117
    and Bedan penitentials, 69–72,
        107–109
    date of, 74–75, 77
    manuscripts of, 72, 75, 107–
        109, 113, 130, 131, 132, 169
    and penitential of Theodore,
        76, 77
    and Peter Damiani, 148
    prologue to, 71, 74, 75, 106, 143,
        178
    sources and structure of, 72–
        75. *See also* Pseudo-Egbert,
        tradition of
Elene, 182, 188, 190–192

England and the continent:
  eighth-century contact, 95–96
  tenth-century contact, 122–124,
    127–132
éric, 44
Ethelbert (king), laws of, 79, 80
Ethelred (king), laws of, 146
Eucharist, 6, 65, 81, 82, 143, 146
Excerpts from a Book of David, 19, 21
Excommunication, 5, 40
Exegesis, Irish, 50, 51, 59
Exeter, 130, 131, 132
Exeter Book, The, 132, 194
Exhortation to Christian Living, An,
    180, 181
Exile, 16, 22, 42, 55, 181, 193
Exorcism, 85

F

Fasting:
  in distraint, 44
  as penance, 6, 9, 16, 22, 56, 111,
    157, 167
  voluntary, 82, 119, 164, 173, 187
Fates of the Apostles, 188
Fear:
  of God, 106, 162, 178–179, 185,
    186, 194
  of shame, 177–178, 194, 195
Finnian (abbot), 21, 30, 50
  Life of, 53
  penitential of, 3 n. 5, 65 n. 13
    date of, 36
    and devotional confession, 87
    and native law, 42
    structure of, 37–38, 57
Fleury, 129
Florilegia, 49, 120
Frankish penitentials, 101–104, 119–
    121. See also Bobbio Peniten-
    tial; Halitgar (bishop), peni-
    tential of; Hrabanus Maurus;
    Poenitentiale Floricense; Poe-
    nitentiale Martenianum;
    Poenitentiale Sangallense;
    Poenitentiale Sangermanense;
    Tripartite penitentials

Freising, statutes of, 100–101
Frisia, 95
Fulk (archbishop), 127

G

Gelasian Sacramentary, 105
Gerbald (bishop), statutes of, 100
Gildas, Preface of, 19
Gloria, 181, 182 n. 21
Glosses, 47, 48–49, 171
Gower, John, Confessio Amantis, 206
Gratian, 202
Gregory I (the Great):
  Libellus Responsionem, 68, 101
    n. 23, 107, 110
  Pastoral Care, 124, 151 n. 1, 154,
    207 n. 24
Grimbald, 127
Guthrum, treaty with Edward, 125

H

Haito (bishop), statutes of, 100
Halitgar (bishop), penitential of:
  date of, 103, 136, 148
  manuscripts of, 106–107, 130, 131,
    132, 133, 137
  and ordo confessionis, 105–106, 116,
    132
  and public penance, 105
  sixth book, "Roman Penitential,"
    of, 104–105, 109, 120
  sources of, 103–104
Handbooks of penance. See
    Penitential
Handlyng Synne, 206–207
Hibernensis: Collectio Canonum Hi-
    bernensis, 41–42, 68, 99, 101
    n. 23, 128–129, 130, 156
Hincmar (archbishop), 111, 127
Homiletic Fragment II, 196
Homilies. See Ælfric (abbot), hom-
    ilies of; Blickling homilies;
    Cambrai Homily; Lent, hom-
    ilies for; Vercelli Book, hom-
    ilies of; Wulfstan (arch-
    bishop), homilies of

Honor, 45, 177–178
Honor price, 44
Hrabanus Maurus, 106, 116

I

Iberia, 26
Ine (king), laws of, 79, 126
Instructions for Christians, 180
Interior spirituality, in penance,
    8–10, 67, 115–119, 156, 158,
    194, 202–208
Interrogationes Examinationis, 100
Iona, 35, 61
Ireland:
    literary culture of, 61–62, 90–91
    social structure of, 33–35, 41, 46
Irish Libellus Precum, 84
Irish missions:
    to the continent, 26–27, 95–96
    to England, 61–63
Isidore of Seville, 86 n. 92, 89 n. 105

J—K

John the Faster, penitential of, 69
Jonas of Bobbio, *Life of Columba-
    nus*, 35, 37
Judgment Day II, 181, 185–187, 194,
    196
Juliana, 182, 188–190, 192
Kinship, degrees of, 43, 46

L

Laity:
    instruction of, 36–37, 81–82, 83,
        112, 113, 120, 143, 172, 173, 175
    penances for,
        on the continent, 120
        in England, 66, 67, 79–84, 137,
            140
        in Ireland, 30, 36–39, 48, 52
Lambeth Commentary, 50
Langland, William, 13, 206
Law, ecclesiastical (canon law), and
        penance, 15, 19, 20, 21
    on the continent, 98–99, 104

in England, 64–65, 128–129
in Ireland, 24, 39–42
in later Middle Ages, 202–203
Law, secular (native law), and pen-
        ance, 11, 15
    in England, 75–77, 78–79, 80, 81,
        125–126, 146–147
    in Ireland, 23–24, 39–49
Laws, English. *See* Alfred (king),
    laws of; Athelstan (king),
    laws of; Cnut, laws of; Ed-
    mund (king), laws of; Ed-
    ward, treaty with Guthrum;
    Ine (king), laws of; Wihtred
    (king), laws of
Laws, Irish, 23–24, 42–44. *See also
    Book of Aicill*; *Cáin Lá-
    namna*; *Críth Gablach*; *Sen-
    chas Már*
Laws of Manu, 22–23
Lazarus, 22, 159
Lent, 5, 16, 82, 112, 146, 157, 163, 164,
        167, 173
    homilies for, 155–156, 157, 159,
        161–162, 163, 164, 165
Leofric (bishop), 132
Lérins, 24, 26
Libelli precum. See Prayers,
    confessional
Libraries, of churches, 110–111
    in early Ireland, 20 n. 3
Loire Valley, 26
Lord's Prayer, The, 175–176, 181, 183, 194
Lorica, 85–86, 89
Lorsch, 72, 110
Lothair, 111–112
Louis the Pious, 101, 111

M

Manaig, 34, 36, 44–45
Manuals of confession (later Middle
        Ages), 8, 204–206
Manuscripts:
    Brussels, Bibliothèque Royale:
        8558–8563: 133 n. 39, 138 n. 57
    Cambridge, Corpus Christi
        College:

Manuscripts (*continued*)
   163: 142 n. 74
   178: 158 n. 24
   190: 132 n. 38, 133 n. 42, 134
     n. 46, 138 n. 57, 142 nn. 73,
     75, 164 n. 41, 171 n. 57
   201: 139 n. 64, 141 n. 68, 175–
     176 n. 2
   265: 132 n. 37, 133 n. 40
   272: 169 n. 53
   320: 131 nn. 30–31, 163–164
     n. 40
  Cambridge University Library:
   Gg 3. 28: 160 n. 32
  Cologne, Dombibliothek:
   91: 101 n. 23
  Copenhagen, Kongelige
    Bibliothek:
   NY. Kgl. S. 58: 101 n. 23
  Karlsruhe, Badische
    Landesbibliothek:
   Aug. CCLV: 108 n. 49
  London, British Library:
   Arundel 155: 171 nn. 59, 61
   Cotton Galba A. xiv: 172 n. 62
   Cotton Nero A. i: 141 n. 72
   Cotton Tiberius A. iii: 164 nn.
    42–43, 171 n. 59, 172 n. 63
   Cotton Tiberius C. i: 165 n. 44,
    171 n. 60, 173 n. 65
   Cotton Vespasian D. xv: 132
    n. 36, 171 n. 58
   Cotton Vespasian D. xx: 132
    n. 35, 170 n. 56, 171 n. 60
   Harley 7653: 85 n. 87
   Royal 2 A. xx: 85 n. 87
   Royal 2 B. v: 171 n. 59
   Royal 5 E. xiii: 108 n. 49, 130
    nn. 26–27
  Munich, Staatsbibliothek:
   Clm 6311: 73 n. 50
  Oxford, Bodleian Library:
   Barlow 37: 132 n. 37
   Bodley 311: 130 nn. 24–25, 169
    n. 52
   Bodley 516: 131 n. 29
   Bodley 718: 131 nn. 32, 34, 170
    nn. 54–55, 172 n. 64

   Junius 121: 133 n. 41, 134 n. 46
   Laud Misc. 482: 133 n. 41, 138
    n. 57, 163–164 n. 40
  Paris, Bibliothèque Nationale:
   Lat. 943: 131 n. 33
   Lat. 2341: 72 n. 46, 108 n. 48,
    109 n. 55
  St. Gall, Stiftsbibliothek:
   550: 110 n. 58
   682: 108 n. 49
  Vatican City, Biblioteca Aposto-
    lica Vaticana:
   Pal. Lat. 294: 71 n. 42
   Pal. Lat. 485: 107 n. 45, 108
    n. 46, 109 n. 54, 113 n. 67
   Pal. Lat. 554: 70 n. 36, 72 n. 47
  Vesoul, Bibliothèque de la ville:
   73: 110 n. 56
  Vienna, Nationalbibliothek:
   2171: 108 n. 47
   2223: 70 n. 36, 73 nn. 48, 50, 107
    nn. 44–45
Martin of Tours, 26
Martyrdom, 28–29
Martyrology of Oengus, 32
Medical metaphor, 30–31, 62, 84,
   85, 87, 89, 159, 187
Memory, 50–51, 112 n. 64
Mercia, 62, 84, 134, 153
Monastery of Tallaght, 32, 35, 36, 43,
   48, 54, 58, 113
Monasticism, Irish:
  as centers of penance, 35–39
  discipline in, 27–30
  Egyptian influence on, 25–27
  and native society, 32–35
Monastic Rules. *See* Benedict of
   Nursia; Columbanus, rules
   of
Mortification, 28–29, 52, 139
Mute dog, theme of, 151

N

Nantes Chronicle, 128
Nicholas (pope), 3 n. 6, 104
Nithard, *Chronicle* of, 112

Nobility, piety of, 15–16, 34, 62, 83–84, 95, 111, 114–115, 172
Norman conquest, 147–148

O

Old English Handbook ("A Late Old English Handbook for the Use of a Confessor," ed. Fowler):
and commutations, 140–141
date of, 139
introduction (ordo) to, 140, 163, 167–169, 170
and public penance, 141
sources and structure of, 139–140
Old English Penitential (Die altenglische Version des Halitgar'schen Bussbuches, ed. Raith):
and commutations, 138, 141
date and authorship of, 133–135
manuscripts of, 133–134
and the Old English "Scrift boc," 136–138
and public penance, 138, 141
sources and structure of, 135, 136–137, 148
Old English "Scrift boc" (Das altenglische Bussbuch, ed. Spindler):
and commutations, 141
date of, 134–135, 136–137, 154
and Egbert, 133–134
introduction (ordo) to, 135, 162, 163, 164, 166, 168, 172 n. 62, 173
manuscripts of, 133–134
and public penance, 138, 141, 157
sources and structure of, 136, 148
Old-Irish Penitential, 2 n. 5, 32, 37
manuscript form of, 58
and native law, 43–44
and reform movement, 43, 54, 59, 113
structure of, 38–39, 50, 58
and Theodore, 68
Old-Irish Table of Commutations, 32, 54–55, 113

Ordo confessionis (private penance):
in Double Penitential, 117–118
early forms of, 105, 118, 165–166
in English manuscripts, 131, 132, 166–170
in Halitgar's penitential, 105–106
purpose of, 105–106, 117–119
techniques used in, 164–169, 194. See also Penance, public, liturgy of; Prayers, confessional
Origin, 21, 25
Osgar (abbot), 129
Oswald (bishop), 122–123
Oswiu (king), 78

P

Paderborn, Capitula of, 111
Parts of the body. See Anatomical motif
Paruchia, 41, 46
Penance:
dual system of, 6, 52, 141
private:
early history of, 6–7
Irish origins of, 5–6, 19–25
later medieval developments in, 202–204
and repentance, 12–13, 154, 156–157
and sacramental tradition, 8, 156, 182
theology of, 9–10, 114–116. See also Bede; Columbanus, penitential of; Cummean (abbot), penitential of; Egbert (archbishop); Finnian (abbot), penitential of; Halitgar (bishop), penitential of; Hrabanus Maurus; John the Faster, penitential of; Robert of Flamborough, penitential of; Theodore (archbishop), penitential of
public:
continental revival of, 97–98, 105, 111–113
early history of, 5–6, 97

Penance (*continued*)
  in England, 66, 83, 138, 141–
    142, 146, 150, 157–158,
    161–162
  in Ireland, 4, 41–42, 51–52, 87
  liturgy of, 52, 87, 113, 119, 141–
    142, 146, 150, 168, 169–170
  and private penance, 6–7, 36,
    141, 145
  for sick and dying, 143, 146
Penances:
  harsh or extreme, 16–17, 54–55,
    111, 201
  vicarious, 81, 201–202. *See also*
    Almsgiving, as penance;
    Commutations of penance;
    Exile; Fasting; Prayer
Penances (tariffs) for individual
    sins:
  anger, 48, 50, 56
  avarice, 56
  disobedience, 27–28, 47
  gluttony, 56
  heresy, 66
  injury, 42
  languor, 56, 65
  lying, 67
  murder, 7, 16, 40, 42, 43, 51, 55,
    67, 75, 76–77, 80, 111–112,
    138, 140, 146
  perjury (and false witness), 45, 56,
    75, 125
  sexual offenses, 2–3, 11, 15, 40, 55,
    56, 65, 66–67, 75, 80, 118,
    140, 201
  sins of thought, 28, 65–66, 149
  Sunday observance, 66, 79
  superstition (and magic), 11, 67,
    74, 140
  theft, 43, 56, 75
Penitential (handbook of penance):
  controversies about, 1–3, 94–97,
    148–149
  function and purpose of, 7–10,
    17–18, 148
  historical importance of, 4, 13–17,
    198–201
  as a manuscript, 58, 110

  origins of, 19–25, 57
  use of, required, 74, 100–101, 112,
    119, 143
Penitential literature, 11–13, 152,
    179–182, 205, 208
Penitential motif, 176, 183, 194
Penitentials. *See* Bede; Columba-
    nus, penitential of; Cum-
    mean (abbot), penitential of;
    Egbert (archbishop); Fin-
    nian (abbot), penitential of;
    Halitgar (bishop), peniten-
    tial of; Hrabanus Maurus;
    John the Faster, penitential
    of; Robert of Flamborough,
    penitential of; Theodore
    (archbishop), penitential of
Penitentials, anonymous. *See Bobbio*
    Penitential; *Poenitentiale*
    Floricense; *Poenitentiale Mar-*
    tenianum; *Poenitentiale San-*
    gallense; *Poenitentiale San-*
    germanense; Tripartite
    penitentials
Penitent's Prayer. See Resignation
Perfection (monastic ideal), 27–30
Peter Damiani, 148
Peter Lombard, 202
Pilgrimage, 35, 67, 181
Poenitentiale Floricense, 105 n. 37, 118
    n. 85, 165–166
Poenitentiale Martenianum, 102 n. 26
Poenitentiale Sangallense, 105 n. 37,
    118 n. 85
Poenitentiale Sangermanense, 131
Pontifical Romano-Germanique, 113,
    118, 142
Prayer:
  during confession, 87–88,
    169–170
  among laity, 83, 112–113, 172
  in monastery, 27
Prayers:
  catechetical, 83, 84, 160, 161, 169,
    172, 173
  confessional:
    continental versions of, 89–90,
    113–115

English versions of, 87–90, 131–132, 169–173
Irish ("Celtic" style), 84–87. *See also* Anatomical motif; Confession, devotional (to God alone)
Preaching, 10, 63, 74, 83, 113–114, 144–145, 151–153, 156, 160–161, 164
Precepts, 194–195
Psalms, 21, 27, 54, 55, 90–91, 114
Beati (Psalm 118), 55, 90–91
Pseudo-Bede, tradition of, 69, 92, 109
Pseudo-Cummean, penitential of, 92, 101, 102, 110
Pseudo-Egbert, tradition of, 83 n. 83, 133–134, 150
Pseudo-Egbert *Excerptiones*, 129
Pseudo-Theodore, penitential of, 132–133
Pseudo-Wulfstan, homily of, 164

R

Reform councils, Frankish, 98–100
Regino (bishop), *Ecclesiastical Discipline*, 118, 119
Regularis Concordia, 150
Remission of sins:
seven, 103
twelve, 20–21, 87, 135, 173
Resignation, 181
Resignation B, 193–194, 196
Rheims, 127–128, 169
Robert of Flamborough, penitential of, 202–203
Rodulf (bishop), *Capitula* of, 100
"Roman penitential." *See* Halitgar

S

Saints' lives, Irish, 35, 53–54
Samthan, *Life* of, 53
Scripture, 20–21, 32, 98
Seafarer, The, 180–181, 193, 195–196
Seasons for Fasting, The, 128, 180, 183
Senchas Már, 39–40, 46

Shame, 162, 177–179, 183, 184
Sherborne Pontifical, 131
Sins (eight chief ones), lists of, 18, 38, 50, 58, 66, 88, 100, 102–103, 120, 156, 167
Sir Gawain and the Green Knight, 205
Social classes, in penitentials, 8, 11, 14, 15, 16, 47, 66–67, 79–81, 117, 135, 147
Social control, theory of, 3–4, 200–201
Soul and Body, 187–188, 206
"Soul-friend," 31–32, 58
Statutes, Frankish, 100–101, 131. *See also* Freising, statutes of; Gerbald (bishop), statutes of; Haito (bishop), statutes of; Vesoul, statutes of; Waltcaud (bishop), statutes of
Stowe Missal, 52
Summons to Prayer, A, 180, 181
Superstition, 11, 67, 74, 80–81
Synods:
First Synod of St. Patrick, 40–42, 51–52
of Hertford (672), 63
of Toledo (589), 97
of Tribur (895), 117, 118 n. 86

T

Theodore (archbishop):
achievement of, 62–64
penitential of, 2–3
and authorship ("Discipulus Umbrensium"), 63, 64, 68
date of, 63
manuscripts of, 68–69, 101, 107, 130, 131, 132, 163
and native law, 78–81
and penitentials of Bede and Egbert, 75–77
and public penance, 66
structure of, 64–65. *See also Canones Gregorii*; Pseudo-Theodore

Theodulf (bishop):
  and confession, 112, 186
  First and Second *Capitula* of,
    102, 109, 113, 156, 157
    in Old English, 121, 144, 164
  and penitentials, 102–103
Tours, 114
Tripartite penitentials, 101–102, 130

V

Vercelli Book, homilies of, 152–154,
    156–157, 164
Vernacular tradition:
  continental, 112–113, 119–120
  English, 83, 114, 123–124, 149–
    150, 169–170, 172
  Irish, 37, 51, 59, 113
Vesoul, statutes of, 100–101
Vetus Gallica, 68, 99, 101 n. 23

W

Waltcaud (bishop), statutes of, 100
Wanderer, The, 181, 193, 195–196
Wareham, 128
Warfare, penance for, 76, 111–112
Wife's Lament, The, 193–194
Wihtred (king):

  laws of, 79
  Privilege of, 84
Wilfrid, 95
Willibrord, 95
Winchester, 122, 123, 128
Wisdom tradition (in Old English
    poetry), 193–195
Women:
  as confessors, 53
  in monasteries, 56–57
  penances for, *versus* status under
    native laws, 11, 66–67
Worcester, 122, 123, 130, 131, 132, 133
Wulfstan (archbishop), 6
  achievement of, 123
  and Ælfric, 143–144, 163
  ecclesiastical legislation of:
    Canons of Edgar, 144, 175
    Institutes of Polity, 144–145
    Northumbrian Priest's Law,
      145–146
  homilies of, 161–163, 177–178
  and native law, 146–147
  and public penance, 141–142, 146,
    161–162, 163

Y

York, 126, 145